KIERKEGAARD'S METAPHORS

by Jamie Lorentzen

MERCER UNIVERSITY PRESS / 2001

ISBN 0-86554-731-9   MUP/H548

The paper used in this publication meets the minimum requirements
of American National Standard for Information Sciences—
Permanence of Paper for Printed Library Materials, ANSI Z39.48-1984.

Library of Congress Cataloging-in-Publication Data

Lorentzen, Jamie.
    Kierkegaard's metaphors / by Jamie Lorentzen.
        pp.   cm.
    Includes bibliographical references and index.
    ISBN 0-86554-731-9 (alk. paper)
        1. Kierkegaard, Søren, 1813–1855.
        2. Metaphor. I. Title.
B4378.M48 L67 2001
198'.9—dc21

                                              2001030526
                                                  CIP

Contents

Acknowledgments

Acknowledgment is gratefully made to Independent School District 256, Red Wing, Minnesota, Superintendent Clayton Hovda, and its 1996 board members for granting me a sabbatical during the 1997–1998 academic year to compose the lion's share of the manuscript. Publication has been generously supported by grants from the Minnesota Humanities Commission, the Kierkegaard House Foundation, and Robert and Carolyn Hedin.

Many thanks also go to Gordon Marino and Cynthia Lund for their support and kind friendship in and out of the Howard V. and Edna H. Hong Kierkegaard Library, St. Olaf College, Northfield, Minnesota. Thanks to Gordon Marino and Carol Holly for scrutinizing segments of the manuscript's early drafts, and to Marjorie Hakala for help compiling the index. Edna and Howard Hong, Matt Peterson, John Graber, Dan Dietrich, and my dear wife, Jane, have given helpful criticism of the manuscript on the whole and in detail—especially Jane, whose repeated readings and constant support have been gifts beyond measure. Finally, a quiet thanks to the late Reverend Dr. Louis H. Valbracht, who preached with great passion and wisdom (and with continual reference to Kierkegaard) to unwitting confirmands like me years ago at St. John's Lutheran Church, Des Moines, Iowa.

In the end, this book is a striving born of gratitude for the support of those listed above as well as other friends and family members who have helped me grow along the way.

To

Howard Hong and Edna Hong

one a poet-philosopher,
the other a "somewhat" theologian,
together a lovingly coupled gift
to many a friend and pupil

with gratitude

Abbreviations

Unless otherwise indicated, the following abridged titles (left column) will signify citations from the Kierkegaard Writings series (Princeton NJ: Princeton University Press, 1978–1998) and Søren Kierkegaard's Journals and Papers series (Bloomington: Indiana University Press, 1967–1978).

Early Writings	KW I. *Early Polemical Writings*
Irony	KW II. *The Concept of Irony*
Either/Or I	KW III. *Either/Or* I
Either/Or II	KW IV. *Either/Or* II
Eighteen Discourses	KW V. *Eighteen Upbuilding Discourses*
Fear & Trembling	KW VI. *Fear and Trembling*
Repetition	KW VI. *Repetition*
Fragments	KW VII. *Philosophical Fragments*
Climacus	KW VII. *Johannes Climacus*
Anxiety	KW VIII. *The Concept of Anxiety*
Prefaces	KW IX. *Prefaces; Writing Sampler*
Three Discourses	KW X. *Three Discourses on Imagined Occasions*
Stages	KW XI. *Stages on Life's Way*
Postscript I, II	KW XII. *Concluding Unscientific Postscript to* Philosophical Fragments I, II
Corsair	KW XIII. *The Corsair Affair*
Two Ages	KW XIV. *Two Ages*
Various Spirits	KW XV. *Upbuilding Discourses in Various Spirits*
Works of Love	KW XVI. *Works of Love*
Christian Discourses	KW XVII. *Christian Discourses*
Crisis	KW XVII. *The Crisis and a Crisis in the Life of an Actress*
Without Authority	KW XVIII. *Without Authority: The Lily in the Field and the Bird in the Air; Two Ethical-Religious Essays; Three Discourses at the Communion on Fridays; An Upbuilding Discourse; Two Discourses at the Communion on Fridays*

If I imagined two kingdoms bordering each other, one of which I knew rather well and the other not at all, and if however much I desired it I were not allowed to enter the unknown kingdom, I would still be able to form some idea of it. I would go to the border of the kingdom known to me and follow it all the way, and in doing so I would by my movements describe the outline of that unknown land and thus have a general idea of it, although I had never set foot in it. And if this were a labor that occupied me very much, if I were unflaggingly scrupulous, it presumably would sometimes happen that as I stood with sadness at the border of my kingdom and gazed longingly into that unknown country that was so near and yet so far, I would be granted an occasional little disclosure.
  —*Either/Or* I, 66

Forget the metaphorical for the actual. . . .
  —*Eighteen Discourses*, 130-31

What is the good? It is God. Who is the one that gives it? It is God. Why is the good a gift and this expression not a metaphor but the only real and true expression?
  —*Eighteen Discourses*, 134

Preface

Halfway up a hill between two buildings on the St. Olaf College campus in Northfield, Minnesota, I began reading Danish thinker and writer Søren Aabye Kierkegaard (1813-1855). To the south, Holland Hall (patterned after the fortress monastery of Mont St. Michel on the Normandy coast) housed the philosophy department; the Howard and Edna Hong Kierkegaard Library nested on its top floor facing east. To the north, Rølvaag Library (roughly similar in architectural design to Holland Hall and no less imposing) housed the English department.

Both departments shaped my formal undergraduate education. The true locus of my education, however, was outside of (yet still between) the two academic camps. There, I nursed a notion that interdisciplinary approaches to literature and philosophy made images richer and ideas subtler. I uncomfortably yet doggedly attended to poetics sporadically evident in philosophy and to philosophical ideas in literature. During days surrounding autumnal and vernal equinoxes of my college years, I went so far as to drag a desk out of doors and between the two buildings. There, on an old, gray Royal typewriter, I would hammer out philosophical essays for the English department and literary essays for the philosophy department, even though I knew the compositions probably would meet with lukewarm receptions at the thresholds of both departments. English papers subsequently were criticized for their philosophical content; philosophy papers, due to their literary bent, were criticized for not adhering to the rigor of philosophical method. In the strict scope of their disciplines, my professors' red ink was justifiable. Nonetheless, I maintained my bivouac in the ambiguous and sometimes tense no-man's land between the two academic castles. It was a worthy place from which to view the world and time. Meanwhile, Kierkegaard and the Hongs legitimated my camp on the hill by encouraging a dynamic, symbiotic relationship between literature and philosophy.

In 1992, more than a decade after my graduation ceremonies, the Hong Kierkegaard Library moved from the top floor of Holland Hall to the basement of Rølvaag Library, several floors below the many-windowed English department and near the bedrock of the building. I interpreted the move as a good sign that philosophy and literature could live undivided under one roof, where both disciplines could join in an ongoing construction project of mutual upbuilding, where stylistic and substantive tensions between concrete images coexisting with abstract philosophical ideas might no longer be a detriment to sound inquiry but rather a clear advantage. In a September 1985 CBC radio interview, Howard Hong cited D. H. Lawrence: " 'The novel and philosophy was one with Plato and became divided to the detriment of both.' " This assertion continues to sustain my interpretation of the Hong Kierkegaard Library's move. Literature built without a philosophical bedrock will not endure. Philosophy without poetry lacks literary windows through which actual, daily cares and struggles of human existence may be viewed more concretely and thereby addressed more deliberately.

Kierkegaard knew the need for such a union between literature and philosophy, for he knew how humans hunger for the concrete-actual in literature and the abstract-ideal in philosophy to sustain a healthy and fully human existence. Further, Kierkegaard was acutely aware of the importance of bridging such a divide to protect the fully human from impending advances of industrialism, materialism, and consumerism that threaten the import of literature and philosophy in human development. Against long odds and a contemporary culture that largely misunderstood his own interdisciplinary approach to both the world of everyday and the world of ideas, he thus built a many-windowed esthetic upon a firm bedrock of ethical, philosophical, and religious presuppositions. Metaphor—that darling trope of English departments—is the focus of the present discussion not only because it most easily and effectively conjoins literary image with philosophical idea, but because, for Kierkegaard, it consistently is the concrete literary mortar to the abstract philosophical bricks of his thought.

Kierkegaard does not construct an overt, developed concept of metaphor beyond a brief but compelling paragraph opening the "Second Series" of *Works of Love*. The content and style of his entire authorship nevertheless may be said to rely heavily upon an intimate understanding of metaphor and of how he uses metaphor. Metaphor for Kierkegaard is an all-in-one tool he uses to conjoin thoughts on esthetics and imagination with ethical-religious concerns. The end product is virtually seamless, for how Kierkegaard uses metaphor not only informs but also imi-

tates many of his esthetic, ethical, psychological, existential, philosophical, and religious thoughts on what it means to be human.

Kierkegaard scholars on both ends of the past quarter-century decry
the relative neglect of critical discussion of the relationship between Kierkegaard's poetic style and his ideas. Louis Mackey wrote in the early
1970s that Kierkegaard's artistry, "while often praised, has seldom been
sufficiently appreciated, and that its integral relationship to his thought
has never been clearly seen."[1] In particular, Mackey notes that
Kierkegaard's

> use of pseudonyms, of metaphor, and of more complex literary forms to con-
> vey his ideas dictates the way in which these ideas are to be understood and
> appropriated. Like the unity of the corpus of a poet, the unity of Kierke-
> gaard's writings is a metaphoric rather than a literal unity; his thought is
> analogically one rather than univocally one; and his dialectic is a dialectic
> of images (in the largest critical sense) rather than a dialectic of concepts in
> the abstract.[2]

Twenty-five years later, G. Heath King echoed Mackey:

> Kierkegaard's description of himself as "poet and thinker" (e.g., *Journals*,
> VI, X[1] A 281, April 25, 1849, 148; IX A 213, n.d. [1848], 38-39) is well
> known, and one speaks abstractly of the "poetic qualities" of Kierkegaard's
> style, but no attempt has been made to ask how these qualities may aid in
> shedding light on certain concepts, whose inner implication for one another
> may at first not be fully recognized, because not systematically expounded.
> . . . The most revealing, if also the most neglected, poetic feature of Kierke-
> gaard's prose [is] his use of metaphor. Taking Kierkegaard's own
> communicative ideal—"the reduplication of the contents [of a presentation]
> in the form" [*Postscript* I, 333]—as a guiding clue, access will be sought to
> a leitmotiv of Kierkegaard's philosophical writings.[3]

* * *

---

[1] Louis Mackey, *Kierkegaard: A Kind of Poet* (Philadelphia: University of Pennsylvania Press, 1971) xi.

[2] Ibid., xi-xii.

[3] G. Heath King, *Existence, Thought, Style: Perspectives of a Primary Relation Portrayed through the Work of Søren Kierkegaard* (Milwaukee: Marquette University Press,
1996) 11, 14.

The present discussion contributes to the growing dialogue among critical readers of Kierkegaard regarding how lyrical and imaginative elements of his writings inform his esthetic, ethical, philosophical, and religious point of view. Although many scholars in past decades have referred to Kierkegaard's panache for the poetic to greater or lesser extents, much criticism continues merely to footnote his literary genius (how he writes) in deference to analyses of his philosophical genius (what he writes). Bypassing Kierkegaard's poetic style, however, neglects much of the essence of his writings, especially given Kierkegaard's conscious and persistent self-scrutiny throughout his journals and published writings about how (and not only what) he writes.

An author's greatness often is measured by his coupling of form and content. How the author writes informs the content of composition. This is especially true in Kierkegaard's case, given his treatment of ethics throughout his writings (overtly in his Climacus writings) that consistently asserts a similarly formulated existential premise, namely, how a human being exists is as essential as the "whatness" or purpose of that person's existence. Just as, according to Chaucer, "The wordes moote be cosyn to the dede,"[4] so too personal authenticity presupposes a likeness between words and deeds, form and content, the "how" of personal style and the "what" of the personality portrayed. Form imitates or is "cosyn to" content—indeed, form is a metaphor for content. Form thereby establishes an indirect yet concrete and more readily available path by which the meaning of content may be understood, appropriated, and internalized.

Instead of an orthodox form of didacticism, Kierkegaard ascribed to a highly stylized and personal form of indirect communication (even, primarily because of metaphor, in much of his signed religious works). For Kierkegaard, then, style and form became no less essential than content and thought. Kierkegaard perhaps may be sought more effectively along the path of style than the path of philosophical abstraction, for just as a person "essentially puts his whole personality into his communication," Kierkegaard writes, so too "an author puts his whole soul into his style."[5]

* * *

---

[4]Geoffrey Chaucer, *Chaucer's Major Poetry*, ed. Albert Baugh (Englewood Cliffs NJ: Prentice-Hall, 1963) 254 ("General Prologue," *The Canterbury Tales*, l. 742).

[5]*Two Ages*, 103.

Dialogue on Kierkegaard's metaphoric style has emerged slowly. Sub-
stantive and sensitive discussions have been published, including Louis
Mackey's *Kierkegaard: A Kind of Poet* (1971), sections from Ronald J.
Manheimer's *Kierkegaard as Educator* (1977), the introduction to
Thomas C. Oden's *Parables of Kierkegaard* (1978), David J. Gouwens's
Kierkegaard's Dialectics of the Imagination (1989), M. Jamie Ferreira's
Transforming Vision: Imagination and Will in Kierkegaardian Faith
(1991), Sylvia Walsh's *Living Poetically: Kierkegaard's Existential
Aesthetics* (1994), and G. Heath King's *Existence, Thought, Style: Per-
spectives of a Primary Relation Portrayed through the Work of Søren
Kierkegaard* (1996). This list is by no means exhaustive, although it is
representative of the breadth of the dialogue.

The Mackey and Walsh texts discuss Kierkegaard's esthetics with
attention toward his imaginative processes, of which they suggest his
metaphoric process is a part. Ferreira and Gouwens focus more sharply
on Kierkegaardian imagination than upon his esthetics in general, and a
discussion of Kierkegaard's metaphoric style becomes more substantive.
Manheimer and, to a greater extent, Oden and especially King, examine
and illuminate Kierkegaard's metaphoric style; they discuss various
aspects of metaphor that inform particular and selected metaphorical
themes or assertions about metaphor that Kierkegaard employs. (Manheimer discusses metaphor relative to Kierkegaard as an educator; Oden
presents thoughts about metaphor in the strict scope of Kierkegaard's
parables; King addresses metaphor as it applies to specific metaphorical
patterns in Kierkegaard's writings, such as "sea" and "light" metaphors.)
The present discussion is a sustained and comprehensive consideration of
metaphor in relation to Kierkegaard's entire authorship. As such, it may
be placed between the more general discussions of metaphor relative to
esthetics and imagination (Mackey, Walsh, Ferreira, and Gouwens) and
the more particular discussions of specific metaphorical constructions and
intentions of Kierkegaard (Manheimer, Oden, and King).

The above-cited critical discussions of Kierkegaard's esthetics, imagination, and metaphor (as well as strictly literary discussions focused
specifically on metaphor) have in the main helped challenge and affirm
aspects of the present discussion. I am indebted to those writings. In addition, critical literary considerations of metaphor are addressed in the
present discussion when they elucidate Kierkegaard's use of metaphor or

offer other windows from which to re-view and question various established concepts and theories of metaphor.

In Janet Soskice's *Metaphor and Religious Language*, the second chapter is entitled "Problems of Definition." In it, Soskice instinctively takes Socrates' advice in the *Phaedrus* by attempting to know and define what it is one is deliberating about before one begins deliberation, so as not to go utterly astray.[6] Soskice begins the chapter as if advancing Socrates' own sense of irony and humor toward scholastic pretense:

> Anyone who has grappled with the problem of defining metaphor will appreciate the pragmatism of those who proceed to discuss it without giving any definition of it at all. One scholar claims to have found 125 different definitions, surely only a small fraction of those which have been put forward, for not only is the subject matter elusive, but a definition of metaphor useful to one discipline often proves unsatisfactory to another.[7]

Soskice then offers a working definition:

> *metaphor is that figure of speech whereby we speak about one thing in terms which are seen to be suggestive of another.* . . . We can here briefly clarify some of our terms; "speaking" is intended to mark that metaphor is a phenomenon of language use (and not that it is oral). Similarly, "thing" signifies any object or state of affairs, and not necessarily a physical object; the moral life, the temperament of the Russian people, and the growth of the soul are all equally "things" in this sense. Finally, "seen to be suggestive" means seen so by a competent speaker of the language.[8]

There are, as Soskice notes later, virtues of elasticity in such a skeletal definition. In the case of the present discussion, Soskice's definition will be used as a point of departure. Her definition will be qualified throughout the discussion to address and focus upon Kierkegaard's own uses of and thoughts on metaphor that (1) take the form of, for example, simple metaphor, simile, and narrative or extended metaphors such as parables, fables, allegories, and satire; and (2) point to issues including

---

[6]See Plato, *The Dialogues of Plato* I, trans. B. Jowett (New York: Random House, 1937) 242 (*Phaedrus*, 237c).

[7]Janet Soskice, *Metaphor and Religious Language* (Oxford: Clarendon Press, 1985) 15.

[8]Ibid.

indirect communication and to examples of comparison and contrast, existential collision, contradiction, opposition, tension, paradox, dialectic, and reduplication. Soskice's own assertion that metaphor is strictly a figure of speech also will be reconsidered in the context of Kierkegaard's existential and religious inquiry.

The present discussion begins with an introduction maintaining that metaphor—more than abstract thought in isolation—offers what Kierkegaard calls a "truer impression" of an idea. Metaphors frame the abstract concretely, and thereby serve as hooks onto which ideas may be hung[9] and may more easily be grasped and perceived. Metaphor also helps define Kierkegaard as a poet-philosopher who, ethically, strives toward the religious.

Chapter 1 considers Kierkegaard's indirect communication (what Kierkegaard calls the *maieutic*), that is, communication about certain individual experiences and relationships that—according to Kierkegaard in an early journal entry—"cannot be expressed in words."[10] Metaphor figures centrally in such communication from the beginning of his authorship. Not only does metaphor strive to overcome inadequacies of direct communication, but Kierkegaard's multivoiced pseudonymity is structured upon metaphor. Metaphor also is used often by Kierkegaard in his polemics, satire, humor, irony, and dialectics—and for good reason: metaphor is born of relationships that often are ambiguous, contradictory, and rife with tense opposition.

Chapter 2 addresses Kierkegaard's esthetic stage of existence and his primary model of the self-deceiver: the romantic esthete. The esthete's self-deception relies largely on his intellectual admiration of the poetics of metaphor while ignoring the ethical requirement that appropriates metaphor as a guide to or a map of ethical action. The esthete thereby avoids earnest interactions or collisions with his actual self—interactions or collisions that otherwise would offer a foundation upon which the self may be made ethically concrete. Lacking earnestness, a romantic estheticism that isolates the self from ethical-religious contexts foreshortens and hides actuality; such esthetic passion is fantastical when pitted against concrete ethical-religious passion. In other words, Kierkegaard's esthete

---

[9]I am indebted to Howard Hong for this sturdy "hook" image.
[10]*Journals* I, I A 327, January 1837, 252.

becomes entangled in metaphor instead of allowing metaphor to help disentangle his life by clarifying the ethical. The discussion includes how the romantic tradition prefigures not only Kierkegaard's portrayals of Constantin Constantius and the young man in *Repetition*, but also A and Johannes the Seducer in *Either/Or* I. Finally, Kierkegaard's treatment of Danish theologian, pastor, and writer Adolph Peter Adler (1817–1869) and other less-than-earnest stewards of Christendom are considered against a similar romantic-esthetic view of metaphor.

Chapter 3 considers Kierkegaard's ethical stage and the ethicist's obligation to address conflicts or collisions of the self by disclosing both limits and possibilities of the self. The ethicist uses and analyzes metaphor to achieve a balanced relationship between the "possible" self and the "actual" self of an individual. Discussion focuses upon (1) ethical disclosure of esthetic self-deception, concealment, and denial; (2) a consideration of what conventional esthetic poetry conceals versus what ethical poetry discloses; (3) the terrifying, yet matter-of-fact task of ethics to practice what one preaches, and how metaphor points to both ethical practice and preaching; and (4) how metaphor, viewed ethically, is composed so that readers may imagine themselves within certain contexts of existence for purposes of existential appropriation. Further, ethical revelation through metaphor provides awareness of the universality of human freedom, choice, and responsibility. Ethical disclosure through use of metaphor offers foundations for the kind of existential collision that inspires spiritual upbuilding.

Chapter 4 considers Kierkegaard's religious stage. The manifestation of existential collision is enacted by the literalization of metaphor, rendering the self ultimately concrete. Discussion includes (1) an analysis of Kierkegaard's "concept" of metaphor as described at the outset of the "Second Series" of *Works of Love*; (2) how metaphor ultimately must be rejected, annulled, or revoked to embrace fully its existential significance; and (3) a consideration of examples from Kierkegaard of how the *telos* or goal of the religious self (imitation, suffering, atonement) completes itself through the revocation and literalization of metaphor.

For consistency, Kierkegaard passages incorporated in quotations borrowed from scholars who cite earlier Kierkegaard editions have been requoted from the Kierkegaard's Writings series and the Søren Kierkegaard's Journals and Papers series (unless a requoted passage substantively alters the interpretation of the cited scholar). "Aesthetics" or "æsthetics" in passages quoted from critical works has been changed to "esthetics." Finally, third-person masculine singular pronouns (he, him, his, himself) are treated in the present discussion as inclusive-language usage.

Introduction

A Truer Impression: Kierkegaard's Metaphors

A. Prologue. Two Views of One Caricature

One of many derisive caricatures of Søren Kierkegaard published in Denmark's satirical weekly *Corsair* portrays him darkly etched in silhouette against a light, celestial background.[1] He stands on thin legs atop a cloud. His hat weighs heavy upon his brow, further exacerbating the curvature of his spine. His cane appears to support him, but not as a cane usually supports, with its tip on firm ground. Rather, it is wedged fast and perpendicularly under his arm: a ramrod straight crossbeam suspending a crooked crucifix in midair.

The cartoon intended to parody both Kierkegaard and, apparently, the creation of light. Rays emanate from all sides of the author, illuminating and transferring life to orbiting celestial and worldly bodies. Those satellites include the sun and other stars, the earth, the moon, an angel, people, faces, churches, a house, other buildings, a horse, a donkey, a bird, a crown, a boot, bottles, rocks. Encompassed within its circular frame, the caricature is a ribald portrait of a self-centered artist. The unsigned article accompanying the artwork, entitled "The Great Philosopher," solicits further malicious joy at Kierkegaard's expense: "the heavens, the sun, the planets, the earth, Europe, and Copenhagen revolve around Søren Kierkegaard, who stands silent in the middle and does not once take off his hat in recognition of the honor shown to him."[2]

Kierkegaard has suggested that an individual's life constantly moves between two extremes of identity, one reflecting the ideal of that person and the other reflecting that person's caricature.[3] Just as most caricatures

---

[1]See title page, above (iii). Also see *Corsair*, Supplement, 133.

[2]*Corsair*, Supplement, 131, 133.

[3]*Letters & Documents*, 49.

(no matter how justly inspired or grossly misconceived) have a fingerhold upon some trivial truth of physical or psychological flaws, so also, according to Kierkegaard, "every artistic conception always retains something of the ideal, even in caricature."[4] Subsequently, behind the glib satirical facade of the *Corsair*'s caricature there reside profounder truths about the "essential" Kierkegaard for readers, namely, his works. Those truths, embedded in his texts, offer an alternative way to view the caricature. The "ideal" of Kierkegaard's persona as Christian ethicist is retained. Such an alternative interpretation of the *Corsair*'s caricature suggests a "happy"[5] Kierkegaard amassing a fortune of meaningful ideas by witnessing the ongoing cavalcade of physical objects and actual events from the "little world that surrounds [him]"[6] before he bequeaths that fortune en masse to readers. Instead of portraying the writer as godlike, condescendingly transmitting life's essence into objects, the caricature instead depicts the author charged by a joyful, terrifying universe. From this perspective it is not difficult to imagine the man in the silhouette vanishing from sight, becoming nothing after ultimately dis-charging his findings in print.

Kierkegaard's darkened figure in the caricature not only aptly suggests his stated hope to become nothing, but also befits the pose he intends to strike in his entire authorship. Unlike detailed portraits that prompt viewers to attend to distinctive personal features (and the personal life of the one portrayed), Kierkegaard's silhouetted figure invokes a sense of nothingness for which his personality as an author always strived. Authority from which a reader might presume the author to speak is radically diminished. Such powerfully charged negativity is intended to cast a reader's eye away from temporal concerns about the author's life and toward what Kierkegaard calls the "decisive issue"[7] of the reader's personal ethical-religious development. Kierkegaard goes to great lengths to become like a silhouette throughout his pseudonymous and signed works, to be no more solid than the cloud upon which he stands in caricature. He intends for readers to be left alone as ethically free and inde-

---

[4]*Letters & Documents*, 63.

[5]*Corsair*, 46.

[6]*Corsair*, 46. This comment from Kierkegaard became grist for the *Corsair*'s mill that resulted in the caricature.

[7]*Various Spirits*, 123.

pendent agents in order to read and then judge for themselves the veracity or falsity of his texts.

"My whole life is an epigram to make men aware," Kierkegaard writes in one journal entry.[8] With this statement, he portrays his whole life's literary output as an epigrammatic text appended to the main body of a larger text: a reader's life and self-awareness. Such figurative speech portrays his life's work as insignificant—virtually nothing, a jest, a mere "epigram"—when compared to individual human lives. Kierkegaard's comparison here is put forth not so much as rhetorical posturing by which the reader may come to see humble, self-effacing qualities of a conscientious genius living in the mid-1800s in Europe. Rather, the comparison strikes to the core of Kierkegaard's position on ethics, for it "is unconditionally true of the ethical that it cannot be taught"[9] but instead must be appropriated existentially by the learner.

Kierkegaard takes his cue from Greek philosopher Socrates' maieutic or indirect form of communication that "makes the reader or hearer himself active."[10] He maintains—through words of his pseudonymous writer Johannes Climacus—that any historical personage who also is something of a teacher has to be made "accidental, a vanishing point, an occasion"[11] by which the learner could come to know of inwardness. Similarly, pseudonymous author Anti-Climacus writes that the art of indirect communication creates a "dialectical knot" that only the hearer of the communication can unravel: "the art [further] consists in making oneself, the communicator, into a nobody . . . an absentee, an objective something, a nonperson. . . . If anyone wants to have anything to do with this kind of communication, he will have to untie the knot himself."[12] Such a Socratic teacher, according to Johannes Climacus, is nothing more than an occasion for a pupil's self-learning: "if [the teacher] gives of himself and his erudition in any other way, he does not give but takes away."[13] Kierkegaard hopes that by positioning himself negatively (inconspicuously) as an author, readers more likely would examine for themselves what it means to be human. "We shall not pursue further what has been

---

[8]*Journals*, V, VIII[1] A 549, n.d. [1848], 435.
[9]*Journals*, I, VIII[2] B 88, n.d. [1847], 301.
[10]*Journals*, IV, VII[1] A 74, n.d. [1846], 210.
[11]*Fragments*, 11.
[12]*Practice*, 133.
[13]*Fragments*, 11.

developed here," Johannes Climacus writes, quelling one of his own arguments to promote readerly self-knowledge, "but leave it up to each person to practice coming back to the idea from the most diverse sides, to practice using his imagination to uncover the strangest instances of relative differences and relative situations in order to figure it all out."[14]

The *Corsair* thus fundamentally misjudges the ethical relationship Kierkegaard establishes with his readers. But the tabloid's infractions do not end there. It also betrays its own ignorance of and unhappy admiration for Kierkegaard when it takes offense at his reluctance to "take off his hat" to be recognized publicly. In the context of a sharply focused and pointed religious idea that he served, Kierkegaard was not interested in writing to be admired, much less admired as an egotist. Rather, he wrote to help readers recognize how difficult—how glorious—it is to be human. Near the end of his heated battle with the *Corsair*, Kierkegaard writes in his journal of how he cannot understand people who become offended by his aversion to being admired:

> The only thing I wanted was to be of benefit to them. . . . Here is a young girl. Her only desire is one thing, to kneel adoringly at my feet—and the only thing I want is least of all this. I will simply say to her: Go into your room, lock your door, pray to God, and you will have infinitely much more than the paltry fragment of admiring me. —And that is why I am called an egotist.[15]

In this context, the *Corsair*'s claim that Kierkegaard "stands silent in the middle and does not once take off his hat in recognition of the honor shown to him" does not point to a self-centered arrogance on Kierkegaard's part. On the contrary, it points to a centeredness of self in the service of an idea that he believes promises a vast and transformative wonder for human beings. According to Kierkegaard, readers need only strive as individuals toward an earnestness worthy of the ethical-religious instead of passively and collectively admiring others' strivings. "With respect to a merely human prototype. . .there is no time for admiration—get busy right away at the task of imitating him," Kierkegaard writes.

[14]*Fragments*, 98. See also *Late Writings*, 279, for a similar conclusion.
[15]*Journals*, V, VII¹ A 184, n.d. [1846], 353.

"The ethical truth of the matter is just this—that admiration is suspiciously like an evasion."[16]

How does Kierkegaard ethically strive toward such a religious vanishing point in his authorship? How does he blacken or negate himself from his literary palate, suspended between heaven and earth, while simultaneously coloring the vacillating human thought-patterns he witnesses around him? How does he deliberately, repeatedly, persistently, and convincingly help his reader understand for himself what it means to be human in all its varied, tragic, joyful tones? How do the orbiting objects in the *Corsair*'s caricature—and the many thousands of other vehicles for thought and symbol that the caricature implies—better inform Kierkegaard's method and thought, and thereby better inform his readership?

By the thousands (more than ten thousand in his published and unpublished writings, and his journals and papers available in English), Kierkegaard expresses his ideas with metaphor. As unwittingly portrayed in the *Corsair*'s caricature, metaphor encircles and frames Kierkegaard's thought.

B. A Truer Impression

Before he constructs one metaphor in parable, Kierkegaard directly yet with calculated understatement explains why he uses metaphor: "My listener, I have something more I would like to say, but I shall cast it in a form that at first glance you may find not quite solemn. Yet I do it deliberately and advisedly, for I believe that precisely in this way it will make a truer impression on you."[17] Kierkegaard perceives the metaphoric style of parable as "not quite solemn" in contrast to the solemn tone of objective, systematic philosophical discourse then in vogue. This latter style shrewdly portrays truths—no matter how subjective—in such a way as to *appear* "true" in an objective, demonstrable sense, thus offering the veneer of objective authority.

Kierkegaard, however, does not believe that truth—or love or faith for that matter—could be demonstrated in any objective sense.[18] The

---

[16]*Journals*, IV, X^1 A 134, n.d. [1849], 295.

[17]*Self-Examination*, 85.

[18]See, e.g., *Irony*, 204; *Either/Or* I, 59; *Either/Or* II, 15; *Eighteen Discourses*, 27; *Fragments*, 39, 42-43, 62, 68; *Stages*, 90, 158-59; *Postscript* I, 28-30; *Works of Love*, 13-14; *Sickness*, 87, 95, 103-104, 129; *Practice*, 26ff.; *Self-Examination*, 68; *Judge for*

solemn form or style in which such demonstrations are portrayed by writers of whom Kierkegaard was critical subsequently range from presumptuous to disingenuous to pompous to hypocritical. For Kierkegaard, then, a primary problem with the style (as well as content) of systematic or direct communication is what it does *not* offer the reader. It fails to offer the reader the ability to gain a "truer impression" of an idea, given that it naturally limits, if not outright denies, the reader's subjective or existential response. In other words, direct communication distances the reader from himself by not offering opportunities for the reader to respond to objective text within the largely subjective context of individual human existence and linguistic experience. The reader, for instance, is not able to appropriate the content of the text after private deliberation. In addition, the reader is excluded from taking personal responsibility for personal choices, and from embracing joys and suffering regrets for those choices. Systematic or direct communication does not offer these kinds of opportunities because such discourse is more intent upon demonstrating truths intended to make life more understandable and hence easier for people.

Deeds and ideas that Kierkegaard would intimate by indirect communication in general and metaphor in particular are instead far more difficult to emulate than the ease that comes from following the "modern rote-method which says everything the sooner the better and all at one time, which awakens no self-action but only leads the reader to rattle [objective discourse] off like a parrot."[19] The "not quite solemn," more humorous, and irreverent tone of metaphor offers readers situations derived from daily existence from which they are encouraged to choose and judge for themselves what is and is not true. The deliberateness with which Kierkegaard advises himself to provide, via metaphor, a "truer impression" of what is and is not true and of what it means to be a human being is born from his commitment to prompt individual readers to accept the burden of deliberately and actively making their own individual choices.

Johannes Climacus surveys the world around him and finds—much like twentieth-first-century transit systems, not excluding the information highway's virtual transit system—

Yourself! 191-92, 194-96, 203; *Journals*, I, IV A 108, n.d. [1843], 4; VIII¹ A 547, n.d. [1848], 153.

[19]*Journals*, IV, VII¹ A 74, n.d. [1846], 210.

many benefactors of the age who know how to benefit mankind by making life easier and easier, some by railroads, others by omnibuses and steamships, others by telegraph, others by easily understood surveys and brief publications about everything worth knowing, and finally by the true benefactors of the age who by virtue of thought systematically make spiritual existence easier and easier and yet more and more meaningful.

Climacus then comprehends his task:

suddenly this thought crossed my mind: You must do something, but since with your limited capabilities it will be impossible to make anything easier than it has become, you must, with the same humanitarian enthusiasm as the others have, take it upon yourself to . . . make difficulties everywhere.[20]

Like all of Kierkegaard-Climacus's humor, there is a deep earnestness here that places the burden of existence squarely upon each individual by disclosing the human failure to recognize that an "easier" life exacts a deleterious price from human life. An "easier" life relaxes an individual's need to discern, discriminate, judge, and choose. An "easier" life allows a person to flee from ethical demands by fleeing from the ultimate individual responsibility of personal choice. For all its lack of solemnity and apparent irreverent humor, then, metaphorical constructions surface on almost every page of Kierkegaard's authorship as "fruitful, instructive, and suggestive"[21] agents of his indirect communication. Kierkegaard's metaphors make life more difficult for his readers—but for all that, they make life existentially richer by encouraging readers to understand more fully and become more responsible for their own lives through ethical appropriation of metaphorical meaning.

Elsewhere, the pseudonymous writer Judge William points to Kierkegaard's deeper ethical concerns regarding the less than solemn philosophical tone implicitly struck by metaphorical constructions. The judge claims to offer metaphors to make a truer existential impression, something he calls earnestness: "If what I say [in the form of metaphor] should lack stringency, then perhaps it has a little more earnestness."[22]

---

[20]*Postscript* I, 186, 187.
[21]*Works of Love*, 203.
[22]*Either/Or* II, 173.

In a similar vein, yet with greater irony and less sympathy for impatient people, Johannes Climacus introduces one parable this way:
"Suppose there was a king who loved a maiden of lowly station in life—
but the reader may already have lost patience when he hears that our
analogy begins like a fairy tale and is not at all systematic."[23] In *For Self-
Examination*, Kierkegaard shares Climacus's acerbic wit:

> Let me give [a metaphorical] example, fashioned on those old tales about
> what a person in former times had undergone in intense suffering, something
> these untried sagacious times presumably will regard as a fable that at most
> has some poetic value.[24]

There is abundant irony and jesting humor in the above passages.
They entertain the earnest reader who, living in a world of didacticism,
appreciates a meaningful kind of indirect communication to which metaphor points. They also stir and challenge the contrived voices of less-
than-earnest readers who depend upon "modern rote methods." In a
journal entry developing notes for potential lectures on communication,
Kierkegaard says that

> The right kind of earnestness (absolutely in respect to ethical communica-
> tion, and partially in respect to ethical-religious communication) . . . contains
> much . . . irony and what belongs to irony. . . . The really right kind of
> earnestness, especially as regards ethical communication, would certainly
> appear to most people to be jesting.[25]

Against systematic discourse, the more poetic and figurative speech of
metaphor (Greek: *metapherein*, to transfer, change) or metaphorical
(Danish: *overført*, carried over) speech is the memorable *impress* with
which Kierkegaard leaves readers to "transfer" or "carry over" to themselves "a truer impression" of what it means to be human.

According to Philip Wheelwright, metaphor etymologically implies
both change (*meta*) and motion (*phora*), "the reference being to semantic
motion of course, not physical."[26] However, linguistic change and motion

---

[23]*Fragments*, 26.

[24]*Self-Examination*, 78.

[25]*Journals*, I, VIII² B 88, n.d. [1847], 301.

[26]Philip Wheelwright, *Metaphor and Reality* (Bloomington: Indiana University Press, 1962) 69.

indicated by metaphor also carry metaphysical and ontological implications. Readers of metaphor internally may move or change themselves based upon a change of perception that they individually experience by appropriating a particular metaphor's meaning. Given that Kierkegaard maintains that "the most tremendous thing conceded to man is—choice, freedom,"[27] the freedom that metaphor offers individuals is not insignificant. Rather, it is a freedom to appropriate meaning into a personal context instead of to "parrot" directives manufactured through the systematic discourse of others.

Just as the motto above the stage of the Royal Theater in Copenhagen proclaims dramatic performances to be "instructive and refining, not only for entertainment,"[28] Kierkegaard's metaphors are not simply for esthetic ornamentation. They are essential to his authorship and compelling to readers seeking (1) to understand themselves as beings endowed with freedom and (2) to develop their own humanness.

> When all is said and done [writes Anti-Climacus], whatever feeling, knowing, and willing a person has depends upon what imagination he has, upon how that person reflects himself—that is, upon imagination. . . . The imagination is the possibility of any and all reflection, and the intensity of this medium is the possibility of the intensity of the self.[29]

By inviting readers to begin to imagine themselves through metaphorical constructions, Kierkegaard prompts them to think for themselves in a qualitative way, then *become* human on ethical and religious levels in the etymological sense of "existence" (*existo* [stand forth], *ex* [out] + *sto* [stand])—or, according to Howard Hong, to " 'stand out' beyond immediacy, beyond the givenness of subsistence."[30]

Metaphor also is Kierkegaard's imaginative tool of choice because it commonly and universally may be embraced and understood by everyone while simultaneously allowing for different, particular, and personal levels of interpretation. Use of metaphor is an educational, Socratic means to aid the uninitiated by coupling familiar situations with unfamiliar ideas about life. Soskice writes that metaphor "has the virtue . . . as Aquinas says, of

---

[27]*Journals*, II, X² A 428, n.d. [1850], 69.
[28]*Repetition*, 154 and n. 50.
[29]*Sickness*, 31.
[30]*Either/Or* I, Notes, 658.

being accessible to the uneducated."[31] Here Soskice offers an egalitarian rationale for metaphor to which Kierkegaard subscribes. In a broader sense of the word "uneducated," however, the sentiment that she shares with Aquinas also points to the elucidating power of metaphor for "educated" people who nonetheless are "uneducated" in personal existence—that is, those who instinctively may understand the literal-figurative relationship of metaphor but may fail to accomplish the ethical requirement, namely, to appropriate and personalize the metaphorical expression into their own lives.

There is another significant reason why metaphor is an appropriate vehicle by which human beings may come to know and define themselves. The essential elements that make up metaphor are analogous to the essential elements that make up a human being. Anti-Climacus writes:

> A human being is a synthesis of the infinite and the finite, of the temporal and the eternal, of freedom and necessity, in short, a synthesis. A synthesis is a relation between two. Considered in this way, a human being is still not a self.[32]

Similarly, simple metaphor synthesizes two dissimilar or contrasting things: a tenor, or primary subject (e.g., "imagination"), and a vehicle, or a secondary subject suggesting or illuminating particular aspects of the primary subject that otherwise may not readily be apparent (e.g., "wings"). In the simple metaphor "Imagination has wings," the tenor (imagination) is an idea, an abstraction. The vehicle (wings) denotes a particular, actual object. Although not all metaphors are so dialectically cogent, this particular form of metaphor, like a human self, is a synthesis of the abstract and the actual, of the universal and the particular. The simple metaphor that collides the abstract and the actual, fashioning the two parts into a single dynamic idea, becomes a choice tool for any existential wordsmith and dialectician, for its form and content more closely imitate the human self and human existence than systematic discourse.

In effect, metaphor offers up a situation or a story—however brief ("Imagination has wings")—about which readers are invited to inquire ("What common attributes of wings suggest the nature of imagination?"),

---

[31]Janet Soskice, *Metaphor and Religious Language* (Oxford: Clarendon Press, 1985) 24.

[32]*Sickness*, 13.

and to which they are invited to recognize and respond ("Imagination can help a person internally transcend or 'rise above' a purely physical existence"[33]). As such, metaphor makes the writer's position more familiar to the reader by the reader's own processes of inference, for "the leap of inference," Kierkegaard writes, is evident both in "induction and analogy."[34] Analogies, Johannes Climacus writes, in fact are what "awaken the mind to an understanding."[35] Further, metaphor closes any communicative gap by making the writer's position more familiar to the reader from the reader's own basis of common knowledge and without forcing the writer's position onto the reader under dubious auspices of presumed authority. Like a poet's argument, Mackey notes, Kierkegaard's metaphorically constructed arguments "cannot be taken as the ground of a merely theoretic assent. It must be imaginatively relived by the reader and, to have its full effect, must be met with a personal response, an existential 'reduplication' or an equally existential refusal."[36] This kind of "intimacy," as Ted Cohen calls metaphor's relation to the reader,[37] invites readers to examine limitations and affirm possibilities of their own personal positions. Such examination is required to reject or develop personal thoughts and thereby refine or transform personal beliefs about existence.

The "intimacy" that metaphor achieves when binding together a writer and reader's shared knowledge also extends to telling jokes, something to which Cohen also compares metaphor. Jokes, Cohen notes, require a recognition on the hearer's part that what is being said by the speaker *is* a joke.[38] Perhaps a more significant commonality between metaphors and jokes, however, is that the element of contradiction is implied in both metaphor and jokes. In metaphor, where two *dissimilar* things are compared, a logical misrelation or contradiction exists between

---

[33]In one journal entry, Kierkegaard writes: "Man, too, has wings, he has imagination, intended to help him *actually* rise aloft" (*Journals*, III, XI² A 210, n.d. [1854], 391; my emphasis).

[34]*Journals*, III, V C 7, n.d. [1844], 19.

[35]*Fragments*, 26.

[36]Louis Mackey, *Kierkegaard: A Kind of Poet* (Philadelphia: University of Pennsylvania Press, 1971) xii.

[37]See Ted Cohen, "Metaphor and the Cultivation of Intimacy," in *On Metaphor*, ed. Sheldon Sacks (Chicago: University of Chicago Press, 1979) 1-10.

[38]Ibid., 8.

tenor and vehicle. In the metaphor about imagination and wings, for instance, human imagination does not logically equate with actual wings, just as much as X does not mathematically equal Y. In a joke, a logical misrelation exists between "what is and what ought to be." (Howard Hong offers this cogent formula for laughter: laughter "arises essentially from an awareness of contradiction, opposites, basic contrasts. Laughter means discrimination, the distinction between appearance and reality, what is expected and what is, what is and what ought to be."[39]) In the joke about the man who slipped on a banana peel, the stereotypical character of a sophisticated man suggests that he is not *supposed* to slip on a banana peel. But poetic justice (that always allies itself with contradictions embedded in irony and humor) invokes laughter, especially if, prior to slipping, the man's nose is so arrogantly high in the air that he is ignorant of what is in plain view in front of him.

Similarly, a full appreciation of metaphor requires the discernment of significant differences and the awareness of contradiction, opposites, and basic contrasts. More than discursive philosophy, metaphor—especially parables, fables, and satire—allows for moral philosophizing under the auspices of normative ethics. Both jokes and metaphors intimately engage readers because readers are invited to discover in their own particular lives possible moral or ethical contradictions that mirror universal contradictions implicit in metaphors or jokes. Such discoveries are precisely occasions in which "truer impressions" occur, where recognition of contradiction initiates individuals into a deeper knowledge of others and of themselves.[40] Kierkegaard, according to Gregor Malantschuk, interprets life from the viewpoint of two contrasting principles (dualism, contradiction) instead of from the viewpoint of unity (monism), because incongruities are rife in concrete life.[41]

---

[39]Howard V. Hong, "The Comic, Satire, Irony, and Humor: Kierkegaardian Reflections," *Midwest Studies in Philosophy* 1 (1976): 99.

[40]It is no wonder, then, that Kierkegaard's two transitional stages into higher spheres of human existence (irony, between esthetic and ethical spheres of existence; and humor, between ethical and religious spheres) are based upon revelations of existential contradictions in one's life. If the contradictions are understood as contradictions and then ethically addressed, they prompt an individual to choose to appropriate higher spheres of existence, to choose to become *more* meaningfully human. See *Journals*, II, III B 19, n.d. [1840-41], 264-65.

[41]*Journals*, I, Commentary, 522.

The ethical misrelationship or contradiction one may witness between what *is* and what *ought to be* thus is borne out in many of Kierkegaard's metaphors. Such metaphors point to misrelations in the actual world and petition for an ethical or ethical-religious response. Anti-Climacus's metaphor of the basement inhabitant is one example:

> Imagine a house with a basement, first floor, and second floor planned so that there is or is supposed to be a social distinction between occupants according to floor. Now, if what it means to be a human being is compared with such a house, then all too regrettably the sad and ludicrous truth about the majority of people is that in their own house they prefer to live in the basement. Every human being is a psychical-physical synthesis intended to be spirit; this is the building, but he prefers to live in the basement, that is, in the sensate categories. Moreover, he not only prefers to live in the basement—no, he loves it so much that he is indignant if anyone suggests that he move to the superb upper floor that stands vacant and at his disposal, for he is, after all, living in his own house.[42]

Readers may be attracted to—or offended by—this metaphor because it considers how one who lacks the courage to become spirit may exist. Readers also may be attracted to—or offended by—the metaphor because it constructs a concrete image of human capability for personal upbuilding. An ethical reader is prompted to consider and act upon other, higher possibilities for his life by learning to reject a strictly sensate life when it is pitted against higher stages of life and found wanting.

In another metaphor, Anti-Climacus portrays the pathetically ludicrous nature of a sensate person unaware of himself:

> There is a story about a peasant who went barefooted to town with enough money to buy himself a pair of stockings and shoes and to get drunk, and in trying to find his way home in his drunken state, he fell asleep in the middle of the road. A carriage came along, and the driver shouted to him to move or he would drive over his legs. The drunken peasant woke up, looked at his legs and, not recognizing them because of the shoes and stockings, said: "Go ahead, they are not my legs."[43]

Readers again may be attracted to—or offended by—this parable by its comic representation of a person lacking fundamental self-knowledge.

---

[42]*Sickness*, 43.
[43]*Sickness*, 53.

They also may be attracted to—or offended by—the very tragedy and pathos of the universality of human ignorance. The parable represents a contradiction from which all individuals to some degree suffer. (As Howard Hong notes, Kierkegaard's humor "is not the funny, the comic, but is the sadly benevolent recognition of difference in sameness, sameness in difference, born of radically penetrating insight into temporal actuality in the context of the eternal."[44]) Difficult as it may be to stare directly at ourselves in a moral context, it is just as difficult not to stare at what may be a likeness of ourselves that portrays sad and desperate efforts to make sense of contradictions.

Metaphor thus is capable of intimately attracting or drawing, as if by gravitational pull or magnetic force, the reader closer to issues to which the author points. "The speaker [of a metaphor] has performed a task by yoking what the hearer has not yoked before," Wayne Booth suggests, "and the hearer simply cannot resist joining him; they thus perform an identical dance step."[45]

Nonetheless, a dual intent of Kierkegaard's metaphors is in another sense the opposite, namely, to distance readers from the author so that they assume responsibility for their own actions after rejecting or appropriating such knowledge. Johannes Climacus, referring to the subtitle of *Repetition* ("An Imaginary Psychological Construction") comments upon such distance between author and reader. Metaphor's innate indirect communication, he suggests, offers individuals settings to which they personally may respond and upon which they may act:

> By taking place in the form of an imaginary construction, the communication creates for itself an opposition, and the imaginary construction establishes a chasmic gap between reader and author and fixes the separation of inwardness between them, so that direct understanding is made impossible. The imaginary construction is the conscious, teasing revocation of the communication, which is always of importance to an existing person who writes for existing persons, lest the relation be changed to that of a rote reciter who writes for rote reciters.[46]

---

[44]*Journals*, VI, Notes, 591.

[45]Wayne C. Booth, "Metaphor as Rhetoric: The Problem of Evaluation," in *On Metaphor*, ed. Sheldon Sacks (Chicago: University of Chicago Press, 1979) 52.

[46]*Postscript* I, 263-64.

Climacus then uses an analogy to support this position:

> If a man were to stand on one leg or, in a droll dancing posture, swing his
> hat, and in this pose recite something true, his few listeners would fall into
> two classes, and he would not have many, since most of them would
> probably abandon him. The one class would say: How can what he says be
> true when he gesticulates that way? The other class would say: Well, it
> makes no difference whether he performs an entrechat or stands on his head
> or turns somersaults; what he says is true, and I will appropriate it and let
> him go.
>
> So it is with the imaginary construction. If what is said is earnestness
> to the writer, he keeps the earnestness essentially to himself. If the recipient
> interprets it as earnestness, he does it essentially by himself, and precisely
> this is the earnestness.[47]

In this way, Kierkegaard's literary voice strives to disappear in
metaphor by imaginatively constructing situations to which anyone may
approach or resist on their own terms and without overt, direct interpretation by the originator. This particular form of indirect method ultimately
leaves the reader—and the author—to contend freely with issues invoked
by metaphor. Kierkegaard writes:

> The words of John the Baptizer, "I am a voice" [Matt. 3:3, Mark 1:3], could
> be applied to my work as an author. To prevent any mistaken identity and
> being taken for the extraordinary, I always withdraw myself, and the voice,
> that is, what I say, remains. But I always withdraw myself in such a way
> that I do own up to [my own] striving [toward the religious]. Thus I am like
> a voice, but I always have one more auditor than speakers generally have:
> myself.[48]

Much to the *Corsair*'s chagrin, then, Kierkegaard does not take off
his hat in the previously discussed caricature because worldly recognition
is not his goal. Rather, his ultimate goal as an author is to vanish so that
both reader and author may come to terms with their own selves. Metaphor, as an Achilles-like shield in his arsenal of indirect communication,
is a substantive means to that goal. Such poetic laissez-faire, however, is
not necessarily the goal of all writers of metaphor. Nevertheless, few

---

[47]*Postscript* I, 264.
[48]*Journals*, VI, X^2 A 281, n.d. [1849], 268.

writers deliberately and self-advisedly invest more energy into and make more demands upon both their subject matter and their readership than Kierkegaard. He makes the investment because his main subject *is* his reader.

C. Framing the Abstract in Concrete Terms

As philosopher, Kierkegaard appreciates the significance of the world of ideas, that scholarly landscape of abstraction and ideality. As an existential dialectician, however, he—like Socrates with his ideas—demands that those ideas "become visible through the immediately concrete" for readers to appropriate them more readily.[49] Metaphors make his ideas visibly concrete everywhere and permeate all fundamental stages of human life depicted in his thought: the esthetic stage (an existence of sensate immediacy standing prior to choice), the ethical stage (an existence of deliberate choice, resolve, responsibility), and the religious stage (an existence of joyful grace amid profound spiritual suffering). A primary reason for Kierkegaard's poetic style, according to David Swenson, is Kierkegaard's poetic visualization:

> His thinking is not only sharply defined as is that of few philosophers in the history of thought, but it is at the same time present in the situation, concrete, and poetically imaginative. He possesses as much imagination as he possesses dialectic, and as much dialectic as imagination. In this respect we have to go back to Plato to find a genius which parallels his.[50]

Even Kierkegaard's pseudonym Judge William, the ethical pragmatist, is as poetically equipped to take off on esthetic flights of the imagination and metaphor as any other esthetic, ethical, or religious pseudonym in Kierkegaard's authorship. And although the judge hates "all imaginary constructing,"[51] he nonetheless "is not an unwilling participant in little

---

[49]*Irony*, 267. Henry David Thoreau makes a similar claim, but even more quickly to the point: "All perception of truth is the detection of an analogy; we reason from our hands to our head" (Henry David Thoreau, *The Journal of Henry David Thoreau* II, ed. Bradford Torrey and Francis H. Allen (Salt Lake City: Gibbs M. Smith, Inc., 1984) 463 (5 September 1851).

[50]David Swenson, *Something about Kierkegaard*, rev. and enl. ed. (Minneapolis: Augsburg Publishing House, 1945) 27-28.

[51]*Either/Or* II, 123.

imaginary constructions"[52]—especially when the metaphor points to strict ethical and ethical-religious jurisprudence. The quantity of metaphors Judge William deliberately constructs demonstrates his willingness to participate in metaphoric style, for he arguably develops as many metaphors in *Either/Or* II as Kierkegaard's pseudonymous writer and poetic esthete, A, constructs in *Either/Or* I (not to mention the scores of metaphors he constructs in his "Reflections on Marriage" in *Stages on Life's Way*). When Judge William offers reasons for his broad use of metaphor, he reflects Kierkegaard's own general reasoning of how best to philosophize: "Abstraction is ideality's first expression, but concretion is its essential expression."[53]

Just as the concrete self is the essential expression of the ideal self, metaphors (insofar as they render abstractions linguistically concrete) are "essential" expressions for all of Kierkegaard's thoughts on ideality. Those concrete images, in turn, invoke the abstractions from which they were inspired, thus *re*calling and guiding the reader back into Kierkegaard's more abstract syntax of ideality. Kierkegaard's metaphoric method surfaces in one journal entry: "as a poet and philosopher, I have presented everything in the medium of imagination."[54]

One of Kierkegaard's metaphors is particularly applicable to such method. Just as one who rows a boat turns his back to the goal toward which he is working—for otherwise he could not row well[55]— so too a reader of metaphor arrives at the metaphor's conceptual destination (tenor) not by looking directly and objectively at an abstract formulation of the idea but rather by plying through personal knowledge with oars of imagination to experience subjectively the concrete formulation of the idea (vehicle). By dint of metaphorical construction, the concrete form of the vehicle mimics the abstract idea. Simply understanding the abstract expression does not reflect the total value of the boat ride. Life itself is played out in the plying away and the ongoing appropriation of existential meaning, just as a life with a *telos* (a goal or purpose) charges the "plying away" with meaning.

---

[52]*Either/Or* II, 105.
[53]*Stages*, 114.
[54]*Journals*, V, VIII^1 A 650, n.d. [1848], 447.
[55]See *Christian Discourses*, 73-74.

The Western cultural tradition often teaches, as Roger Shattuck asserts, that one must deal with *ideas* as the highest form of knowledge. But Kierkegaard's interest in individual spirit demands something that metaphor, especially narrative metaphor, offers. Shattuck notes that

> the process of abstraction by which we form ideas out of observed experi-
> ence eliminates two essential aspects of life that I am unwilling to relin-
> quish: time and individual people acting as agents. At their purest, ideas are
> disembodied and timeless. We need ideas to reason logically and to explore
> the fog of uncertainty that surrounds the immediate encounter with everyday
> living. Equally, we need stories to embody the medium of time in which
> human character takes shape and reveals itself to us, and in which we
> discover our own mortality.[56]

Kierkegaard's metaphors implicate readers in time and recruit readers as agents of their own human freedom. His imaginative constructions are vignettes about the reader and mirrors of the reader's human nature. To objectify the stories too overtly betrays the very nature of the subjective single individual for whom Kierkegaard wrote. It seems natural for readers to defend themselves from themselves with abstractions when envisioning the terrifying gap that metaphor cuts between what *is* and what *ought to be*. But the attention Kierkegaard pays to his metaphorical constructions—attention that prompts readers to draw moral comparisons to themselves by seeing themselves in the metaphor—also may tend to help mitigate that gap, between readers' actual and potential selves, between readers' egotistical, selfish selves and the better angels of their ethical selves. "Soon you realize," Thomas Oden writes of Kierkegaard's parables, "that it is not you who are interpreting the parable but the parable that is interpreting you."[57] Readers close the book and return to existence, consciously choosing or not choosing to take the hint and attend both to possibilities that metaphor discloses for them and to limita-tions to which abstract thinking necessarily is shackled.

Here again, intimacy is essential in Kierkegaard's metaphors—in this case, an intimacy of commonly shared esthetic sensations. "What Aristotle saw as the merit of metaphor," King maintains, was a means by

---

[56]Roger Shattuck, *Forbidden Knowledge* (New York: St. Martin's Press, 1996) 9.

[57]Thomas C. Oden, *Parables of Kierkegaard* (Princeton NJ: Princeton University Press, 1978) ix.

which "to transport the reader into the condition of immediate sensa-tion."[58] Similarly, Kierkegaard's metaphors constitute challenging points of departure into a reader's ethical and religious self by way of the immediate senses and life of the reader. The esthetic not only is an effec-tive avenue through which the ethical and religious may be illuminated, but also is a legitimate avenue—if navigated with the care of a dialec-tician-ethicist like Kierkegaard. Esthetic immediacy, John R. Donahue writes, plays a significant role both in metaphor and the religious:

> Metaphor is especially suited to express two necessary qualities of religious experience: immediacy and transcendence. A religious experience—the sense of awe in the face of the holy or of being grasped by mystery—is always immediate and individual, and in the great religious literature of human history it is expressed in physical and sensuous imagery. At the same time, religious experience involves a sense of being drawn out of oneself to the transcendental and confesses the limits of language to express the experi-ence. Jesus thus spoke a language of the familiar and concrete which touched people in their everyday lives but which pointed beyond itself and summoned people to see everyday life as the carrier of self-transcendence.[59]

As a religious poet, Kierkegaard constructs his metaphors with similar intent, illuminating the extraordinary within the context of daily, ordinary human existence.

Johannes Climacus addresses the significance of such concretization in human becoming while highlighting the abstract thinker's limitations. Without the concrete, the abstract thinker cheats himself out of confront-ing contradictions inherent in being human. As he hypothesizes the genesis of the "absentminded professor," Climacus indirectly advocates metaphorical usage to usher the abstract thinker into the concrete:

> In the language of abstraction, that which is the difficulty of existence and of the existing person never actually appears; even less is the difficulty explained. Precisely because abstract thinking is *sub specie aeterni* [under the aspect of eternity], it disregards the concrete, the temporal, the becoming of existence, and the difficult situation of the existing person because of his

---

[58]G. Heath King, *Existence, Thought, Style: Perspectives of a Primary Relation Portrayed through the Work of Søren Kierkegaard* (Milwaukee: Marquette University Press, 1996) 26. King cites Aristotle, *Rhetoric* 3.10.
[59]John R. Donahue, *The Gospel in Parable* (Philadelphia: Fortress Press, 1988) 9-10.

being composed of the eternal and the temporal situated in existence. If abstract thinking is assumed to be the highest, it follows that scientific scholarship and thinkers proudly abandon existence and leave the rest of us to put up with the worst. Yes, something follows from this also for the abstract thinker himself—namely, that in one way or another he must be absentminded, since he, too, is an existing person.[60]

Climacus identifies the task of the subjective, existing individual as having the opposite task of the abstract thinker. The main focus of metaphor thus shifts from an individual desiring *only* intellectually to understand the idea or tenor to an individual striving to appropriate the pathos of the existential activity as portrayed by the vehicle:

Instead of having the task of understanding the concrete abstractly, as abstract thinking has, the subjective thinker has the opposite task of understanding the abstract concretely. Abstract thinking turns from concrete human beings to humankind in general; the subjective thinker understands the abstract concept to be the concrete human being, to be this individual existing human being. . . . Existential pathos results from the transforming relation of the idea to the individual's existence.[61]

It is no wonder, then, that Kierkegaard so prolifically uses metaphor as a primary communicative means by which he rows toward tenors of his esthetic, ethical, social, individual, psychological, philosophical, and religious thought. He takes advantage of the light, ironic, humorous, jesting, or seemingly "not quite solemn" elasticity of metaphor to tug readers confidently into deep, heavy, and earnest currents of his philosophic patterns of thought and readers' own existences. His hope is that those earnest ideas ultimately may buoy up, lighten, and enlighten readers, all to prepare readers for the task of becoming human.

Kierkegaard's metaphors thus require the author's insistence on authorial distance after knowledge is intimately transmitted through metaphor. His metaphors package unique thought in common images. They also exemplify Kierkegaard's passion for the personal, the particular, the individual within the context of day-to-day actuality, for "in and with the dailiness begins the religious."[62]

---

[60]*Postscript* I, 301.
[61]*Postscript* I, 352, 387.
[62]*Journals*, VI, IX A 471, n.d. [1848], 79.

Nothing in Kierkegaard's liberal field of perception is thus trivial or extraneous. Mackey notes that, when apprehended by a reader, any object in Kierkegaard's figural writing may function as a possibility both as a term of knowing and as a challenge to action.[63] Thus, any object of the physical or the actual that he could see or imagine—a bird, an alehouse keeper, a royal coachman, peat—points through metaphor to the overwhelming question that Kierkegaard repeatedly, albeit indirectly, demands his readers to ask: What does it mean to be a human being on the stage of time and finitude, with the infinite backdrop of eternity over one's shoulder? In this context, what Albert Hofstadter says of Martin Heidegger may also be said about Kierkegaard and the latter's influence on the former:

> In order to say what he must say, reporting what he sees, relaying what he hears, the author has to speak of the gods, mortals, the earth, shoes, the temple, the sky, the bridge, the jug, the fourfold, the poem, pain, the threshold, the difference, and stillness as he does. In truth, this is not philosophy; it is not abstract theorizing about the problems of knowledge, value, or reality; it is the most concrete thinking and speaking about Being, the differing being of different beings and the onefoldness of their identity in and with all their differences; and it is one with the being of the thinker and speaker, himself.[64]

What Kierkegaard claims Socrates to have understood also applies to Kierkegaard: "every single thing was a metaphorical and not inappropriate symbol of the idea."[65] Metaphor may even introduce the possibility of seeing God. Johannes Climacus writes:

> Nature, the totality of creation, is God's work, and yet God is not there, but within the individual human being there is a possibility (he is spirit according to his possibility) that in inwardness is awakened to a God-relationship, and then it is possible to see God everywhere.[66]

---

[63]Mackey, *Kierkegaard: A Kind of Poet*, 285.

[64]Albert Hofstadter, introduction to Martin Heidegger, *Poetry, Language, Thought*, trans. Albert Hofstadter (New York: Harper & Row, 1971) xi.

[65]*Irony*, 18. Gregor Malantschuk nevertheless makes an important note: "According to Kierkegaard's view Plato did not go beyond the stages of metaphorical and abstract thought" (*Journals*, II, Commentary, 613).

[66]*Postscript* I, 246-47.

Later in the *Postscript*, Climacus qualifies his assertion about "seeing God" by distinguishing between two distinct religious views:

> The religious person . . . joins the conception of God together with everything and sees the contradiction [that is, sees the finite and the infinite simultaneously], but in his innermost being he relates himself to God, whereas immediate religiousness rests in the pious superstition of seeing God directly in everything.[67]

Of his own ability to see *metaphors* anywhere, Kierkegaard nevertheless writes that

> it is easy to find partially or totally analogous situations on a small scale in everyday life, and that the situations are smaller, not in any valid sense crucial, not world-historical, not historic, makes no essential difference; an arithmetic problem is the same whether it involves millions or pennies.[68]

This sentiment of course is heartfelt by many writers and poets who, for the most part, consciously employ metaphor, but as Oden notes:

> No writer in [the Western tradition] has made more persistent use of parables, stories, and narrative metaphors than has Søren Kierkegaard . . . [who] ranks among the best of the great parabolists of the Western tradition.[69]

No single writer also has made more persistent use of metaphor in the service of the religious.

D. The Poet-Philosopher

More important than the quantity of Kierkegaard's metaphors is the quality of his metaphorical usage, which is measured by the integrity of dialectical tension between tenor and vehicle. In the case of many of Kierkegaard's metaphors, situations from two existence-spheres—for example, esthetic/ethical, esthetic/religious, and ethical/religious spheres— are dialectically pitted against each other. Metaphor that suspends the reader between tenor and vehicle with such tension also encourages the

---

[67]*Postscript* I, 505.
[68]*Eighteen Discourses*, 281.
[69]Oden, *Parables of Kierkegaard*, vii.

reader to allow the tenor to nourish an understanding of the vehicle and vice versa. The image is not unlike what Mark Taylor writes of translation, in which host and parasite "are bound in a symbiotic relationship which is mutually nourishing. The host feeds the parasite which, in turn, renews the life of the host. . . . Through translated representation, the parasite enlivens the host."[70] Given a communicative need for abstractions to be translated into concrete forms to be effective, expressions of a wide and varied constellation of ideas required not only the head of a philosopher but the pen of a poet.

Kierkegaard's literary task, then, was to adopt and refine the means of translation that would distill or ground abstract ideas into a form more easily embraced by readers. The task means to achieve such an end without losing in translation the tense dialectical essence of any given idea. Metaphor is Kierkegaard's primary translator in his indirect communication, for the ethicist's metaphor is obliged to see both the tenor of a philosophical idea (original or host) and the vehicle of an image derived from actuality (derivative or parasite). As ethicist-philosopher, Kierkegaard constructs ethical counterweights to offset purely esthetic conceptions of metaphor. He is neither solely poet—what G. K. Chesterton calls a lover of the finite—nor solely philosopher—what Chesterton calls a lover of the infinite.[71] Rather, Kierkegaard is both. His deep sympathetic love and passion for the finite and the actual is demonstrated repeatedly by his metaphorical constructions. His poetical talent, however, extends beyond estheticism and remains a caring partner and translator of the philosopher-theologian's love for the infinite and the religious. In one journal entry, Kierkegaard's definition of himself as an *ethical-religious* poet incorporates not only the philosopher-theologian's love of the infinite but also the finite actions of a human being who is the true existential participant of the poem: "This poet loves the ideal; he differs from the usual [esthetic] poet to the extent that he is ethically

---

[70]Mark Taylor, "Reinventing Kierkegaard," *Religious Studies Review* 7/3 (July 1981): 203-204. "Translation" is a fitting analogue here, given its relationship, at least in German, to the very word "metaphor." Paul de Man notes that the word "translate" is *übersetzen* in German, which itself translates the Greek *meta phorein* or "metaphor." Paul De Man, "The Epistemology of Metaphor," in *On Metaphor*, ed. Sheldon Sacks (Chicago: University of Chicago Press, 1979) 15.

[71]G. K. Chesterton, *The Man Who Was Thursday* (London: Penguin, 1986) 176.

aware that the task is not to poetize the ideal but to be like it."[72] Mackey elucidates the symbiotic relationship between poetry and philosophy that informs Kierkegaard's own love, a love that does not deny the powerful presence either of things or of ideas:

> Both poetry and philosophy use signs to embody and communicate meaning. The difference between poetry and philosophy is a function of the duality that is latent in every sign. Every sign has two dimensions: it is both a thing (*res*) itself and a significance (*signum*); as thing it reposes ontologically in itself, as significance it points beyond itself to its referent. Philosophy strives toward pure *theoria*, and so stresses the significance of its signs. Poetry aims at pure *poiesis*, and so looks upon the sign chiefly as thing. Yet neither poetry nor philosophy can afford to neglect the other dimension.[73]

Nor does Kierkegaard ethically neglect either poetry or philosophy, just as the maker of a good metaphor does not neglect the oppositional roles of tenor and vehicle that create the necessary tension or collision for the metaphor to engage. Such a tension signifies, according to Ronald J. Manheimer, "a border region" for Kierkegaard "where fact and value meet. . . . Kierkegaard finds in metaphor language's capacity to transfer speakers and listeners to a threshold of meaning."[74]

What Kierkegaard says of Socrates *qua* ironist—that he "is lighter than the world, but on the other hand he still belongs to the world; like Mohammed's coffin, he is suspended between two magnets"[75]—could also be said of Kierkegaard as poet-philosopher. He exists in suspension between the finitude of actuality and the infinitude of ideality. He knows that to weigh in too heavily on one side or the other would render his authorship undialectical, one-sided, disingenuous. Anti-Climacus writes:

> To become oneself is to become concrete. But to become concrete is neither to become finite nor to become infinite, for that which is to become concrete is indeed a synthesis. Consequently, the progress of the becoming must be

---

[72]*Journals*, VI, X³ A 152, n.d. [1850], 324.

[73]Mackey, *Kierkegaard: A Kind of Poet*, 267.

[74]Ronald J. Manheimer, *Kierkegaard as Educator* (Berkeley: University of California Press, 1977) 196.

[75]*Irony*, 152.

an infinite moving away from itself in the infinitizing of the self, and an infinite coming back to itself in the finitizing process.[76]

Dialectics implicit in metaphor comprise a synthesis of tenor and vehicle, of idea and image, of the universal and the particular. Similarly, according to Kierkegaard's pseudonymous writer Anti-Climacus, the dialectical makeup of a human being "is a synthesis of the finite and the infinite, of the temporal and the eternal, of freedom and necessity."[77] Such dialectics must be sustained for the sake of the tension that legitimately transfers the onus of existential choice onto individual readers. Greatest existential action is derived from addressing tense contradictions of existence resulting from the greatest sustained balance of opposites. Kierkegaard knows this and, like other religious poets such as Chaucer and Milton, he has sympathies for and critical reservations about both esthetic and religious forms of discourse. Subsequently, he is capable of envisioning the most extreme instances of contradiction and collision.

---

[76]*Sickness*, 30.
[77]*Sickness*, 13. See p. 10 of the present discussion.

Chapter 1

DECEIVING INTO THE TRUTH:
METAPHOR AND INDIRECT COMMUNICATION
(THE MAIEUTIC)

A. Kierkegaard's Early Thoughts on Metaphor

Through the use of metaphor Kierkegaard asserts, attacks, displays, exemplifies, compares, contrasts, persuades, invites, teases, jokes, appeals, satirizes, critiques, upbuilds—and by doing so, he prompts his reader to participate in the religious inquiry to which his metaphors point. Nonetheless, Kierkegaard often warns against the deceptive attraction of maieutic or indirect communication to which metaphor subscribes. He thus persistently strives in his authorship to admonish readers to judge the subject matter for themselves, lest readers come to admire the author solely for his poetic wit or dialectical intelligence instead of actively appropriating thoughts of his texts into their own lives—or rejecting them. "Have I . . . the right to use my art in order to win over a person, is it not still a mode of deception?" Kierkegaard asks in one journal entry. "When he sees me moved, inspired, etc., he accepts my view, consequently for a reason entirely different from mine, and an unsound reason."[1]

Kierkegaard's repeated claim across his authorship that he writes "without authority"[2] is in keeping with his need to let readers judge for

---

[1] *Journals*, I, V A 47, n.d. [1844], 253.

[2] Howard Hong writes in *Without Authority* (Historical Introduction, ix) that Kierkegaard "saw himself as one who 'has something of a poet in his nature, in other respects is a thinker, but—yes, how often I have repeated this, to me so important and crucial, my first statement about myself—*without authority*' (*Papirer*, IX B 10)." Hong then notes numerous other references to Kierkegaard's use of the phrase, including *Eighteen Discourses*, 5, 53, 107, 179, 231, 295; *Without Authority*, 99, 165; Supplement to *Without Authority*, 216, 226-27, 235 (*Papirer*, IX B 22, n.d. [1848]; VIII² B 9:17, n.d. [1847]; X¹ A 328, n.d. [1849]); *Self-Examination*, 3; *Point of View*, 6, 12, 15, 78, 87, 118; *Journals*,

themselves. Write what he will or how he will, Kierkegaard's implied covenant with the reader is one that protects the reader's freedom to think and choose for himself, wholly independent of other individuals, while at the same instant wholly *dependent* (in a religious context) upon God as the genesis of human freedom. Any attempt on Kierkegaard's part to control or make decisions for the reader would invalidate his entire authorship. Rather, his task is to prompt by simply presenting his metaphors before withdrawing from the reader to allow the reader to accept or reject the message of the metaphor.[3] Although Kierkegaard seeks "to breathe some interiority into" individuals, he leaves it up "to each one whether he will use it."[4] This is the limit of Kierkegaard's intentions as an author.

Aware of the risks involved in any form of indirect communication— risks that may offend a reader or turn a reader against the author—Kierkegaard nonetheless asserts an ethical claim to use such a form:

> Compel a person to an opinion, a conviction, a belief—in all eternity, that I cannot do. But one thing I can do, in one sense the first thing (since it is the condition for the next thing: to accept this view, conviction, belief), in another sense the last thing if he refuses the next: I can compel him to be aware.
>
> That this is a good deed, there is no doubt, but neither must it be forgotten that this is a daring venture. By compelling him to become aware, I succeed in compelling him to judge. Now he judges. But what he judges is not in my power. Perhaps he judges the very opposite of what I desire. Furthermore, that he was compelled to judge perhaps makes him infuriated, ragingly infuriated—infuriated with the cause, with me—and perhaps I become the victim of my daring venture.[5]

II, X^2 A 159, n.d. [1849], 65-67; VI, IX A 189, n.d. [1848], 36; X^2 A 375, n.d. [1850], 281-82.

[3]The ethical act of withdrawal from potentially influencing another's decision-making capabilities is critical for Kierkegaard, who maintains, as noted earlier, that "the most tremendous thing conceded to man is—choice, freedom" (*Journals*, II, X^2 A 428, n.d. [1850], 69). The author's act of withdrawal also mimics—albeit imperfectly, as Kierkegaard would be quick to add—God's withdrawal that, according to Kierkegaard, constitutes human freedom. See especially *Journals*, II, VII^1 A 181, n.d. [1846], 62-63. See also *Irony*, 189-90; *Fragments*, 42-43; *Stages*, 144; *Various Spirits*, 29, 30; and *Journals*, I, X^5 A 22, n.d. [1852], 100 and X^4 A 473, n.d. [1852], 105.

[4]*Journals*, VI, X^2 A 375, n.d. [1850], 282.

[5]*Point of View*, 50.

Kierkegaard suggests here that using methods of indirect communication such as metaphor bears potential rhetorical risks that he is willing to take under certain ethical imperatives—risks that he was willing to take ever since he began thinking of writing as a way of life.

In a journal entry written during his early twenties, at the outset of his writing career, Kierkegaard already intimates both the practical and ethical influence metaphor will have on his entire authorship: "There could be some very interesting investigations of the various uses of metaphor in various languages and at various levels of development."[6] Donald Davidson maintains that what distinguishes metaphor is not meaning but use,[7] and in the journal entry above, the first aspect that Kierkegaard understands about metaphor is that it is a tool to be used as means to an end that, for him, is to be found beyond mere esthetic-poetic appreciation. Metaphor, in other words, has various uses in various languages and at various stages of development. Specifically, Kierkegaard's metaphors have different uses and meanings in the context of different languages (e.g., religious versus secular) and in the context of various stages of development (e.g., esthetic, ethical, and religious). Although Kierkegaard never overtly, directly, or objectively investigates metaphorical usage (with the exception of his brief discussion of metaphorical speech in religious language at the outset of the "Second Series" of *Works of Love*), his conscious and prolific use of metaphor in various languages and at various stages of development *indirectly* investigates, scrutinizes, and conceptualizes itself. Both the meaning of metaphor and the purpose of his use of metaphor eventually are made manifest by Kierkegaard's collective use of metaphor throughout his authorship.

Even in the first entry of his monolithic journal, twenty-year-old Kierkegaard not only intimates that a concept of metaphorical usage

---

[6]*Journals*, III, I A 251, n.d. [1836], 3.

[7]Donald Davidson, "What Metaphor Means," in *On Metaphor*, ed. Sheldon Sacks (Chicago: University of Chicago Press, 1979) 41. Davidson argues that metaphor belongs exclusively to the domain of use, and not to meaning. As a rhetorical device for existential, ontological and theological discourse, metaphor indeed has its uses, although such discourses also would be hard-pressed to exclude metaphor, as indicated by Davidson, from meaning. See, e.g., Janet Soskice, *Metaphor and Religious Language* (Oxford: Clarendon Press, 1985) 28.

generates understanding and knowledge, he also portrays that concept metaphorically:

> In order to see one light determinately we always need another light. For if we imagined ourselves in total darkness and then a single spot of light appeared, we would be unable to determine what it is, since we cannot determine spatial proportions in darkness. Only when there is another light is it possible to determine the position of the first in relation to the other.[8]

What Kierkegaard states here about the very nature of acquiring knowledge implicates metaphor as a substantive tool to acquire that knowledge. The vehicle of a metaphor illuminates its tenor, just as one light is determinately envisioned by another. The suggestion of light in relationship with knowledge illuminates knowledge in a way that previously may not have been understood. Determination of meaning is rendered by comparison and contrast or, in the case of comparisons and contrasts constructed with the aid of the imagination, determination of meaning is rendered in large part by metaphor.

Young Kierkegaard's predilection for and scrutiny of the metaphoric is suggested again as he deliberates in a letter to his sister Petrea's brother-in-law, natural scientist Peter Wilhelm Lund, about the course of his interests and his eventual life's work:

> Naturally every man desires to be active in the world according to his own aptitudes, but this again means that he wishes to develop his aptitudes in a particular direction, namely, in the direction best suited to his individuality. But which direction is that? Here I stand before a big question mark. Here I stand like Hercules, but not at the crossroads—no, here there are a good many more roads to take and thus it is much more difficult to choose the right one. It is perhaps my misfortune that I am interested in far too much and not decisively in any one thing; my interests are not subordinated to one but instead all stand coordinate.[9]

Given the path of authorship that he ultimately chooses for himself, Kierkegaard advances his interests in many other fields by using the knowledge he has gained from those fields to construct metaphors that elucidate points he makes in his authorship. In effect, the ethical master

---

[8]*Journals*, II, I A 1, April 15, 1834, 518.
[9]*Journals*, V, I A 72, June 1, 1835, 21. See also *Letters & Documents*, 43-44.

of "either/or" ironically (but not unethically) chooses all his interests by becoming a metaphorist, for such a profession obliges him to invest time at least attending to his other interests for the sake of constructing durable metaphors that depict his primary interest. In addition, he gains both knowledge about and sympathy for the multifariousness of life and what life offers every human being. His choice not only makes him become a better writer of the human condition in all its diversity and sameness, but helps him strive to become what he ultimately identifies as a religious personality. In the *Point of View*, Kierkegaard discusses his younger years that led to him becoming both religious author and, along the way, a penitent:

> I had to become and did become an observer, as an observer and as spirit was extraordinarily enriched with experiences by this life, came to see very close at hand that epitome of desires, passions, moods, feelings, etc., and had practice in entering into and coming out of a person and also in imitating him. My imagination and my dialectic continually had plenty of material to work on and plenty of time, free of all activity, to be idle. For long periods I have done nothing but practice dialectical exercises with an admixture of imagination, testing my mind and spirit as one tunes an instrument—but *I* was not really living. . . . Instead of having been young, I became a poet, which is youth a second time. I became a poet, but with my religiously oriented background, indeed, with my definite religiousness, the same fact became for me a religious awakening also.[10]

Satisfying all of his interests through his construction of metaphors in the service of the religious, Kierkegaard understandably chooses "both-and": both a religious disposition and an esthetic style as metaphorist. Through his poetic talents, his use of metaphor, and his pseudonymous authorship, he recruits his wide range of interests in the same way Shakespeare recruits his interests—all in the service of a single occupation and, in Kierkegaard's case, a single idea: the religious.[11] Like Shakespeare,

---

[10] *Point of View*, 82, 84.

[11] "In the hour of my death I shall repeat again and again, if possible, what every word in my writings testifies to: . . . I have been convinced that my striving has served to illuminate what Christianity is" (*Journals*, II, X¹ A 646, n.d. [1849], 283). Elsewhere, Kierkegaard writes: "Just as one versed in natural science promptly knows from the crisscrossing threads in a web the ingenious little creature whose web it is, so an insightful person will also know that to this authorship there corresponds as the source someone who *qua* author

Kierkegaard did not need to know a lot about everything; he simply needed to know a lot about his craft, and then something about a lot of things, activities, relationships, and occupations. Then, through his craft, he describes the essence of each thing, activity, relationship or occupation with *seeming* expertise—which is precisely the point of confluence of Shakespeare's and Kierkegaard's genius: they both were penetratingly observant citizens of the world who also understood and were prolific users of metaphor. (What nonetheless distinguishes Kierkegaard from Shakespeare is that Shakespeare, according to Anti-Climacus, never addresses the religious sphere, although Shakespeare's depiction of the human, worldly, esthetic, and ethical spheres are, Anti-Climacus notes, of the highest order: "But even Shakespeare seems to have recoiled from essentially religious collisions. Indeed, perhaps these can be expressed only in the language of the gods. And no human being can speak this language. As a Greek has already said so beautifully: From men, man learns to speak, from the gods, to be silent."[12])

Even at age 21, Kierkegaard already has made sense of properly combining all of his interests into a seamless whole through figurative styles in which metaphor comes to play a significant role (the figurative style of metaphor comparable to "sauce" in the following journal entry):

> The difference between an author who picks up his material everywhere but does not work it up into an organic whole and one who does that is, it seems to me, like the difference between mock turtle and real turtle. The meat from some parts of the real turtle tastes like veal, from other parts like chicken, but it is all together in one organism. All these various kinds of meat are found in mock turtle, but that which binds the separate parts is a sauce, which still is often more nourishing than the jargon which takes place in a lot of writing.[13]

Although the young Kierkegaard suggests in his letter to Lund that the finitude and physicality of the natural sciences is "coordinate" with and not "subordinated" to the infinite and psychical underpinning of theology, a pecking order is established for the fledgling religious author.

'has willed only one thing' " (*Point of View*, 6. See also *Journals*, V, V B 148:5, n.d. [1844], 252-53; 524; VI, IX A 171, n.d. [1848], 27; X^2 A 106, n.d. [1849], 234; X^6 B 4:3, June 1, 1851, 418; *Various Spirits*, 24-25; *Point of View*, 6, 12, 23, 41, 53, 55).

[12]*Sickness*, 127.

[13]*Journals*, V, I A 32, November 22, 1834, 8.

In the same letter, he concludes that natural science merely offers him a "substratum" of "details . . . that can be observed from a side that does not involve insight into the secrets of science."[14] In Kierkegaard's own anticipation of what he considers to be the greater challenge, namely, a vocation in theology, he writes: "Christianity itself has such great contradictions that a clear view is hindered, to say the least."[15] Such an assertion, in the context of his letter to Lund, precurses his implementation of metaphor as an effective agent of indirect communication to address those contradictions. Theology becomes the fulcrum for his Archimedean point to move worlds of dialectical thought toward spheres of existential action; metaphor becomes a substantive lever for both the dialectic and the human condition that it serves. In other words, the esthetic poet and observer in Kierkegaard does not disengage himself from the "substratum" and "details" of finitude, the world of actuality, or the natural sciences, for such details can be useful vehicles in metaphorical constructions that, in turn, serve to clothe (and, in the case of much of his pseudonymous authorship, *cloak*) his religious corpus.

Given the inability to express through direct communication ideas of heaven, eternity, and the infinite—ideas that pass all understanding—Kierkegaard effectively *evokes* those ideas through the indirect, poetic language of metaphor. "Things" in the finite and physical world of actuality, if articulated ethically and through metaphor, offer *negative* representations of heaven, eternity, and the infinite by their very opposition and contrast.[16]

---

[14]*Journals*, V, I A 72, June 1, 1835, 22. See also *Letters & Documents*, 44-45.

[15]*Journals*, V, I A 72, June 1, 1835, 23. See also *Letters & Documents*, 45.

[16]For a metaphorical example of this, see the first of the three epigrams cited at the outset of the present discussion. The pseudonymous writer A, harboring a passion for music but claiming not to understand it, constructs a parable of speaking about music from the standpoint of a writer instead of a musician. The metaphor, however, also may reflect Kierkegaard's own desire to speak about eternity despite his necessary inability to understand eternity. It represents the indirect or negative communication about some thing by describing what that thing is *not* instead of positively describing what it is. It also implies the necessity of the metaphoric when access to positive description is impossible. In *Fragments* (26), for instance, Johannes Climacus maintains that "no human understanding can provide an analogy" to describe Christ's infinitely sorrowful understanding of the unrequited love between God and humans, "even though we shall suggest one here [through the use of metaphor] *in order to awaken the mind to an understanding of the divine*" [my emphasis]. Here, Kierkegaard recognizes both the imperfection and the need

Just as the similarity between Christ and Socrates, according to Kierkegaard, consists essentially in their dissimilarity,[17] it is possible through metaphor to illuminate the eternal negatively by pitting it against time, the heavens negatively by pitting them against earth, the infinite negatively by pitting it against the finite. Johannes Climacus states that "opposites show up most strongly when placed together."[18] Mackey notes that no finite image can contain God and that "the negative, in earthly and human relations, is the sign of the positive, in matters heavenly and godly."[19] Similarly, Kierkegaard as dialectician surfaces in one journal entry: " 'spirit' can never be represented directly; there must always be a negation first, and the more 'spirit,' the more care is taken that the negation is the negation of the very opposite."[20] "There is an analogy," young Kierkegaard writes in his dissertation, "only because there is a contrast."[21] One such contrast between human and divine governance is evident in the following parable:

> Once upon a time there was a rich man. At an exorbitant price he had purchased abroad a team of entirely flawless, splendid horses, which he had wanted for his own pleasure and the pleasure of driving them himself. About a year or two passed by. If anyone who had known these horses earlier now saw him driving them, he would not be able to recognize them: their eyes had become dull and drowsy; their gait lacked style and precision; they had no staying power, no endurance; he could drive them scarcely four miles without having to stop on the way, and sometimes they came to a standstill just when he was driving his best; moreover, they had acquired all sorts of quirks and bad habits, and although they of course had plenty of feed they grew thinner day by day.
>
> Then he called in the royal coachman. He drove them for a month. In the whole countryside there was not a team of horses that carried their heads so proudly, whose eyes were so fiery, whose gait was so beautiful; there was

---

of metaphor to gain understanding of the divine.

[17]*Irony*, 6.

[18]*Fragments*, 91.

[19]Louis Mackey, *Kierkegaard: A Kind of Poet* (Philadelphia: University of Pennsylvania Press, 1971) 257.

[20]*Journals*, II, XI¹ A 152, n.d. [1854?], 510.

[21]*Irony*, 15. Roger Shattuck defines metaphor similarly: "Similarity with a difference means metaphor." Roger Shattuck, *Proust's Binoculars* (Princeton NJ: Princeton University Press, 1983) 58.

no team of horses that could hold out running as they did, even thirty miles in a stretch without stopping. How did this happen? It is easy to see: the owner, who without being a coachman meddled with being a coachman, drove the horses according to the horses' understanding of what it is to drive; the royal coachman drove them according to the coachman's understanding of what it is to drive.[22]

Kierkegaard follows up this parable with a direct explanation of meaning (the parable brings to a conclusion a religious discourse, that is, a discourse in which Kierkegaard feels at greater liberty to speak directly of the religious). He withholds direct interpretation within the framework of the parable proper, however, for he keeps the nature of the royal coachman hidden. Kierkegaard, wanting the reader to understand the parable while reading it, thus prompts the *attentive* reader to infer the presence of divine governance in the parable from the adjective "royal." Such is the game of Kierkegaard, for the game of writing in such a way is as deep and earnest a pleasure as Wordsworth made metaphor writing out to be: "chief . . . causes upon which the pleasure received from metrical language depends . . . namely, the pleasure which the mind derives from the perception of similitude in dissimilitude."[23]

The withholding of direct communication or interpretation thus renders Kierkegaard comparable to Shakespeare's clownish servant, Launce, who says (borrowing freely from Matthew 13:34): "Thou shalt never get such a secret from me but by a parable."[24] It also renders him comparable to words of Nicholas of Cusa: "If I strive in human fashion to transport you to things divine, I must need use a comparison of some kind."[25] In other words, manufacturing positive, direct demonstrations or defenses of the religious only weakens or disparages faith—faith that comes from within instead of externally.[26] Later in his life, after having tested and retested the art of indirect communication as the essential way to evoke truth in the context of subjectivity, Kierkegaard continues to ask

---

[22]*Self-Examination*, 85-86.

[23]William Wordsworth, *Selected Poems and Prefaces*, ed. Jack Stillinger (Boston: Houghton Mifflin, 1965) 460 (from "Preface to *Lyrical Ballads*").

[24]*The Two Gentlemen of Verona*, 2.5.39-40.

[25]G. Heath King, *Existence, Thought, Style: Perspectives of a Primary Relation Portrayed through the Work of Søren Kierkegaard* (Milwaukee: Marquette University Press, 1996) 148. King cites from *The Vision of God*, trans. E. G. Salter (New York, 1960) 3.

[26]See 5-6n.18, above.

God for support in the matter: "keep my deepest concern silent in my innermost being, understood only by you, so that I may never speak directly of it to anyone."[27]

B. The Pseudonyms: Metaphoric Thought-Experiments, Godly Satires, and Structuring a Maieutic Authorship in a World of Direct Communication

Suggestive not only of the ambitious metaphorical range Kierkegaard commands in his early years, but also prefiguring his need to establish his literary voice within metaphorical constructs, twenty-five-year-old Søren writes in a letter to his close friend Emil Boesen:

> I need a voice as piercing as the glance of *Lynceus*, as terrifying as the groan of the giants, as sustained as a sound of nature, extending in range from the deepest bass to the most melting high notes, and modulated from the most solemn-silent whisper to the fire-spouting energy of rage. That is what I need in order to breathe, to give voice to what is on my mind, to make the *viscera* of both anger and sympathy tremble.[28]

Such a complex voice is not possible using the univocal construct of direct communication. The dominant philosophic language of the time (in particular, Hegel's objective-speculative logic) not only was generally incompatible with Kierkegaard's stylistic instincts but also with his ethical, philosophical, and religious convictions. "Using parables," Oden notes, places Kierkegaard's "philosophical intentions in stark contrast to the stilted, nonexperiential Hegelian logic against which he is struggling."[29] Ethics and human freedom without imaginatively constructed examples playing an essential role in the means of their communication (examples that *de facto* are to some degree metaphoric) command little

---

[27]*Christian Discourses*, 211. Kierkegaard's "First and Last Declaration" in his *Postscript* and, more thoroughly, his *Point of View* and *Journals and Papers* nevertheless conspire against this prayer to God.

[28]*Letters & Documents*, 54. For another memorable metaphoric medley, executed in rapid-fire succession by Kierkegaard, of some two dozen similes about what writing a preface is like, see *Prefaces*, 5-6.

[29]Thomas C. Oden, *Parables of Kierkegaard* (Princeton NJ: Princeton University Press, 1978) x.

or no vocalization, much less aspire to the literary voice Kierkegaard desired. Kierkegaard writes:

> Regrettably one finds almost no examples of the ethical in logic, which arouses in my thought a suspicion about logic and serves to support my theory of the leap, which is essentially at home in the realm of freedom, even though it ought to be metaphorically suggested in logic and should not be explained away, as Hegel does.[30]

What systematic communication failed to offer Kierkegaard was, as Oden notes, a communicative avenue on which a concept of human capability (and thereby a normative approach to ethics and freedom) may be driven, "even though [systematic discourse] may succeed very well in communicating information."[31]

Kierkegaard in effect responds to a looming eclipse of the heart's poetic-subjective discourse by his own culture's fashionable speculative-objective discourse. In the following journal entry, he intimates a growing decadence advanced by speculative philosophical language: "Philosophical terminology and its usage simply degenerate to the ridiculous. I wonder what someone would say if I were to speak of an earthquake in the old terminology."[32] Kierkegaard inquires here if such eras invested primarily in data and information gathering effectively abandon the figurative for the literal, the subjective-religious for the objective-scholarly, and thereby reject a sense of the metaphoric and the rich ambiguities and possibilities that such a language offers individuals. The enervation of a poetically informed epistemology that Kierkegaard witnessed in the nineteenth century is not unlike what T. S. Eliot eulogizes in the twentieth: "Where is the wisdom we have lost in knowledge? / Where is the knowledge we have lost in information?"[33]

For the sake of individual existence informed by the "old [ethical-religious] terminology," then, Kierkegaard surveyed more closely the landscape of poetic, literary, and figurative forms of writing that would give renewed breath to a personal voice and would not shy from but

---

[30] *Journals*, III, V C 12, n.d. [1844], 20.

[31] Oden, *Parables of Kierkegaard*, xvi.

[32] *Journals*, V, IV A 37, n.d. [1843], 216.

[33] T. S. Eliot, *Complete Poems and Plays* (New York: Harcourt, Brace and World, 1971) 96 (from "Choruses from 'The Rock' " I, 15-16).

rather espouse the ineluctable aspects and infinite wealth of human existence. Indirect communication became, according to Kierkegaard, his "native element,"[34] for such discourse conveys, as Mackey notes, "the most intensely subjective content by means of the most objective linguistic correlates of image, simile, and metaphor."[35]

Kierkegaard eventually constructs a formidable constellation of pseudonyms—what he later dubs his "godly satire"[36]—that serves to offer a plenitude of metaphoric points of illumination regarding various stages of existence. They represent, according to Carole Anne Taylor, "metaphoric truth[s] about the *way* to approach the eternal."[37] Each pseudonym is a vehicle to which a reader (including Kierkegaard himself[38]) may compare personal and particular habits, partialities, anxieties, passions. All pseudonyms ultimately point metaphorically to ways in which it is possible for the reader to become more fully human by helping evoke the reader's self-examination of personal similarities and differences between reader and pseudonym. "A comparison has its significance, of course," Kierkegaard writes in 1838, "only insofar as it leads back to a deeper understanding of that for the sake of which it appeared."[39] The "sake" for which the vehicle of pseudonymity appears in Kierkegaard is the tenor of the individual personality, the "I" and its attendant ethical-religious "eye" that was fast developing cataracts by eyewitnessing the nineteenth century's accelerated growth of cultural and industrial collectivism, mass production, and the infinite minutiæ of information even then being tabulated, calculated, and computed en masse:

> One of the tragedies of modern times is precisely this—to have abolished the "I," the personal "I." For this very reason real ethical-religious communication is as if vanished from the world. For ethical-religious truth is related essentially to personality and can only be communicated by an *I* to an *I*. As soon as the communication becomes objective in this realm, the truth has become untruth. Personality is what we need. Therefore I regard it as my

---

[34]*Journals*, VI, X^2 A 195, n.d. [1849], 251.

[35]Mackey, *Kierkegaard: A Kind of Poet*, 272.

[36]*Point of View*, 17.

[37]*Kierkegaard and Literature*, ed. Robert Schleifer and Robert Markley (Norman: University of Oklahoma Press, 1984) 176.

[38]See *Point of View*, 12: "I regard myself rather as a *reader* of the books, not as the *author*."

[39]*Early Writings*, 86.

service that by bringing poetized personalities who say *I* (my pseudonyms) into the center of life's actuality I have contributed, if possible, to familiarizing the contemporary age again to hearing an *I*, a personal *I* speak. . . . But precisely because the whole development of the world has been as far as possible from this acknowledgement of personality, this has to be done poetically. The poetic personality always has something which makes him more bearable for a world which is quite unaccustomed to hearing an *I*. Beyond this I admittedly do not go. I never venture to use quite directly my own *I*. But I am convinced that the time will come when an *I* stands up in the world, someone who says *I* directly and speaks in the first person. Then, for the first time, he will also in the strictest sense rightly communicate ethical and ethical-religious truth.[40]

Malantschuk notes that it was the German theologian Friedrich Schleiermacher (1768–1834) who gave Kierkegaard the idea of using persons as representatives (or metaphoric vehicles) for various tenors of life-views instead of presenting them abstractly.[41] He cites one particular journal entry in which twenty-two-year-old Kierkegaard states that Schleiermacher

constructs a host of personalities out of the book itself and through them illuminates their individuality, so that instead of being faced by the reviewer with various points of view, we get instead many personalities who represent these various points of view. But they are complete beings, so that it is possible to get a glance into the individuality of the single individual and through numerous merely relatively true judgments to draw up our own final judgment. Thus it is a true masterpiece.[42]

"Here," Howard Hong notes, "is the seed of Kierkegaard's indirect method, the use of imaginary constructions, 'experiments,' rather than actual descriptions or formal discursive arguments."[43] Hong then cites an entry from 1845, ten years later, in which Kierkegaard states explicitly:

Later I again found illumination of the meaning of imaginary construction [*Experiment*] as the form of communication. If existence is the essential and

---

[40]*Journals*, I, VIII² B 88, n.d. [1847], 302.

[41]*Journals*, IV, Commentary, 627.

[42]*Journals*, VI, I C 69, October 1835, 13.

[43]Howard V. Hong, "Tanke-Experiment in Kierkegaard," in *Kierkegaard: Resources and Results*, ed. Alistar McKinnon (Montreal: Wilfrid Laurier University Press, 1982) 48.

truth is inwardness . . . it is also good that it is said in the right way. But this right way is precisely the art that makes being such an author very difficult. . . . If this is communicated in a direct form, then the point is missed; then the reader is led into misunderstanding.[44]

Hong writes:

the poet is "one who makes," who construes, constructs, and composes hypotheses as do the philosophers and the scientists. What distinguishes the poet is a kind of imagination that shapes the possibles in palpable form, in the form of "idea; actuality." The poet's mode is not the discursive, demonstrative, didactic mode of the scientist and philosopher or the strict narrative mode of the historian. His mode is that of imaginative construction in the artistic illusion of actuality, or, to borrow a phrase from Climacus in *Fragments*, it is to construct imaginatively or to hypothesize *in concreto* [*Fragments*, 78] rather than to use the scientific and philosophic mode of abstraction in his presentation.

The poet in this view is an imaginative constructor [*Experimentator*] who presents the possible in experiential verisimilitude, and for the existential philosopher "the portrayal of the existential is chiefly either realization in life or poetic representation, *loquere ut videam* [speak that I may see]" [*Journals*, I, X² A 414, n.d. (1850), 461; cf. *Stages*, 398 and n. 430]. Kierkegaard is therefore the poetic *Experimentator* who makes or fashions the various pseudonymous, poetic, imaginative constructors who in turn imaginatively shape characters, scenes, situations, and relations expressive in various ways of the hypothesis(es) in-forming the work. *Experimentere* is therefore a transitive verb: imaginatively and reflectively to construct a hypothesis and imaginatively to recast it and its implications in the constructed poetic illusion of experiential actuality.[45]

The deception implicit in imaginatively constructing "in the artistic illusion of actuality" or the "poetic illusion of experiential actuality" requires little explanation from an esthetic poet's point of view, given that artistic or poetic illusion is inherent to that kind of poet's job. But such esthetic language for Kierkegaard *qua* ethical-religious poet requires further examination. For, given that Kierkegaard himself writes of his pseudonymity's illusive quality, he indirectly yet persistently prompts the reader to visit and revisit hazards implicit in indirect communication:

---

[44]*Journals*, I, VI B 40:45, n.d. [1845], 259-60.
[45]Hong, "Tanke-Experiment in Kierkegaard," 47.

[F]rom the total point of view of my whole work as an author, the esthetic writing is a deception, and herein is the deeper significance of the *pseudo-nymity*. But a deception, that is indeed something rather ugly. To that I would answer: Do not be deceived by the word *deception*. One can deceive a person out of what is true, and—to recall old Socrates—one can deceive a person into what is true. Yes, only in this way can a deluded person actually be brought into what is true—by deceiving him.[46]

C. "The Fork"

Danish author and historian Troels Frederik Troels-Lund (1840–1921) recounts a childhood anecdote that may have been Kierkegaard's "first, childish expression" of his eventual polemical posture.

He was called "the Fork." According to his sister's account this stems from an incident in which he was asked what he would most like to be, and he answered, "A fork." "Why?" "Well, then I could 'spear' anything I wanted on the dinner table." "But what if we come after you?" "Then I'll spear you."[47]

The pet name/metaphor for Kierkegaard the polemicist and rhetorician extends to Kierkegaard the literary stylist and metaphorist. His childhood name in the family home speaks first to one form of metaphoric writing, namely, satire. In specific reference to his nickname, Kierkegaard's niece, Henriette Lund, considers her uncle as having a "precocious tendency to make satirical remarks."[48] But the metaphor for Kierkegaard the author need not end there. "The Fork" befits his metaphoric style: it has more than one prong to "spear anything" one wanted, just as a good metaphor has more than one "prong" (at least one tenor and one vehicle) in which to "spear" any meaning more fully than a univocally communicative form. Metaphor offers Kierkegaard the poetically forked tool by which to spear with greater effect ideas in any sphere of existence. Further, the "forked tongue" implication of the nickname exposes Kierkegaard as one who entertains, if not traffics in, acts of deception.

---

[46]*Point of View*, 53.

[47]Bruce H. Kirmmse, *Encounters with Kierkegaard* (Princeton NJ: Princeton University Press, 1996) 3.

[48]Ibid., 151.

Iris Murdoch claims that language is a machine for making false-hoods.[49] In this context, metaphor is an obvious cog to such a linguistic machine because it is a figure of speech that says one thing in terms of another and, by doing so, manufactures logical contradictions that (especially to the literal-minded) may be considered false. To John Locke, metaphor and other figurative language are "perfect cheats" because, among other reasons, such language exists only to "insinuate wrong ideas, move the passions, and thereby mislead judgment."[50] And although Kier-kegaard would not disagree that metaphor evokes passion ("Without passion, no poet, and without passion, no poetry,"[51] pseudonymous author Frater Taciturnus writes), Kierkegaard's specific use of the metaphoric instead guides or prompts good judgment by establishing imaginative landscapes with which readers may experiment and test their abilities to judge the truth against deceit. Knowledge of the good, in this context, presupposes knowledge of deceit.

The task of Kierkegaard as religious ethicist and guide is no less dangerous than the wily Odysseus navigating his ship safely between Scylla and Charybdis. The writer must steer his poetic "deceptions" toward religious truths "with all the craftiness and subtlety at [his] disposal."[52] On the one hand, Kierkegaard must take care not to crash upon the esthetic stage of existence from which his metaphoric style derives charm, power, and momentum. On the other hand, he strives not to drown in a whirlpool the requirement that prompts readers to judge for themselves. Kierkegaard suggests how such potentially horror-ridden navigations are achieved when admonishing his reader not to ignore the religious good but instead to remember to "carry over" the religious ("carry over" in the following context as in carrying over the digits in arithmetic calculation to the next column):

> But above all do not forget one thing, the number carried [*Mente*] that you have, that it is the religious that you are to have to come forward. Or, if you are able to do so, portray the esthetic with all its bewitching charm, if

---

[49]See Owen Thomas, *Metaphor and Related Subjects* (New York: Random House, 1969) epigram to text (from Iris Murdoch's *A Severed Head*).

[50]John Locke, *An Essay Concerning Human Understanding*, ed. Peter Nidditch (Oxford: Oxford University Press, 1975) 508 (bk. 3, chap. 10, §34).

[51]*Stages*, 405.

[52]*Point of View*, 88.

possible captivate the other person, portray it with the kind of passionateness whereby it appeals particularly to him, hilariously to the hilarious, sadly to the sad, wittily to the witty, etc.—but above all do not forget one thing, the number carried that you have, that it is the religious that is to come forward. Just do it; do not fear to do it, for truly it can be done only in much fear and trembling.[53]

Artistic or poetic illusion is inherent in an esthetic poet's task. But *appearing* to speak with a forked tongue for the reader's sole ethical-religious good while avoiding outright duplicity requires subtle dialectical agility—agility with which Kierkegaard fortunately was endowed. "If I had been only [an esthetic] poet," Kierkegaard reflects in one journal entry much later in his life,

> I may well have ended up in the nonsense of merely poetizing Christianity without perceiving that it cannot be done, that one has to take himself along and either existentially express the ideal himself (which cannot be done) or define himself as one who is striving. Had I not been a poet I may well have gone ahead and confused myself with the ideal and have become a zealot. What, then, has helped me in addition to what is of greatest importance, that a Governance has helped me? The fact that I am a dialectician.[54]

From first to last for Kierkegaard, purity of heart is to will one thing, and that "thing" is the religious.[55] In true "dialectical interaction . . . the religious [is] the crucial, the esthetic the incognito"[56]—the latter of which "becomes a means of communication."[57] Subsequently, to strive effectively toward eternal validity of the religious within the context of the world and time, Kierkegaard fights worldly duplicity with the intrinsic duplicity of metaphor. "A poet is not an apostle," pseudonymous writer Johannes de Silentio asserts: a poet "drives out the devil only by the power of the devil."[58] Duplicitous poetic constructs of metaphor—when used attentively, dialectically, and ethically in forms ranging from parable to pseudonyms—manufacture the most liberal of linguistic possibilities for Kierkegaard's religious message. "Though analogy is often misleading,"

---

[53]*Point of View*, 46.
[54]*Journals*, VI, X^2 A 375, n.d. [1850], 282.
[55]See 31n.11, above.
[56]*Point of View*, 53.
[57]*Point of View*, 49.
[58]*Fear & Trembling*, 61.

Samuel Butler reportedly maintained, "it is often the least misleading
thing we have."[59] How Henry VIII (according to the *Oxford English
Dictionary*) coined the word "metaphor" in a 1533 letter reflects the same
dialectical power that Murdoch, Butler, Kierkegaard, and many other
poet-philosophers ascribe to the trope: "And rather than men would note
a lye when they know what is meant, they will sooner by allegory or
metaphor draw the word to the truth."

" 'Direct communication' is," according to Kierkegaard, "to communicate the truth directly; 'communication in reflection' is: *to deceive
into the truth*."[60] But as Anti-Climacus notes, imagination can be deceptive without being detrimental, it can "deceive . . . into the truth."[61] In
one journal entry, Kierkegaard elucidates the ethical-religious underpinnings of his mode of deception in which (as he notes in *Point of View*
with respect to "the communication of truth") a temporary suppression of
something may lead to the true becoming more true[62]:

> To "deceive" belongs essentially to the essentially ethical-religious com-
> munication. "To deceive into the truth." . . . Ethical communication in char-
> acter always begins with placing a "deception" in between [the teacher and
> the learner], and the art consists in enduring everything while remaining
> faithful to character in the deception and faithful to the ethical.[63]

Elsewhere, Kierkegaard writes that "all *true* communication of truth must
always begin with an untruth. This is partly because it is impossible to
tell the whole truth in one minute or an even shorter time. On the
contrary, it takes perhaps a long, long time for that."[64]

Kierkegaard's views of both indirect and direct communication, as
Howard Hong notes, thus are predicated on the conception of his ethical-
religious task:

> "It is Christianity that I have presented and still want to present; to this
> every hour of my day has been and is directed" [*Journals*, VI, IX A 171,

---

[59]Thomas, *Metaphor and Related Subjects*, 6 (from Samuel Butler's *Notebooks*).
[60]*Point of View*, 7.
[61]*Practice*, 190.
[62]*Point of View*, 89.
[63]*Journals*, I, VIII[2] B 85, n.d. [1847], 288. See also *Journals*, VI, X[2] A 196, n.d.
[1849], 252.
[64]*Adler*, 170.

n.d. (1848), 28]. With the Socratic method of indirection, he used a pseudonymous, esthetic approach because of what he regarded as the illusion of "Christendom." "Thus in a certain sense I began my activity as an author with a *falsum* [deception] or with a *pia fraus* [pious fraud]. The situation is that in so-called Christendom people are so fixed in the fancy that they are Christians that if they are to be made aware at all many an art will have to be employed. If someone who otherwise does not have a reputation of being an author begins right off as a Christian author, he will not get a hearing from his contemporaries. They are immediately on their guard, saying, 'That's not for us' etc." [*Journals*, VI. IX A 171, n.d. (1848), 27].[65]

The upshot of Kierkegaard's adoption of metaphoric styles that may be considered deceptive is to bring an individual into a personal relation to actuality so that the individual may deliberately and personally begin to choose and appropriate the ethical-religious. "As soon as a person can be brought to stand at the crossroads in such a way that there is no way out for him except to choose," Judge William maintains, "he will choose the right thing."[66] The presupposition from which the optimistic judge renders his opinion is the same presupposition from which Kierkegaard's "deceptions" work, namely, that one will choose "the right thing" when choosing "the wrong thing" is understood as a choice made under a delusion—hence, no deliberate, reasonable, real choice at all:

[T]hat someone is under a delusion and consequently the first step, properly understood, is to remove the delusion—if I do not begin by deceiving, I begin with direct communication. But direct communication presupposes that the recipient's ability to receive is entirely in order, but here that is simply not the case—indeed, here a delusion is an obstacle. That means a corrosive must first be used, but this corrosive is the negative, but the negative in connection with communication is precisely to deceive.

What, then, does it mean "to deceive"? It means that one does not begin *directly* with what one wishes to communicate but begins by taking the other's delusion at face value.[67]

---

[65] *Point of View*, Historical Introduction, x-xi.

[66] *Either/Or* II, 168.

[67] *Point of View*, 54. Kierkegaard is emphatic on the issue of initially taking the learner's delusion at face value. Elsewhere in *Point of View* (45), Kierkegaard writes: "*If one is truly to succeed in leading a person to a specific place, one must first and foremost take care to find him where he is and begin there.* This is the secret in the entire art of helping."

Indirect communication, a primary agent of which is metaphor, resides within the relation between the esthetic writing as the beginning and the religious as the *telos* (goal).

> It begins with the esthetic, in which possibly most people have their lives, and now the religious is introduced so quickly that those who, moved by the esthetic, decide to follow along are suddenly standing right in the middle of the decisive qualifications of the essentially Christian, are at least prompted to become *aware*.[68]

All that is required of the reader is to develop the maieutic imaginatively, for "imagination is what providence uses to take men captive in actuality, in existence, in order to get them far enough out, or within, or down into actuality. And when imagination has helped them get as far out as they should be—then actuality genuinely begins."[69] Kierkegaard's indirect communication thus is not unlike, according to Kierkegaard, God's own ability to upbuild when it comes to prompting an individual to walk confidently into existential moments of choice:

> [S]o it is in fact with God's upbringing: he deceives a man into the truth. [The individual] grasps the truth in imagination—it looks so inviting, he cannot escape it, he goes along—and now he stands right in the middle of actuality, and the matter is altogether different.[70]

The individual finds that truth is a fork, with various prongs extending from its handle—prongs poised to pierce the individual into self-awareness.

D. Language's Inadequacies, Existentialist Writing, and Becoming Human through a Persona

Just as subjectivity informs Kierkegaard's existentialism and, in general, existentialist writing—so, too, does his attention to the metaphorical. Kierkegaard's use of the poetic-metaphoric attempts to correct the failure of systematic communication to illuminate the nuances of human perceptions—a failure Kierkegaard saw in the philosophical discourse of his

---

[68]*Point of View*, 7; cf. *Point of View*, 43-44.

[69]*Journals*, II, XI^1 A 288, n.d. [1854], 313-14.

[70]*Journals*, IV, X^4 A 264, n.d. [1851], 9.

time, and a failure that late-nineteenth-century and twentieth-century existential thinkers also perceived. The inadequacy of direct communication to articulate intimately human matters has inspired and continues to inspire esthetic and religious poets. In turn, metaphor (because it is indirect, suggestive, evocative) always has been the preferred form with which to venture beyond language's denotative limits.

Esthetically, metaphor establishes access to the inexpressible by virtue of its indirect communicative force. Shattuck cites the preference of symbolist poet Stéphane Mallarmé (1842–1898) toward metaphor and, by extension, indirect communication: " '*To name* a thing is to destroy three-quarters of the poem's enjoyment, which consists in getting at something little by little, in gradually divining it. The ideal is *suggestion*.' "[71] Shattuck's subsequent comments on Mallarmé echo Kierkegaard's attack upon systematic thought and the latter's reasons for communicating indirectly. According to Shattuck, Mallarmé implies

> that there are feelings and states of mind so delicate as to be best approached indirectly, by mere hints, by evocation in sound and sense. . . . Another poet, Paul Valéry, drew the full conclusion: "To see a thing truly is to forget its name." The most exciting enterprise of language is to avoid using language according to its conventional forms. Don't make anything too clear. The imagination needs a milieu of mystery to work in.[72]

Theologically, "metaphor and parable become the language par excellence," writes John Donahue, "since they point beyond what is expressed to what is beyond expression."[73] Just as Shattuck understands Mallarmé's esthetic symbolism ("Someone told me as a child how to see a star at night: Don't look directly at it; look slightly to one side of it. . . . This indirect approach to the subtleties and complexities of the world lies at the heart of symbolism described by Mallarmé"[74]), so, too, Kierkegaard understands both the impossibility of confronting the religious directly and the possibility of intimating by indirection the divine: "To see [God] is like looking at the sun; we can look at the sun only indirectly; if one wants to stare at it directly, he will see nothing but

[71]Roger Shattuck, *Forbidden Knowledge* (New York: St. Martin's Press, 1996) 120.
[72]Ibid.
[73]John Donahue, *The Gospel in Parable* (Philadelphia: Fortress Press, 1988) 13.
[74]Shattuck, *Forbidden Knowledge*, 121.

black spots before his eyes."[75] To see even oneself and one's relatively trivial worldly worries, for example, Kierkegaard maintains that one needs to divert one's eyes from oneself and, in the following instance, consider the lilies and the birds:

> When the eyes are staring, they are looking fixedly ahead, are continually looking at one thing, and yet they are not actually seeing, because, as science explains, the eyes see their own seeing. But then the physician says: Move your eyes. And thus the Gospel says: Divert your mind—look down at the lily and quit staring at the worry; look up at the bird and quit staring at the worry. Then when the tears stop while the eyes are looking down at the lily, is it not as if it were the lily that wiped away the tears! When the wind dries the tears in the eyes that watch the bird, is it not as if it were the bird that wiped away the tears! . . .
>
> This is what we dare to call a *godly diversion*, which does not, like the empty or worldly diversion, incite impatience and nourish the worry, but diverts, calms, and persuades the more devoutly one gives oneself over to it.[76]

Here Kierkegaard considers an individual who, so fixed upon temporal worry, cannot gain distance from worry in order to displace the worry therapeutically. In this context, nature offers what Kierkegaard calls "godly diversions" so that individuals may come to see themselves and companion worries with clearer vision. Such "godly diversions" as the lilies and the birds are in effect metaphorical vehicles in nature to which viewers may compare and (more importantly in this case) contrast themselves, thereby existentially seeing themselves more clearly by indirection, then "by indirections find directions out."[77]

In the past century and a half, the inadequacy of the language of systematic communication also has inspired existentialist thinkers of all orientations to appropriate a less philosophical and more poetic style to promulgate their ideas about the human condition—ideas that are best viewed with the "side of the eye" or by diversionary indirection that metaphor offers. Such is the case with Kierkegaard, the so-called "father of existentialism." King, for example, discusses how even "trivialities" of the human condition, free of philosophical jargon, accentuate the depth

---

[75]*Journals*, II, II A 663, September 6, 1837, 519.
[76]*Various Spirits*, 184.
[77]*Hamlet* 2.1.63.

of an existential message. A "teasing, sovereign humor integral to the existential illumination, to which the closely united poetic and essayistic forms well lend themselves" appears in place of elaborate, didactic, and systematic proofs. King continues:

> In the writings of the skeptic Kierkegaard, in which these forms reach their highest degree of fusion, the diversionary nature of intellectual discourse in the face of the misfortunes of existence is also conveyed through a similarly random reference to human trivialities. And here, too, we find these misfortunes not to be a "specific something" that can be rectified [see *Postscript* I, 449], but . . . a perennial part of the ebb and flow of the human condition as such.[78]

"As early as 1835," Malantschuk notes, "Kierkegaard wrote in his journal that he did not want to base the development of his thought 'on anything called objective' (*Journals*, V, I A 75, August 1, 1835, 35) but wanted to concentrate on his own personal actuality. This marked interest in personal existence (subjectivity) in contrast to an external, objective knowledge Kierkegaard retained all his life."[79] Portraying personal existence without the use of objective language, however, required an esthetic built upon indirect communication in general and the metaphoric in particular.

Sylvia Walsh illuminates Kierkegaard's interest in personal existence—and by extension, existentialism—in the context of his esthetics. Similar to traditional esthetics, Kierkegaard's existential esthetics

> is an "esthetics" in the sense of involving a concept of beauty and artistic representation, but it is "existential" and therefore nontraditional in that it emphasizes the representation of the esthetic ideal in human life rather than in external or material works of art. In Kierkegaard's thought the term "existential" always connotes the concrete or historical actualization of those factors that are essential to the formation of human personality or the qualitative life of the individual (*Journals*, I, IX A 382, n.d. [1848], 458-59; X^2 A 439, n.d. [1850], 461-62; X^2 A 606, n.d. [1850], 463; X^3 A 725, n.d. [1851], 463-64; X^4 A 5, n.d. [1851], 464). These factors are to be realized in the individual's own being and personal relations, not merely in the form of a conceptual, or ideal, actuality envisioned by the imagination and represented in external

---

[78]King, *Existence, Thought, Style*, 140-41.
[79]*Journals*, IV, Commentary, 712.

products of art. For Kierkegaard, therefore, it is the human self in its
historical or concrete beauty, rather than an abstract beauty, that constitutes
the esthetic ideal; and the goal of his esthetics is to reduplicate that ideal in
human life, not merely to produce a semblance of it in works of art.[80]

The concrete "semblance" of life through metaphoric constructions
(such as fictitious parables and analogies in works of art) may prompt a
viewer to strive to reduplicate the ideal in human life. Such poetic-metaphoric "fiction" is Kierkegaard's stylistic trademark and a standard form
in his existentially esthetic and ethical-religious thought patterns. The
poetic-metaphoric also is central to existentialist writing beginning with
Kierkegaard; such fiction intimates not only what *is* in human existence
but also points to human freedom and capability, or what *can be* in
human existence. Fictions are not "true" or "real" as weighed by a
historical literalist or Christian empiricist (who, as Soskice notes, "should
have no place for [metaphorical] modes at all"[81]); their truth or reality
nonetheless is evident when they become analogues to the reader,
especially the receptive reader seeking either metaphoric models by which
to appropriate and live or to observe and understand models that ethically
would be better left unappropriated and unlived. "Like the multiplicity of
wave formations that appears on the surface of the sea," King writes,
Kierkegaard's existential communication "yields the varied configuration
of life's way, not, however, as mere esthetic charm, but as possibilities
that may take one further."[82]

In the context of Kierkegaard as existentialist writer, the "possibilities" to which King refers essentially are metaphorically constructed
situations. In one journal entry, Kierkegaard indirectly makes a case for
composing metaphorical constructions that create "situations" to which
the reader may existentially respond: "to apprehend ethical and ethical-
religious truth in particular requires a situation, and the same is true of
communicating ethical and ethical-religious truth."[83] As Edith Kern
writes, existential thought and the possibilities it offers has, from its

---

[80]Sylvia Walsh, *Living Poetically: Kierkegaard's Existential Aesthetics* (University
Park PA: Pennsylvania State University Press, 1994) 5.
[81]Soskice, *Metaphor and Religious Language*, 148.
[82]King, *Existence, Thought, Style*, 143.
[83]*Journals*, I, VIII^2 B 88, n.d. [1847], 297.

inception, felt at home in fiction with its metaphorical or imaginary constructions of situations:

> Because of [existentialism's] intense "inwardness" and the "commitment" of its proponents, it has expressed itself more strikingly in imaginative writing than in theoretical treatises. . . . According to modern existentialist thinkers, the paradox and absurdity of life can be more readily deduced from fundamental human situations portrayed in fiction than described in the logical language of philosophy. . . . Indeed, Unamuno considered true philosophy, a philosophy concerned with the concrete man of flesh and blood, to be closer to poetry than to any kind of scientific thought.[84]

Articulating fundamental human situations in close alliance with human existence discloses the potential of imaginary and metaphoric construction in existentialist writing. "In Kierkegaard's writings," King states, "one does not find schematization or general formulas, but, as it were, decipherment of 'situations' of daily experiences which, owing to a peculiarity of tone or appearance, are offered in a given context to the reader as warranting closer consideration."[85] Readers are prompted to recall in their own lives the "pathos of the situation," for, as King adds, "the value of the '*situation*' [is] the stuff of the [reader's] recollection."[86] King further notes that Kierkegaard's existential self "imbibes the sights and sounds of the world" and that "dwelling on the immediately given is reflected in the wealth of imagery in Kierkegaard's prose, in its power to evoke the immediacy of the situation, 'the fragrance of experience.'"[87]

What Kierkegaard achieves with thousands upon thousands of metaphors mined from a lifetime of observing the world about him, of examining personalities with which he has become acquainted, of weighing the personal and professional occupations of humans he has witnessed, and of sympathizing with emotions he and others have experienced, is a comprehensive albeit asystematic *situational* depiction of the world. "Even though I achieve nothing else," Kierkegaard writes, "I nevertheless hope to leave very accurate and experientially based observa-

---

[84]Edith Kern, *Existential Thought and Fictional Technique* (New Haven CT: Yale University Press, 1970) vii.
[85]King, *Existence, Thought, Style*, 112.
[86]Ibid., 28.
[87]Ibid., 40, 41.

tions concerning the conditions of existence."[88] In another journal entry, written a year later, he incorporates the religious in similar understatement. He does not, however, exclude reference to existence-relationships of his metaphoric and imaginary constructions that serve as analogue-maps to the human condition:

> Through my writings I hope to achieve the following: to leave behind me so accurate a characterization of Christianity and its relationships in the world that an enthusiastic, noble-minded young person will be able to find in it a map of relationships as accurate as any topographical map from the most famous institutes.[89]

Kierkegaard's map is not drawn to blaze the trail for the existing individual, but rather to prompt and guide that individual into and through his own journey—even with the ever-present risk or deliberate intent of drowning all maps (just as Prospero deliberately drowns his guiding book in the final act of *The Tempest*). In other words, scholarly or literary contemplation ultimately must yield to the imagination that in turn must yield to the truer experience of actual human existence in the world. Only in such a context does Kierkegaard as ethical-religious poet and metaphorist become an appropriate guide and mapmaker. Scholarly "contemplation," Kierkegaard writes,

> must shorten time considerably—indeed, it actually has to call the mind and thought away from time in order to complete itself in a counterfeit eternal rounding off. In this it is something like the work of an artist in drawing a map of the country. The drawing, of course, cannot be as large as the country; it becomes infinitely smaller, but it also becomes all the easier for the viewer to survey the outlines of that country. And yet if that viewer were suddenly set down in the actuality of that country, where the many, many miles have all their force, he very likely would not be able to recognize the country or gain any notion of it or as a traveler get his bearing in it. . . . What was compacted airtight, as it were, in the completeness of the contemplation must now be stretched out to its full length; it is no longer a rounding off but is in motion. Life is like a poet and thus different from the

---

[88]*Journals*, I, VIII¹ A 127, n.d. [1847], 455.
[89]*Journals*, VI, IX A 448, n.d. [1848], 77-78.

contemplator, who always comes to a finish; the poet wrenches us out into the middle of life.[90]

The ethical-religious poet's indirect communication essentially allows a reader to map out his own actions personally through the appropriation of parables (or any metaphorical speech) into the reader's thoughts, thereby prompting meaning into the reader's deeds. This is overtly displayed in the "Preface" to Kierkegaard's little volume entitled *Three Discourses on Imagined Occasions*—the strength of which lays in Kierkegaard's invitation to the reader to appropriate that which the author calls the "giving" of the book in such a way that the reader may treat the appropriation as a "giving" of oneself. Kierkegaard writes that the book

> quietly waits for that right reader to come like a bridegroom and to bring the occasion [for learning] along with him. Let each do a share—the reader therefore more. The meaning lies in the appropriation. Hence the *book*'s joyous *giving of itself*. Here there are no worldly "mine" or "thine" that separate and prohibit appropriating what is the neighbor's. . . . The appropriation is the *reader's* even greater, is his triumphant *giving of himself*."[91]

Kierkegaard assumes that the value of personal meaning is wedded to the person by appropriation, where a genuine existential or internalizing act for an existing human being involves choice and action inherent in appropriation. In addition, Kierkegaard's above statement about letting both writer and reader "do a share—the reader therefore more" is not unlike Thoreau's famous invitation to appropriate in *Walden*: "we must laboriously seek the meaning of each word and line, conjecturing a larger sense than common use permits out of what wisdom and valor and generosity we have. . . . Books must be read as deliberately and reservedly as they were written."[92] In effect, great existential demands are placed upon the reader to appropriate text slowly, earnestly, and thereby properly, instead of in hazy amazement, admiration, or impatience. As Kierkegaard writes in *Works of Love*: "may your patience in reading correspond to my diligence and time in writing it, inasmuch as, since being an author is my only work and my only task, I have both the

---

[90]*Various Spirits*, 72-73.

[91]*Three Discourses*, 5.

[92]Henry David Thoreau, *Walden*, ed. Walter Harding (New York: Houghton Mifflin Co., 1995) 97, 98 (from "Reading").

ability and the obligation to use a careful—fussy, if you will—but certainly also helpful precision."[93] Impatient reading, Kierkegaard suggests elsewhere, deceives the reader out of the truth while slow reading deceives the reader into the truth.[94] As a prelude to the famous parable of the actor in "An Occasional Discourse," Kierkegaard states his case even more directly:

> [T]he understandableness of this discourse and the listener's understanding are still not the true earnestness and by no means give the deliberation its proper emphasis. To achieve this, the discourse must *decisively* require something of the listener, . . . that he as reader share the work with the one speaking. At this point it must unconditionally require his decisive self-activity, upon which everything depends. So now, my listener, think about the occasion [and] . . . consider your own life . . . [and] allow me . . . to illustrate it with a metaphor.[95]

Kierkegaard informs the religious context of his writings not only contextually but, more significantly, existentially. Johannes Climacus reminds readers forthrightly when (in reference to the concretion versus the abstraction of existence) he prompts a direct, unmediated appropriation of the text by suggesting that the reader *read himself as* the text: "please note that the investigation is not on paper but in existence."[96] The abstract world of words pales in comparison to the concrete, actual deed of existence. Words, in effect, cease to exist if they transform into and become deeds—an idea that, nevertheless, Kierkegaard could best articulate in the following journal entry only through metaphor, because metaphor mirrors the dialectical shift from word to deed: "The essential sermon *is* one's own existence. A person preaches with this every hour of the day and with power quite different from that of the most eloquent speaker in his most eloquent moment."[97] And perhaps this intimate relationship between words and human existence is why Kierkegaard, in prefaces to several of his religious discourses, admonishes his reader to read or sermonize aloud. One's speech becomes one's thought; one's

---

[93] *Works of Love*, 73-74.

[94] *Works of Love*, 3.

[95] *Various Spirits*, 122, 123.

[96] *Postscript* I, 506.

[97] *Journals*, I, X^1 A 650, n.d. [1849], 460; my emphasis. Chapters 3 and 4, below, more fully address this idea.

thought (when appropriated) becomes the basis of one's character that, in turn, may become one's existence. "To reduplicate," Kierkegaard writes, "is to be what one says"[98]—all of which is not simply a fanciful leap or poetic wordplay, but a notion suggested by the very etymology of the word "person." According to Howard Hong, "person"

> epitomizes a metaphysics of selfhood. The Latin *persona* means a mask used by actors to identify the character represented and as an aid in projecting the voice. The word itself is derived from *per*, meaning "through" and *sonare*, "to sound." Therefore the person is the one who sounds through the mask or the various masks seen by others.
>
> The person is not the mask of function, type, class, or social-economic-political relations but is the agent, the responder, the thinker, one who acts . . . , one who bears the external mask or masks that others see. The mask is indeed the person's mask but the person is not synonymous with the mask and is not exhausted by the aggregate of his masks. Language is our best means for trying to get behind the masks.
>
> Socrates is reported to have said to a young man brought as a potential pupil: "*Loquere ut te videam* (Speak so that I may see you)" [Erasmus, *Apophthegmata*, iii. 70: *Opera*, I-VIII (Basel: 1540), IV, 148].[99]

Reading a text aloud, as Kierkegaard recommends at the outset of some of his religious discourses, more effectively helps a reader appropriate and command meaning and significance from the text, so that (as Johannes Climacus writes) "the most ordinary expression comes into existence with newborn originality."[100] Words no longer are simply described as a simile or weak metaphor (e.g., "cosyn to the dede"[101]) but they *become* deed—a truly living word—and the original writer of the text becomes subsumed by the reader's voice . . . and vanishes: "By reading aloud you will gain the strongest impression that you have only yourself to consider, not me, who, after all, am 'without authority,' nor others, which would be a distraction."[102] Coupling word and deed—although plain and simple in an existential context—is not, however, with-

[98] *Journals*, VI, IX A 208, n.d. [1848], 37.
[99] Howard V. Hong, "Trying to Do the Right Thing," *Reece Report* (Northfield MN: Richard Reece) 7/1 (January 1992): 18.
[100] *Postscript* I, 86.
[101] See xiv in preface, above.
[102] *Self-Examination*, 3.

out its own "dialectical knot."[103] A certain honesty is required to wade through the linguistic ambiguity and potential equivocation that such coupling may invoke. Kierkegaard is not loath to help a reader honestly address ambiguity—his metaphoric texts help a reader work and act through a deeper understanding of ambiguous and equivocal contexts to achieve a certain passion that moves a reader toward clearer self-understanding.

E. Language Decay, Ambiguities, Opposition, and the Need for Passionate Tension

Central, then, to Kierkegaard's metaphorical writings is his urgency to address linguistic ambiguities and equivocations that have long been shaping Western thought and culture. Such ambiguities and equivocations are, to apply Howard Hong's words, "the working out of the ecstatic anthropocentric Renaissance view of humankind" that traces "a devolution" of modern man "from divinity, to humanity, to brutality, to technicality and numbers."[104] Kierkegaard was a watchdog of the loosening, relaxation, and decadence of language that typifies this 400-year ebb of spiritual-religious authority in Western culture. What displaced such authority was the onrushing flow of Western secularism and industrialization, replete with a language that stripped its culture of the ability to discriminate between immanent and transcendent categories.

Kierkegaard recognized such linguistic decay of the religious early in life. In an 1836–1837 journal entry, he writes:

At the moment the greatest fear is of the total bankruptcy toward which all Europe seems to be moving and men forget the far greater danger, a seemingly unavoidable bankruptcy in an intellectual-spiritual sense, a confusion of language far more dangerous than that (typical) Babylonian confusion, than the confusion of dialectics and national languages following that Babylonian attempt of the Middle Ages—that is, a confusion in the languages themselves, a mutiny, the most dangerous of all, of the words themselves, which, wrenched out of man's control, would despair, as it were, and crash in upon one another, and out of this chaos a person would snatch, as from a grab-bag, the handiest word to express his presumed thoughts.[105]

---

[103]*Practice*, 133.
[104]Hong, "Trying to Do the Right Thing," 9.
[105]*Journals*, V, I A 328, n.d. [1836–1837], 78-79.

This assertion does not diminish across the course of his pseudonymous authorship, for he revises the journal entry a decade later when Johannes Climacus employs the same ideas while addressing the secularization of Christian language:

> The whole Christian terminology has been confiscated by speculative thought . . . ; even the newspapers use the most sublime dogmatic expression as brilliant ingredients, and while politicians anxiously expect a bankruptcy of nations, a far greater bankruptcy is perhaps impending in the world of mind, because the concepts are gradually being cancelled and the words are coming to mean everything, and therefore dispute sometimes becomes just as ludicrous as agreement. To dispute about loose words and to be in agreement on loose words are indeed always ludicrous, but when even the firmest words have become loose—what then? Just as an old man who has lost his teeth now munches with the help of the stumps, so the modern Christian language about Christianity has lost the power of the energetic terminology to bite—and the whole thing is toothless "maundering."[106]

Given the secularization of religious terms, "it is not even known for sure what Christianity is" anymore, according to Johannes Climacus. "In daily life, when we hear shrimp hawked on the street, we almost think that it is midsummer, when wreaths of woodruff are hawked that it is spring, when mussels are hawked that it is winter. But when, as happened last winter, one hears shrimp, wreaths of woodruff, and mussels hawked on the same day, one is tempted to assume that life has become confused."[107]

According to Climacus, language that helps delineate between, for example, what is relative and what is absolute has been deleteriously "mixed together."[108] Lacking powers of discrimination that otherwise would distinguish esthetic, ethical, and religious categories from one another, Kierkegaard's pseudonymous and esthetic author A recognizes that "language breaks down, and thought is confused"[109]—for, as Johannes Climacus states, "to confuse the [esthetic and religious] spheres is always easier than to keep them separate"[110] (in other words, as Kierke-

---

[106]*Postscript* I, 363.
[107]*Postscript* I, 362.
[108]*Postscript* I, 324.
[109]*Either/Or* I, 230.
[110]*Postscript* I, 454.

gaard himself writes, "unit[ing] contradictions . . . is the ultimate difficulty"[111]). In the larger context of his religious authorship, such confusion is precisely Kierkegaard's argument with established Christendom. Instead of the essentially Christian individual always able to place opposites together[112] in a way that he may still distinguish the distinct nature of each element of a given set of opposites, Kierkegaard suggests that Christendom turns away from the religious and toward the esthetic by making "the finite and the infinite, the eternal and the temporal, the highest and the lowest, blend in such a way that it is impossible to say which is which, or the situation is an impenetrable ambiguity."[113]

For the culture into which Kierkegaard was born, then, "it is very easy to confuse everything in a confusion of language, where estheticians use the most decisive Christian-religious categories in brilliant remarks, and pastors use them thoughtlessly as officialese that is indifferent to content."[114] In one journal entry, Kierkegaard writes:

> Ethics has become completely transformed into the esthetic. We see it and admire it in the theater, in the medium of imagination, but in life it has no home—there it is ridiculous to will even to try to actualize anything of the ethical. In the same way the religious, Christianity, is transposed into the medium of imagination, but to do something about it in life is ridiculous.[115]

In another journal entry, what Kierkegaard calls "Christian wilting" is precisely the result of a confusion of categories spawned by a relaxation of language. "Christian wilting," he writes,

> *artistically* loves tranquility, which is the condition for being able to enjoy life. It mistakes (the better it does this, the more dangerous it is) the artistic for the Christian, human upbringing for Christian character, human cleverness for Christian recklessness, human superiority for Christian worth, the charming magnificence of appearance for the plain dress of everyday truth, a secular, not to say pagan, Sunday-Christianity for New Testament Monday-

---

[111]*Three Discourses*, 77.

[112]*Judge for Yourself!*, 161; cf. *Postscript* I, 505.

[113]*Judge for Yourself*, 123.

[114]*Postscript* I, 269.

[115]*Journals*, I, VIII¹ A 398, n.d. [1847], 417. See also *Point of View*, 130; *Late Writings*, 129; *Journals*, I, VII¹ A 15, n.d. [1846], 408; VI, X¹ A 617, n.d. [1849], 188; X⁵ B 105, n.d. [1849], 206; X⁵ A 119, n.d. [1853], 476.

Christianity; it mistakes artistic seriousness in playing Christianity for the real earnestness of Christianity, the idyllic enjoyment of quiet hours for New Testament painful decision; it mistakes enjoyment for suffering, winning the world for renunciation of the world, heightening life's enjoyment for painfully dying to the world; it mistakes playing over a past event for—what is Christian—making it contemporary, which means that the danger becomes actual and the suffering becomes actual and the offering which is brought is actual, and which means that it does not become, artistically accomplished, an appearance, while the actuality becomes advantage, salary, profit, pride of life, secular-mindedness.[116]

Johannes Climacus agrees:

one responds to the esthetic ethically, to faith intellectually, etc. One is finished with everything, and yet scant attention is given to which sphere it is in which each question finds its answer. This produces even greater confusion in the world of spirit than if in civic life the response to an ecclesiastical matter would be given by the pavement commission.[117]

Implicit in the above pavement commission metaphor, "the whole modern statistical approach to morality"[118] contributes to abuses of metaphor contrived by esthetic and speculative thought. Such linguistic infractions drive the value of religious or absolute language down to pander to man and technological progress instead of up to glorify God and divine wisdom. In the optimistic, confident nineteenth century, Howard Hong writes, Kierkegaard foresaw the progressive dehumanization of humankind's view of itself because of itself.[119] Kierkegaard writes that he was ahead of his time in these matters ("Conditions are still far from being

---

[116]*Journals*, I, X^6 B 233, n.d. [1853], 377.

[117]*Postscript* I, 324.

[118]*Journals* I, VII^1 A 15, n.d. [1846], 408.

[119]Hong, "Trying to Do the Right Thing," 9. Kierkegaard's prophetic vision of humanity's self-dehumanization is especially pertinent in a postindustrial/information/computer age, where the ubiquitous use of metaphors of mechanism pathetically renders humans thinking of themselves existing under the aspect of determinism rather than freedom. (Figures of speech such as "He's a working machine," "Let's interface and network," "My memory banks are so overloaded that I can't compute," and "He's wired" come to mind.) If we are what we say we are through metaphor, then the deterministic metaphor of mechanism is quite capable of corroding uniquely human and ethical concepts such as intimacy, responsibility, accountability, guilt, and (by extension) repentance, forgiveness, and love.

confused enough for proper use to be made of me"[120]), although he also
understood that his writings would be more readily accepted during the
kind of times of which he speaks: "But it will all end, as they shall see,
with conditions getting so desperate that they must make use of desperate
people like me and my kind."[121]

Such a fall or decadence of language mimics even the biblical fall of
man, where, in the most fatal metaphor of the Judeo-Christian tradition,
the serpent tells Eve that she "will be like God"[122] by eating of the tree
of knowledge. Divine language is humanized; the esthetic use of metaphor here illusively raises man to the level of God, renders temporality
on par with eternity, makes the finite tantamount to the infinite. "The fundamental derangement at the root of modern times . . . consists in this,"
Kierkegaard writes, "that the deep qualitative chasm in the difference
between God and man has been obliterated."[123]

Kierkegaard's use of metaphor (as exemplified by the toothless man,
hawking shrimp, and pavement commission metaphors above) are constructed to accent the radical *dissimilarity* between God and man, eternity
and temporality, infinitude and finitude: "Christianity is divine, the
opposite of the human,"[124] Kierkegaard writes. He maintains (instead of
collapses) the absoluteness of that which is absolute, the relativity of that
which is relative. His argument keeps religious and esthetic categories
distinct and separate from one another, and does not confuse the esthetic
and the religious any more than they already have become confused in a
post-lapserian world. With or without a touch of the comic, Kierkegaard
has a point to drive home about his "characterless age":

> As is well known, Heiberg's Councilor Herr Zierlich is so sensitive to
> propriety that he even finds it improper for women's and men's clothing to
> hang together in a wardrobe.
>   We will leave that to Herr Zierlich. But, on the other hand, what in our
> characterless age must of necessity be practiced is the separation, the distinc-
> tion between the infinite and the finite, between a striving for the infinite
> and for the finite, between living for something and living on something that

[120]*Journals*, VI, X³ A 680, n.d. [1850], 367.
[121]*Journals*, VI, X³ A 680, n.d. [1850], 367.
[122]Genesis 3:5.
[123]*Journals*, V, VIII¹ A 414, November 20, 1847, 416.
[124]*Journals*, I, X⁵ A 98, n.d. [1853], 222.

our age—very improperly—has gotten put together in the wardrobe, has gotten blended or made the same, and that, on the contrary, Christianity with the passion of eternity, with the most appalling Either/Or, holds apart from each other, separated by a chasmic abyss.[125]

"The point here as everywhere," Johannes Climacus writes, "is to keep the specific spheres separated from one another, to respect the qualitative dialectic, the tug of decision that changes everything."[126] In a sermon delivered in the pastoral seminary, Kierkegaard considers this particularly important need, informed by metaphor, to separate categories from one another for clear thinking: "In Scripture we find expression and ideas that are used with a special emphasis, metaphorical descriptions that sharply define the contrast between the Christian and the secular and uncompromisingly confirm the separation."[127] Thus, one purpose of religious metaphor is to uphold the separation between the religious and the secular by placing the tenor of the infinite contrastingly aside the vehicle of the finite: "let us not secularize the religious [which would be a deception]," Kierkegaard writes, "but eternally separate the religious and the secular precisely by earnestly thinking about them together."[128]

Such a contradistinction to which religious metaphor ascribes occasionally forces Kierkegaard to disclaim the poetic illusion of a given metaphor in order to keep the religious separate from the secular. While constructing one metaphor about love as an infinite debt, for instance, Kierkegaard overtly interrupts construction of the metaphor, writing that "such talk is all too reminiscent of an actual bookkeeping arrangement."[129] Kierkegaard disclaims in this way specifically to remind the reader of the radical difference between the given tenor (love, God) and vehicle (money, mammon). Further, Kierkegaard disclaims some metaphors even as he writes them to remind the reader that constructing metaphors upon which to *imagine* how to exist is one thing, but that *actual striving* in existence is another. Amid the same love-as-debt metaphorical construction noted above, for instance, Kierkegaard writes: "Love could be described in this way. Yet Christianity never dwells on condi-

---

[125]*Late Writings*, 162.
[126]*Postscript* I, 388.
[127]*Journals*, IV, III C 1, n.d. [1840–1841], 50.
[128]*Various Spirits*, 125.
[129]*Works of Love*, 176.

tions or on describing them; it always hastens to the task or to assigning the task."[130] Kierkegaard suggests here that any religious metaphor—although illuminating on a cognitive level—is ultimately imperfect, for nothing compares with the eternal.

No matter how Kierkegaard tries to separate qualitative categories of existence, however, ambiguities continue to thrive. Nevertheless, by metaphorically defining humans in *contradistinction* to the divine instead of, esthetically, by *comparison* with the divine, Kierkegaard reminds his reader of what it means to be, to become, a human being—what George Eliot calls "a mysterious mixture"[131] and what Anti-Climacus similarly calls "a synthesis" of opposites "of the infinite and the finite, of the temporal and the eternal, of freedom and necessity."[132] This formulation of the contradictory or paradoxical self is not unlike the scenario of the tenor-vehicle relationship of any given metaphor,[133] which is why Mackey claims that

> the ambiguity of human existence is reflected in the analogical (not univocal) unity of [Kierkegaard's] thought, which in turn finds expression in the metaphoric (not literal) mode of utterance. The contradictions of human existence are acknowledged by the distention of all his metaphors.[134]

Metaphor provides Kierkegaard with the dialectical tension and the middle ground—as a kind of no-man's-land—that his indirect communication requires of the reader to struggle with existence itself, to examine not only life but ideas in life that ethically instruct and prompt the reader to choose.

Ambiguities in existence are best depicted by the dialectical balance of opposites, which is where Kierkegaard's imaginative, metaphorical constructions are exercised and regularly tested. "My imagination," Kierkegaard writes, "is not at all prior to the dialectical . . . but follows the dialectical." Kierkegaard adds here that he "can grasp all the Christian qualifications in the most faithful and vital way"[135] because his dialectical

---

[130]*Works of Love*, 177.

[131]George Eliot, *Middlemarch*, ed. W. J. Harvey (New York: Penguin, 1965) 25 (the opening line of the prelude).

[132]*Sickness*, 13.

[133]See 10, above.

[134]Mackey, *Kierkegaard: A Kind of Poet*, 295.

[135]*Journals*, V, VIII^1 A 347, n.d. [1847], 410.

imagination responds to "the essentially Christian [that] always places opposites together."[136] He thereby sustains the tense dissimilarities between the divine and the earthly lest they come to look *like* instead of *unlike* each other. "Why do the opposites have to be kept poles apart, in such frightful tension," Kierkegaard asks, "why can't there be a little scaling down of the miraculous and a little increase of the less divine but more directly human—so as to have a little of the good life in the world?"[137] His wry question is rhetorical; he trusts that the reader would not willingly and deliberately opt for a mediocre existence based upon a mediocre language that likens instead of contrasts the earthly with the divine. "Eternity," writes Kierkegaard, "knows only one procedure: look at everything turned around."[138]

M. Jamie Ferreira notes that " 'of all the factors' of existence [that is, 'thought,' 'imagination,' and 'feeling' (*Postscript* I, 346-47)] it is imagination which is most suited to holding opposites together."[139] Aside from rendering the communicator a "nobody, purely objective," Kierkegaard offers yet another reason for his use of the art of indirect communication in general and metaphor in particular: "The art consists in . . . continually placing the qualitative opposites in a unity."[140] Just as Johannes Climacus notes that the presupposition to all comparison is difference,[141] so too a full appreciation of Kierkegaard's metaphors (and, by extension, his thought) requires not only an understanding of comparison that metaphor evokes, but also the discernment of significant differences and the awareness of contradiction, opposites and basic contrasts—for metaphor essentially is founded upon the principle of contradiction ($X=Y$), not sameness ($X=X$). " 'Where there is metaphor,' " Soskice cites Nelson Goodman, " 'there is conflict.' "[142] Far more than modes of direct communication, metaphors about human existence mirror collisions of heterogeneous elements in human existence, rendering metaphor (as opposed to systematic language) the truer representation of reality.

---

[136]*Judge for Yourself!*, 161.

[137]*Judge for Yourself!*, 162-63.

[138]*Christian Discourses*, 151.

[139]M. Jamie Ferreira, *Transforming Vision: Imagination and Will in Kierkegaardian Faith* (Oxford: Clarendon Press, 1991) 42.

[140]*Practice*, 133.

[141]See *Postscript* I, 594.

[142]Soskice, *Metaphor and Religious Language*, 170.

The synthesis of opposites that occurs by colliding two dissimilar or contrasting things in turn creates paradoxical situations that either are to be believed "by virtue of the absurd"[143] or rejected by actualizing what Anti-Climacus considers "the possibility of offense."[144] ("To believe in the eminent sense," Kierkegaard writes, "corresponds quite rightly to the marvelous, the absurd, the improbable, that which is foolishness to the understanding."[145]) Ferreira notes:

> The centrality and indispensability of imagination is . . . anchored in the importance of *paradoxical choice* in such accounts. It is the distinctive function of imagination to hold elements in tension, and without this activity paradox can neither be perceived nor appropriated. The Kierkegaardian accounts of the ethical provide a stark reminder that development cannot occur except paradoxically, and this explains both the necessity of imagination and the limits of the relevance of theoretical reflection to the process.
>
> Kierkegaard's focus on the paradoxical tension central to the ethical or subjective self is clearly revealed . . . in his insistence that the task of the existing individual is to remain in the great "contradiction"—between finite and infinite, positive and negative, comic and pathetic. The task is not to erase the tension (even if we could), but to sustain it, at the highest pitch possible. In this enterprise theoretical reflection is ineffective, for through such reflection we can only either resolve or reject tension—we cannot live it.[146]

Tension between oppositional forces implicit both in metaphor and human existence especially resonates in Kierkegaard's discussion of contemporaneity in his *Book on Adler*. Just as with Ezra Pound's claim that literature is news "that stays news" (that is, great literature is continually pertinent to, contemporary with, and able to be appropriated in a reader's life), so too Kierkegaard solicits the religious imagination to achieve a contemporaneous status with Christ and the news—the living word—of Christ. Metaphorically constructed situations in fiction and religion call on the reader's imagination to achieve a certain closeness or empathetic contemporaneity with the situation for purposes of appropriation. In effect, Kierkegaard calls upon readers' imaginations to bind time, to

---

[143]See *Fear & Trembling*, 35ff.
[144]See *Sickness*, 83ff.
[145]*Adler*, 47.
[146]Ferreira, *Transforming Vision*, 5-6.

collapse two millennia into a moment, and to render the *extraordinary* in time contemporary and present with the *ordinary* in time—something of which any individual is capable at any time precisely by virtue of human imagination. The intent is to push the primitive existential moment of choice to its crisis by compelling "one either to be offended or to believe," for, "contemporaneity is the tension that does not permit a person to leave it undecided":[147]

> When a person experiences a little event in his life, he learns something from it, and why? Because the event really comes to grips with him. The same person, however, can sit in the theater and see great scenes of tragedy, he can read about the extraordinary in the newspaper, he can listen to the pastor, and it all really makes no impress, and why? Because he does not become contemporary with it, because in the first two instances he lacks imagination; in the last he lacks the inner experience for really becoming contemporary with what is depicted, because he thinks like this: It is, of course, many years since it happened.[148]

The "inner experience" of which Kierkegaard speaks is a passion, a suffering from which the religious life extracts meaning and force. The roles of the imagination in general and metaphor in particular not only conspire largely to inspire and appropriate such passion, but also to possess credentials appropriate for the task: the metaphoric offers existential situations of contemporaneity toward which Kierkegaard points. The metaphoric is composed of elements of ambiguity, opposition, contradiction, and tension that seek natural conclusion in personal and existential choice, an either/or between the wonder of belief and the doubt of offense. In *Adler* (as elsewhere, especially in *Two Ages*), Kierkegaard envisions an age devoid of passion and thereby bereft of the contemporaneous situations that signify the transformative essence of becoming:

> Generally every human being is inclined to imagine a dilemma in relation to the extraordinary if he receives the proper tension-filled impression, has the elasticity to receive the pressure and to react to the pressure. The principle of contradiction has its life and its power in passion. Therefore, as soon as a person is really deeply moved by something, when he is in mortal danger, when the extraordinary appears before him, when he stands im-

---

[147]*Adler*, 41.
[148]*Adler*, 42.

passioned with his future fate in his hands, there is immediately an either/or. But since people nowadays are devoid of passion, flabby as a wet bowstring, since in a spiritual sense their priming powder is damp, then there soon remains only a tradition of the time when human life was tightened by the principle of contradiction. Just as one skeptically reads stories about the times when people became nine hundred years old and were gigantic in stature, so also a slack and dissolute generation will soon hear skeptically and suspect sagaciously the story that people have lived for whom an either/or was actually manifest, people who had their lives in this tension, while the pace of their own lives was like that of an arrow from a tightened bowstring, but this does not mean that for them there was an either/or only once.[149]

Existing, Johannes Climacus writes, cannot be done without passion.[150] Here, Johannes Climacus asserts the kind of existential passion to which Kierkegaard points in *Adler*.

Ferreira, in turn, details how Climacus speaks of such passion in two ways. One of those ways

directly implies the relevance of imaginative activity. He writes, for example, that "only momentarily can a particular individual, existing, be in a unity of the infinite and the finite that transcends existing. This instant is the moment of passion" [*Postscript* I, 197].

Passion, in other words, is generated in the experience or activity of holding or being two elements (infinite and finite) in a tension-in-unity. The centrality of the element of tension to the concept of passion is emphasized repeatedly: passion is precisely what occurs when a person comes "closest to being in two places at the same time" [*Postscript* I, 199]. The reason that the "unity is realized [only] in the moment of passion" is that no existing person can "be in two places at the same time, cannot be subject-object" [*Postscript* I, 199]. The unity is not an identity, but a sustained tension: "When he is closest to being in two places at the same time, he is in passion; but passion is only momentary, and passion is the highest pitch of subjectivity" [*Postscript* I, 199].[151]

Underlying the poetic features of Kierkegaard's writings, according to Walsh, is a poetic passion founded upon an understanding of the poetic

---

[149]*Adler*, 48.
[150]*Postscript* I, 311.
[151]Ferreira, *Transforming Vision*, 31.

as a mode for depicting and relating ourselves to ethical and religious ideals.[152] Just as passion is no ordinary word, then, metaphor—relative to passion—is no ordinary form. Metaphor is capable of inspiring esthetic passion (by concealing collisions with the ethical-religious self) just as much as it is capable of affirming ethical-religious passion (by disclosing and enacting collisions of the self between the esthetic and the ethical-religious), two concerns upon which the next two chapters focus.

---

[152]Walsh, *Living Poetically*, 1.

Chapter 2

CONCEALING COLLISIONS OF THE SELF: THE ESTHETIC POETIZATION OF METAPHOR

A. Reasons for Esthetic Hiddenness

Defining esthetic passion in contradistinction to ethical-religious passion offers an entrance into what the esthetic sphere means for Kierkegaard. Such definition also brings into relief how the esthete's poetized use of metaphor conceals the self from itself and thereby avoids ethical-religious collisions of the self.

Just as George Bernard Shaw compares the passion of a poet to "the bird that presses its breast against the sharp thorn to make itself sing,"[1] so too A begins his "Diapsalmata" of *Either/Or* I (and Kierkegaard officially begins his pseudonymous authorship) with a metaphor of the poet's concealed anguish, an anguish suffered solely *to produce art*:

> What is a poet? An unhappy person who conceals profound anguish in his heart but whose lips are so formed that as sighs and cries pass over them they sound like beautiful music. It is with him as with the poor wretches in Phalaris's bronze bull, who were slowly tortured over a slow fire; to him they sounded like sweet music. And people crowd around the poet and say to him, "Sing again soon"—in other words, may new sufferings torture your soul, and may your lips continue to be formed as before, because your screams would only alarm us, but the music is charming.[2]

---

[1]George Bernard Shaw, *Seven Plays by Bernard Shaw* (New York: Dodd, Mead and Co., 1967) 672 (from *Man and Superman*, act 4).

[2]*Either/Or* I, 19. Lucian reports that Phalaris, a sixth-century tyrant of Argrigentum, received a machine that meted out punishment to those accused while entertaining the accusers. It was a bronze bull that, after placing flutes in its nostrils, a fire under its belly, and the accused locked in its belly, issued sweet music from groans and shrieks of the accused. See *Either/Or* I, Notes, 605-606.

What is significant about such esthetic suffering or passion is that, unlike ethical-religious passion, its goal or purpose is in and for itself—that is, in and for the esthetic production of art—instead of for any existential, ethical, or religious development of the poet or readers' actual lives. As Frater Taciturnus avers, "without passion, no poet, and without passion, no poetry"[3]—the *telos* or goal of the esthetic poet's passion in this formulation is thus the object of poetry itself. According to Johannes Climacus, however, poetry or esthetic production is no *genuine telos* for a poet *qua* human being. What the esthetic poet lacks is a substantive, meaningful, *existential telos*:

> [T]he decisive difference between the poet and the upbuilding [ethical-religious] speaker remains, namely, that the poet has no *telos* [goal] other than psychological truth and the art of presentation, whereas the [upbuilding] speaker in addition has *principally* the aim of transposing everything into the upbuilding. The [esthetic] poet becomes absorbed in the portrayal of the passion, but for the upbuilding speaker this is only the beginning, and the next is crucial for him—to compel the stubborn person to disarm, to mitigate, to elucidate, in short, to cross over into the upbuilding.[4]

In *Two Ethical-Religious Essays*, pseudonymous writer H. H. writes in a similar key as he protests against the purely esthetic artist:

> [A]n artist . . . produces his work of art, but neither he nor his work of art has any *telos* outside. . . . Whether someone writes one page of lyrical poetry or folios of lyrical poetry makes no difference with regard to defining the direction of his work. The lyrical author cares only about the production, enjoys the joy of the production, perhaps often through pain and effort, but he has nothing to do with the others. He does not write *in order to*, in order to enlighten people, in order to help them onto the right road, in order to accomplish something—in short, he does not write: *in order to*.[5]

Metaphor used in the service of the ethical and the ethical-religious (that is, how Kierkegaard understood and used metaphor) thus contrasts sharply with metaphor used in the service of the finite and the purely esthetic. In the latter instance, metaphor embellishes and ornaments itself

---

[3]*Stages*, 405.
[4]*Postscript* I, 257.
[5]*Without Authority*, 107-108.

and its own esthetic production. Just as "physiology spreads out over the plant world and animal world and exhibits analogies, analogies which still are not supposed to be analogies, inasmuch as human life from the beginning, from the first trace, is qualitatively different from the plant kingdom and the animal kingdom,"[6] so also Kierkegaard sees little existential value in the construction of metaphors as purely esthetic constructs. "What then are all these analogies supposed to amount to, especially all the prodigious details of analogies through the use of microscopic observations? . . . *The only certainty is the ethical-religious.*"[7]

Without a substantive ethical-religious *telos* or end in sight—an end that would promote and help structure how time in existence is to be used—the very life and work of the esthete, according to Kierkegaard, is fragmentary. Pure estheticism is like a pier that one of Stephen Dedalus's students in James Joyce's *Ulysses* defines as "a disappointed bridge"[8]—in other words, estheticism does not carry itself or allow itself to be carried over to any other realm and thereby fails to find itself more complete and less fragmented in time and space. The esthete suffers separation from the ethical-religious, a sorrowful *dis*appointment in the context of the ethical-religious. "The artistic striving described by the esthete A in *Either/Or* . . . lies within the temporal," Malantschuk writes, "inasmuch as it has its goal in itself, which is why it is designated as 'fragmentary' (*Either/Or* I, 152). The highest this striving can bring a man is to catch a glimpse of the idea."[9] Lacking a worldview or lifeview to promote such a *telos* that Kierkegaard notes to be "the only true conclusion to every production," every "poet-conclusion" is an illusion.[10] Failing to point away from itself and toward upbuilding the existence of the poet and reader, esthetic production becomes a false or deceptive production for deception's sake, hell-bent on disappointment, doomed (in the romantic sense) to failure. It does not see past the moment of itself, leaving the reader nothing significant to appropriate:

---

[6]*Journals*, III, VII¹ A 186, n.d. [1846], 245.

[7]*Journals*, III, VII¹ A 186, n.d. [1846], 245.

[8]James Joyce, *Ulysses*, ed. Hans Walter Gabler et al. (New York: Random House, 1986) 21.

[9]*Journals*, IV, Commentary, 710. By way of esthetic illustration, see the first epigram (penned by A) of the present discussion.

[10]*Adler*, 8.

Generally the law for all religious communication is that it be true. Why? Because religiously there should be a turning in the direction of acting, doing accordingly, and it is precisely this turning which distinguishes the religious from the esthetic. The esthetic leads into the wild blue yonder, comes like a sneeze and goes like a sneeze. The esthetic is the moment and is in the moment; religiously, it is precisely the next moment which is decisive, for then I am supposed to act, and if I do not attend to that, I have changed that moment . . . into esthetic enjoyment.[11]

In one journal entry, Kierkegaard writes of two instructions in life; the first invokes the esthetic and purely imaginative while the second invokes the ethical-religious and actuality:

The first instruction [in life] is really only a prediction of what will happen. This is the instruction in the medium of imagination, which simply teaches the good but is not particularly attentive to the dialectical introduced when the medium itself (actuality) becomes dialectical. The final instruction [in life] is in the medium of actuality, in the dangers of actuality.[12]

In other words—and in the context of metaphorical usage—the esthetic stage presents metaphors as collisions in existence from which no existential reconciliation or solution may develop. Esthetics presents an individual with various contradictions of human existence. But, given that the esthete neither chooses nor does not choose to address existential collisions, the esthete leaves his reader in mere presentiment and essentially unequipped for deeper personal and ethical development predicated upon the freedom that choice offers. The esthetic poet instead becomes infatuated with constructing riddles and contradictions of human existence through metaphor. Such a poet, according to Kierkegaard, "can understand everything, in riddles, and wonderfully explain everything, in riddles, but he cannot understand himself or understand that he himself is a riddle . . . [whereas] true understanding is the decisive settlement of questions vital to his existence."[13] Without such an understanding, the esthete is able only to go so far as to question his own bondage, but looks no farther than the prison cell of his own making. A asks:

[11]*Journals*, I, XI[2] A 280, n.d. [1853-54], 379.
[12]*Journals*, I, VIII[1] A 143, n.d. [1847], 412-13.
[13]*Works of Love*, 30.

What is it that binds me? From what was the chain formed that bound the Fenris wolf? It was made of the noise of cats' paws walking on the ground, of the beards of women, of the roots of cliffs, of the grass of bears, of the breath of fish, and of the spittle of birds. I, too, am bound in the same way by a chain formed of gloomy fancies, of alarming dreams, of troubled thoughts, of fearful presentiments, of inexplicable anxieties. This chain is "very flexible, soft as silk, yields to the most powerful strain, and cannot be torn apart."[14]

Kierkegaard does not say, however, that the esthetic poet may not be religious—in fact, all he can say in this regard is that *qua* poet the esthete is not religious (implying that *qua* human being the esthete potentially may still develop toward the religious). As an *ethical-religious* poet, however, Kierkegaard is obliged to distinguish between the poetical usage of esthetic and religious poets,

for there certainly are religious poets. But these do not sing about erotic love [*Elskov*] and friendship; their songs are to the glory of God, about faith, hope, and love [*Kjerlighed*]. Nor do these poets sing about love in the sense in which the poet sings about erotic love, since love for the neighbor does not want to be sung about—it wants to be *accomplished*. Even if there were nothing else to prevent the poet from singing about love for the neighbor, it is already enough that beside every word in Holy Scripture a disturbing notice in invisible writing confronts him that says: *Go and do likewise* [Luke 10:37]. Does this sound like a poet-summons that calls upon him to sing?
Thus, the religious poet is a special case.[15]

What surfaces in Kierkegaard's distinction above is his focus in his esthetic works with the Faust theme, of choosing the world instead of God, of gaining the world but losing one's soul.[16] For the sake of esthetic production, the esthetic poet declines to confront being by abandoning his being and thereby also abandoning access to God. Anti-Climacus writes that, religiously understood,

every poet-existence (esthetics notwithstanding) is sin, the sin of poetizing instead of being, of relating to the good and the true through the imagination

---

[14]*Either/Or* I, 34.
[15]*Works of Love*, 46; my emphasis.
[16]See Matthew 16:26; Mark 8:36.

instead of being that—that is, existentially striving to be that. . . . A poet
. . . can have a very profound religious longing, and the conception of God
is taken up into his despair. He loves God above all, God who is his only
consolation in his secret anguish, and yet he loves the anguish and will not
give it up. He would like so very much to be himself before God, but with
the exclusion of the fixed point where the self suffers; there in despair he
does not will to be himself.[17]

If the religious is indeed the religious by passing through and incor-
porating the ethical, Johannes Climacus asserts (furthering Anti-
Climacus's argument), "then it cannot forget that religiously the pathos
is not a matter of singing praises and celebrating or composing song
books but of existing oneself." Climacus then speaks in Socratic terms
about the proper relationship a poet ought to have with his esthetic output
(a relationship for which Kierkegaard strived in his own esthetic production): "Thus the poet-production, if it is not totally absent, or if it is just
as rich as before, is regarded by the poet himself as the accidental, which
shows that he understands himself religiously, because esthetically the
poet-production is the important thing, and the [esthetic] poet is the
accidental."[18]

The esthetic poet's preference for *things* (with which to construct
metaphoric images for the sake of artistic production) instead of prefer-
ring the tenor of *being* explains why Socrates, according to Kierkegaard,
was so critical of esthetic poets: "What Socrates really meant by wanting
to have 'the poets' expelled from the state was that by writing in the
medium of the imagination instead of precipitating men into ethical
realization in actuality, the poets spoiled them and weaned them or kept
them from it."[19] Elsewhere in his journals, Kierkegaard defends Socrates'
ethical stance:

> Socrates . . . explodes existence, which is seen quite simply in his elimi-
> nation of the separation between poetry and actuality. Our lives are such that
> a poet portrays ideally—but actuality is a devil of a lot different. . . .

---

[17]*Sickness*, 77.
[18]*Postscript* I, 388.
[19]*Journals*, IV, X^2 A 229, n.d. [1849], 212. See also *Stages*, 442.

What does it mean to poetize? It means to contribute ideality. The poet takes an actuality which lacks something of ideality and adds to it, and this is the poem. . . .

In order to poetize a man it is surely necessary to understand him. But Socrates himself says: "To understand is to be." O dear poet, if you were able to understand this it would never enter your head to poetize it. . . .

Socrates' whole intention was to put an end to the poetic and to apply the ethical, the whole point of which is that it is actuality.[20]

Romantic and postromantic/modernist poets and writers suffer anxiety when they imagine themselves in relation to their work. Just as A maintains that "the god of erotic love is not in love himself,"[21] John Keats despairs of the radical misrelation he experiences between himself and that poet-existence in which he lives, an existence that constructs metaphors resulting only in poetic-productions. In a letter to Richard Woodhouse, he writes:

As to the poetical Character itself, (I mean that sort of which, if I am any thing, I am a Member; that sort distinguished from the Wordsworthian or egotistical sublime; which is a thing per se and stands alone) it is not itself—it has no self—it is every thing and nothing—It has no character—it enjoys light and shade; it lives in gusto, be it foul or fair, high or low, rich or poor, mean or elevated—It has much delight in conceiving an Iago as an Imogen. What shocks the virtuous philosopher, delights the camelion Poet. It does no harm from its relish of the dark side of things any more than from its taste for the bright one; because they both end in speculation. A poet is the most unpoetical of any thing in existence; because he has no Identity— he is continually in for—and filling some other Body—The Sun, the Moon, the Sea and Men and Women who are creatures of impulse are poetical and have about them an unchangeable attribute—the poet has none; no identity— he is certainly the most unpoetical of all God's Creatures. If then he has no self, and if I am a Poet, where is the Wonder that I should say I would write no more? Might I not at that very instant [have] been cogitating on the Characters of saturn and Ops? It is a wretched thing to confess; but it is a very fact that not one word I ever utter can be taken for granted as an opinion growing out of my identical nature—how can it, when I have no nature?[22]

---

[20]*Journals*, IV, XI[1] A 430, n.d. [1854], 222, 223.

[21]*Either/Or* I, 63.

[22]John Keats, *Selected Poems and Letters*, ed. Douglas Bush (Boston: Houghton Mifflin, 1959) 279.

The letter is penetrating not only because of its philosophical and existential self-scrutiny, but also for its ethical insight. Near the conclusion of the letter, Keats adds: "All I hope is that I may not lose all interest in human affairs—that the solitary indifference I feel for applause even from the finest Spirits, will not blunt any acuteness of vision I may have. . . . But even now I am perhaps not speaking from myself; but from some character in whose soul I now live."[23]

Franz Kafka speaks similarly, but he also details the extent to which his construction of metaphor conspires against the existence of his personal identity:

> Metaphors are one among many things that make me despair of writing. Writing's lack of independence, its dependence on the maid who tends the fire, on the cat warming itself by the stove, even on the poor old human being warming himself. All these are independent activities ruled by their own laws; only writing is helpless, cannot live in itself, is a joke and a despair.[24]

In this context, Kafka considers himself merely as a metaphor-maker, an imitator of life but not one who lives life. He speaks to the esthete's despairing and comical existence, both despairing and comical in the context of contradictions implicit in human nature. He echoes a similar complaint by Thoreau ("How often must one feel, as he looks back on his past life, that he has gained a talent but lost a character!"[25]) and anticipates a similar comical-pathetic, despairing assertion of theatrical actor-existences uttered by the Player in Tom Stoppard's *Rosencrantz and Guildenstern Are Dead*: "we're *actors*—we're the opposite of people!"[26]

Whereas earnestness may call upon the religious poet to "deceive into the truth," the concealed deceit of the esthete (developed to produce esthetic productions as the *telos* of the poet's existence) is attributed in part to a lack of earnestness in himself, an absence of any inward movement in which respect to the soul is paid. "The poet [as esthete] is

---

[23]Ibid., 280.

[24]Franz Kafka, *Diaries 1914–1923* (New York: Schocken, 1965) 200-201.

[25]Henry David Thoreau, *The Journal of Henry David Thoreau* I, 352 (28 March 1842).

[26]Tom Stoppard, *Rosencrantz and Guildenstern Are Dead* (New York: Grove Press, 1967) 63.

the child of eternity but lacks the earnestness of eternity,"[27] Kierkegaard writes, intimating that, although his esthete traffics in the same style of language as sacred language of the religious poet (that is, metaphorical speech), he does not come to understand the ethical-religious demands of such speech. Unable to believe, for instance, that (as the Gospel suggests) he shall be like a bird, the esthetic poet concludes: "I cannot understand the Gospel; there is a language difference between us that, if I were to understand it, it would kill me."[28] In other words, it would kill the esthetic existence of the poet if he were to understand himself as ethically shouldering, Atlas-like, the full weight of actuality—the very actuality from which he escapes by virtue of a purely concealing esthetic imagination. Kierkegaard concludes this idea by weeding out the esthetic poet's metaphor—that "irresistible invention"—from the religious poet's metaphor: "But the Gospel dares to command the poet, dares to order that he *shall* be like the bird. And so earnest is the Gospel that the poet's most irresistible invention does not make it smile."[29]

Unable to reconcile himself with the earnestness of eternity,[30] Kierkegaard's esthete becomes inflamed by poetic beauty instead of simply and purely warmed by the thought that poetry's metaphoric content is capable of ethical or religious upbuilding. Kierkegaard maintains that "the poetic is a dangerous gift both for the man himself and for others, lest that which ought to be a character transformation becomes an esthetic flash fire."[31] In the context of an apparent irreconcilable difference with eternity, the esthetic poet mimics the opening lines of A's trancelike, esthetic, "ecstatic discourse": Construct metaphors, and you will regret it; do not construct metaphors, and you will also regret it; construct metaphors or do not construct metaphors, you will regret it either way.[32] In other words, by constructing metaphors and being esthetically enamored by the very art of metaphors for the sake of the poetic production, one easily may be seduced to turning and turning in vain to the esthetic artifice of metaphor for deliverance from despair—instead of yielding to and becoming wholly dependent upon the religious within existence for

---

[27]*Without Authority*, 8.
[28]*Without Authority*, 8.
[29]*Without Authority*, 9.
[30]*Point of View*, 47.
[31]*Journals*, I, XI^2 A 48, n.d. [1854], 379.
[32]Cf. *Either/Or* I, 38.

deliverance. By not constructing metaphors, however, one may never come to appreciate even a possible relationship with God—a relationship of "cross[ing] over to the upbuilding"[33] to which metaphorical constructions, if existentially appropriated, point.

The esthetic poet who comes to construct metaphors but remains ignorant of how they personally may be appropriated is not unlike W. H. Auden's depiction of the poet who "pretends for fun; he asserts his freedom by lying—that is to say, by creating worlds which he *knows* are imaginary."[34] The simple truth is that avoiding actuality renders esthetic productions poor translations and woefully abbreviated versions of existence—what Kierkegaard calls instances of "foreshortened" actuality. Kierkegaard writes that

> the medium of imagination is a medium of ideality and therefore can express greatness and glory very well, but it cannot express the wretchedness of actuality except on a very foreshortened scale. . . .
> Thus in a certain sense we can say providence has diligently planned actuality this way in order that it can become earnestness, an actual suffering, for everyone individually. If a person could completely anticipate actuality in ideality and imagination and by means of such a movement of the imagination learn how to know himself, develop, etc., equally well as in actuality, then he would really have to say that actuality is superfluous, that God, if I dare say so, has behaved strangely. But this is not the case.[35]

Anti-Climacus writes similarly that

> the power of the imagination cannot depict suffering except in a perfected (idealized), that is, in a mitigated, toned-down, foreshortened depiction. . . .
> With regard to adversities and sufferings, it lacks the actuality of time and of temporality and of earthly life.[36]

Addressing limitations of the poet and the esthete's ultimate rejection of actuality for its idealization, Johannes Climacus writes that "for the poet, actuality is merely an occasion that prompts him to abandon actuality in order to seek the ideality of possibility. Poetic pathos,

---

[33]*Postscript* I, 257.
[34]Henrik Ibsen, *Brand*, trans. Michael Meyer with a foreword by W. H. Auden (Garden City NY: Anchor Books, 1960) 29.
[35]*Journals*, I, IX A 382, n.d. [1848], 458.
[36]*Practice*, 187.

therefore, is essentially fantasy."[37] Similarly, John Elrod maintains that imagination can open up possibilities for existence but cannot legitimately become the medium *par excellence* of existence: "As soon as the self volatilizes itself in its imagination and abandons its strenuous task of remaining in existence while living in the possibilities of the infinite, it becomes fantastical."[38]

Such a phantom-nightmare is that from which the esthete finds it nearly impossible to awake. But to remain in such a stultifying dream is not to become fully human. C. Stephen Evans, for instance, asserts that the esthete's imaginative development is not existential development. "Although both thought and imagination are essential elements of existence, neither is existence itself," Evans writes. "It is possible to imaginatively conceive many possibilities and to have clearly thought through the meaning of these without having in the deepest sense existed. To exist means to choose; choice requires resolution; resolution requires what Climacus calls passion."[39] The moment of existential passion for Johannes Climacus is thus bound up in the unity of the infinite and the finite that transcends existence: "In passion, the existing subject is infinitized in the eternity of the imagination and yet is also most definitely himself."[40] Johannes Climacus further distinguishes between the medium of the poet and the medium of the ethicist, and by doing so points to the eventual abandonment of imaginary constructions for an individual who is becoming an existing person: "the poet's medium is the medium of imagination, is being but not becoming, at most is becoming in a very foreshortened perspective. But take the individual out of this medium of imagination, out of this being, and place him in existence—then ethics immediately confronts him with its requirement."[41]

For all his criticism of the purely esthetic imagination, Kierkegaard nonetheless does not unilaterally dismiss esthetic production as a value-less tool for instruction. Even a bad work of art ethically and critically viewed may indirectly point, by its very contrast, to the good. Further,

---

[37]*Postscript* I, 388.

[38]John Elrod, *Being and Existence in Kierkegaard's Pseudonymous Works* (Princeton NJ: Princeton University Press, 1975) 35.

[39]C. Stephen Evans, *Kierkegaard's Fragments and Postscript: The Religious Philosophy of Johannes Climacus* (Atlantic Highlands NJ: Humanities Press, 1983) 38-39.

[40]*Postscript* I, 197.

[41]*Postscript* I, 420-21.

Kierkegaard's negative evaluations of imagination (and there are many, especially in the pseudonymous works of Johannes Climacus and Anti-Climacus) point primarily to ontological dangers of the esthetic poet or reader who dwells in or is vulnerable to the pitfalls and trappings of the esthetic sphere, for the purely imaginative invests in the forgetfulness of actuality and thereby conceals actuality. Metaphor, as a logical contradiction $(X=Y)$, is capable of manifesting falsehoods that hold the double-potential either of revelation or concealment. The esthetic poet defaults to the latter, what Johannes Climacus calls in reference to *Either/Or* "esthetic hiddenness."[42] Such passionate attention on the esthete's part to conceal existence by bathing in the poetic production of metaphor for its own sake instead of constructing metaphors to prompt individuals to exist is perhaps what is on A's mind when he writes that "I am no friend of figures of speech; modern literature has made them very distasteful to me. It has gone almost so far that whenever I encounter a figure of speech, an involuntary fear comes over me that its true objective is to conceal an obscurity in the thought."[43] A goes so far as to lay a skeptical eye upon the praises given to that literary vehicle that esthetically informs the very brand of egotistic, anguished passion on which he thrives. But then, A is a doubter, and as a doubter, he cannot help but doubt even the tools of his trade. As much as metaphor may conceal for the esthete, it also indirectly may reveal a glimpse of the ethical-religious by virtue of such concealment—an "obscurity" that A understandably fears and from which his fugitive eyes evade. Religious love, too, hides, but what it hides (a multitude of sins) it hides in the service of the religious—which is antithetical to esthetic hiddenness. A, bereft of religious love, hides and ultimately forgets the religious, and by doing so he hides the self from therapeutic collisions with the self that otherwise would serve the good of the self. The self—which is spirit[44]—becomes forgotten amid an ocean of metaphor that egotistically points to and reflects itself, thereby concealing the ethical-religious instead of moving beyond itself to the ethical-religious.

---

[42]*Postscript* I, 268.
[43]*Either/Or* I, 128.
[44]*Sickness*, 13.

B. Sources of Esthetic Hiddenness: the Romantic Tradition

Kierkegaard maintains that the imperfection of everything human involves not being able to see one thing and its opposite *simultaneously*.[45] His assertion implies that the dialectician-ethicist can little afford to forget the opposite nature of a thing or idea just because it temporarily is out of sight or out of mind. Such forgetfulness, after all, breeds an esthetic, sensual partiality for things immediately seen, envisioned, or experienced, thereby succumbing to the temptation of relaxing the tension of opposites and paradox upon which the soundest existential and ethical choices and responsibilities—and the greatness of human characters—are based.

Not so for the esthete, who rather sees great esthetic possibility in forgetfulness for the very same reasons rejected by the ethicist. A maintains that all people desire to forget all unpleasantries. His answer to the problem involves poetry and, indirectly, poetry's syntax, namely, metaphor: "The more poetically one remembers, the more easily one forgets, for to remember poetically is actually only an expression of forgetting.

---

[45]*Journals*, I, III A 112, n.d. [1841], 328. Sartre also intimates this human "imperfection" of which Kierkegaard speaks. His *Psychology of Imagination* in part argues that to imagine or conceive of anything, actuality must be negated, excluded, become nothing in the moment of imagining. When a woman from Warroad, Minnesota, for example, imagines herself on a beach in Bora Bora, the reality of sitting in Warroad imaginatively is canceled or excluded to make way for the imagined actuality of Bora Bora. In dramatic theater, the implied admonition to suspend one's disbelief (dramatic illusion) directs the viewer to exclude or negate one's perception of actuality so that the activity on stage temporarily becomes actuality via the imagination. In an instance of theater-going, the imagination temporarily abandons or rejects actuality; the better the performance, the greater the abandon from the actual world and into an imaginary world—the perceptive, imaginative audience tends to forget or cancel the existence of the auditorium's exit signs, proscenium, other audience members. Theater becomes a form of temporary escape *from* actuality. Audience members with imagination may become "swept away" by the stage action, at least during the dramatic performance; they become, in essence, "out of touch with reality." Just as physics suggests that newly formed matter presupposes the cancellation or transformation of another form of matter, so too imaginatively sustaining an image requires the cancellation or transformation of one's perception of a given actuality for as long as the image is sustained. See Jean Paul Sartre, *The Psychology of Imagination*, A Citadel Press Book (New York: Carol Pub. Group, 1991).

When I remember poetically, my experience has already undergone the change of having lost everything painful."[46]

For the ethicist, metaphor and imaginary constructions are avenues for the disclosure of remembrance (that is, escaping *to* reality), especially if such a person appropriates the metaphor into his own life. But for the esthete (as A suggests above), metaphor deadends in the concealment of forgetfulness (that is, escaping *from* reality). With forgetfulness comes a loosening of conscience and an avoidance of ethical and social responsibilities associated with such a conscience—all for the sake of the immediate conquest of the esthetic production. In this context, Kearney writes that romantic culture conceals the condition of *social* existence at the same time it affirms the condition of *esthetic* existence: "Rejecting the constraints of a dehumanizing social mediation, the romantic individual [seeks] his happiness in and through the immediacy of the creative imagination."[47] The esthetic poet that Kierkegaard developed was derived *from* just such a romantic culture.

Susan Sontag's consideration of the romantic tradition in *Illness as Metaphor* is on par with Kierkegaard's own critique of the esthete when she offers insight into narcissistic effects of the classic romantic poet. Like Kierkegaard's ethical position on metaphor (that is, metaphor's strict poetization must be demythologized and disclosed for metaphor to ally itself with ethical action), Sontag dedicates her own inquiry to the elucidation of particular metaphors of illness "and a liberation from them."[48]

Sickness, Sontag writes, made people "interesting," which is how "romantic" originally was defined and promulgated.

> (Schlegel, in his essay 'On the Study of Greek Poetry' [1795], offers "the interesting" as the ideal of modern—that is, romantic—poetry.) "The ideal of perfect health," Novalis wrote in a fragment from the period 1799–1800, "is only scientifically interesting"; what is really interesting is sickness, "which belongs to individualizing. . . . The romantic treatment of death asserts that people were made singular, made more interesting, by their illnesses. "I look pale," said Byron, looking into the mirror. "I should like to die of a consumption." "Why?" asked a friend, who was visiting Byron

---

[46] *Either/Or* I, 293.

[47] Richard Kearney, *The Wake of Imagination* (Minneapolis: University of Minnesota Press, 1988) 197, 198.

[48] Susan Sontag, *Illness as Metaphor* (New York: Vintage, 1978) 3; my emphasis.

in Athens in October 1810. "Because the ladies would all say, 'Look at that poor Byron, how interesting he looks in dying. . . . ' "

The romantics invented invalidism as a pretext for leisure, and for dismissing bourgeois obligations in order to live only for one's art. It was a way of retiring from the world without having to take responsibility for the decision.[49]

Robert Perkins notes that Kierkegaard, earlier in his authorship, also attempted to focus "the interesting" upon the esthetic persona—a persona that always stands prior to choice and the ethical responsibilities that come with such freedom:

Aage Henriksen has written, "It is not in the word 'love' but in 'the interesting' that [*Either/Or* I] has its center of gravity." The seducer is a master of the interesting. His editor writes, "His life had been an attempt to accomplish the task of living poetically. With a sharply developed talent for discovering the interesting in life, he has known how to find it and after having found it has continually reproduced his experience half poetically" (*Either/Or* I, 304). Thus, the first volume of *Either/Or*, and the "Diary of the Seducer" in particular, is the very model of Romantic literature . . . [for] seduction is a practice of Romantic hiddenness. . . . The seducer deprives the woman of her ethical integrity and victimises her. Hidden beneath the glitter of the seducer's ingratiating charm are the grotesque and diabolical, two further marks of the interesting.[50]

Fallout from the esthete's obsession with the interesting is dictated by the failure of the esthete to upbuild himself ethically or religiously. The indifference he fosters regarding concern for others renders him ethically characterless, no more capable of ethical striving than a kite-flying child. Kierkegaard writes:

There is an apathy about the obligation to have strength of character, a stupidity of characterlessness that is more dreadful than stupidity of mind, perhaps more incurable. And perhaps the most sorrowful thing that can be said about a person is: He cannot be lifted up, his own knowledge cannot lift him up. Like the child who lets his kite go skyward, he lets his knowledge

---

[49]Ibid., 30, 32-33.
[50]Robert L. Perkins, "Abraham's Silence Aesthetically Considered," in *Kierkegaard on Art and Communication*, ed. George Pattison (New York: St. Martin's Press, 1992) 108, 109.

ascend; he finds it interesting, enormously interesting, to watch it, to follow it with his eyes—but it does not lift him up; he remains in the mud, more and more desperately craving the interesting.[51]

What strikes Kierkegaard about the romantics, David Gouwens notes, is their unsatisfied yearnings[52]—yearnings that lack a given *telos* or ideal. Walsh suggests that the romantic poets according to Kierkegaard are engaged in an ideal striving without an ideal, for " 'every ideal is instantly nothing but an allegory hiding a higher ideal within itself, and so on into infinity' (*Irony*, 306)."[53]

Gouwens offers an especially cogent assessment of Kierkegaard's critique of the romantic tradition in his *Kierkegaard's Dialectics of the Imagination*, emphasizing that romantics become victims of their own irony because, although they use concrete images in their poetry, they do not live the concrete. Early in Gouwens' discussion, he quotes from *The Concept of Irony* where Kierkegaard attacks Friedrich Schlegel's novel *Lucinde*:

> "This [letting fantasy alone prevail] is repeated throughout *Lucinde*. Who would be so inhuman as not to be able to enjoy the free play of fantasy, but that does not imply that all of life should be abandoned to imaginative intuition. When fantasy alone gains the upper hand in this way, it exhausts and anesthetizes the soul, robs it of all moral tension, makes life a dream."[54]

Gouwens then suggests that young Kierkegaard's comment is central to his understanding of the romantic imagination: "The imagination is the source of the play of spirit and mind, and as such one can delight in it, but one cannot devote one's whole life to the imagination, for it will in the end make of life a dream."[55] Later in his discussion, Gouwens claims that romanticism tends to view everything as an esthetic object, and that its final flaw is an ethical one, "more amoral than immoral, since the

---

[51]*Late Writings*, 260-61.

[52]David J. Gouwens, *Kierkegaard's Dialectic of the Imagination* (New York: Peter Lang, 1989) 48.

[53]Sylvia Walsh, *Living Poetically: Kierkegaard's Existential Aesthetics* (University Park PA: Pennsylvania State University Press, 1994) 54.

[54]Gouwens, *Kierkegaard's Dialectic of the Imagination*, 15. See *Irony*, 292.

[55]Ibid.

romantic lives too abstractly 'to reach the concretion of the moral and the ethical' (*Irony*, 283)."[56]

The twofold argument Kierkegaard ultimately levels against the romantic imagination is concisely articulated by Gouwens:

(1) The Romantics are guilty of expanding the functions of the imagination to such an extent that they "fantastically" lose contact with finite "actuality," and thus lose themselves in imagination. . . . Contrary to the Romantics' hopes, their failure means that their imagination is not anchored to the finite and actual world, but diffuses the self in a world of endless "possibility." (2) Because the redemption of actuality fails, the actual takes its revenge on the Romantic ironic imagination, rendering it self-contradictory as a life-stance. . . . The ironist becomes the victim of irony. The result is that the Romantic imagination is self-defeating: Romantic irony is not true irony, its feeling is not true feeling, its freedom is not true freedom, its ethics is not ethical, its poetry is unpoetic, and its philosophico-religious speculation ends in confusion.[57]

Later in his cogent discussion, Gouwens summarizes Kierkegaard's opposition to the romantic imagination in the context of how possibility overwhelms actuality, thereby overwhelming itself and any lifeview it may possess:

To live in imagination is to live in possibility, the very opposite of the actuality that gives the self an historical situation (as gift) and an ethical definition (as task). The imagination may attempt to incorporate the actual and finite, but as long as the imagination is itself the medium of that attempt, it is doomed to failure. . . . Central to Kierkegaard's diagnosis of the Romantic imagination's self-contradictions is his conviction that [romantics] lack a consistent principle of form by which to order experience, an organic "lifeview" necessary to both personal and artistic self-integration. In possessing a lifeview an author acquires a depth of outlook that unifies a work of art, delivering it from arbitrariness. Without a lifeview, feeling, freedom, ethics, poetry, and religion become formless and imaginary, and in this inchoate state dissolve into self-contradiction, having at best the negative coherence of a recurring idea.[58]

---

[56]Ibid., 61.
[57]Ibid., 54-55.
[58]Ibid., 70-71.

With Kierkegaard, according to Kearney, comes a definite rupture in the romantic paradigm: "To remain forever within the esthetic phase of creative imagination is, for Kierkegaard, to remain inauthentic; for it is to refuse the either/or choices which constantly confront us in our everyday experience."[59]

C. Becoming Entangled in Metaphor and Acting Fatally

Just as novels sketch out particular situations of imagined characters, Kierkegaard's metaphorical and imaginary constructions invite readers to compare and contrast their own actual or potential situations in life with fictitious characters. The constructions further portray (or at least indicate potential outcomes of) certain human actions, indirectly pointing to ethical decisions that must be made to develop one's humanness. The reader becomes an objective, if not pseudo-clandestine, seer or *voyeur*— not only of the lives of imaginatively constructed characters but also of the reader's own actual and possible lives. When T. S. Eliot's J. Alfred Prufrock muses to himself at the outset of his love song, "Let us go then, you and I," the reader not only secretly witnesses the beginning of a hellish tour of Prufrock's past and potential lives of passivity and inaction (of "decisions and revisions which a minute will reverse"); the reader also may see in Prufrock's testimony shades of the reader's own past and potential lives. *Either* the reader remains a mere *voyeur* and spectator of other actual or imagined lives in an esthetic sense / *Or* he becomes an active participant in his own actuality to which imaginary constructions ethically point. If the reader chooses the *Or*, the issue then turns to *how* he ethically appropriates metaphorical and existential situations in a way that remains true to himself instead of merely pretending to be or to imitate selves portrayed by the metaphorical or imaginary constructions.

Ignoring, denying, or concealing the ethical force of metaphorical constructs—that is, willfully not being alert or not recognizing such constructs—condemns the romantic to willful failure. James Joyce's Stephen Dedalus might never have become an artist had he, instead of being alert to the fate of the son (Icarus) of his paternal namesake and steered away from it, chose to ignore or forget the influence that such a metaphor may otherwise have had on him.

---

[59]Kearney, *The Wake of Imagination*, 201.

In Herman Melville's *Moby-Dick*, Ahab may be said to have consciously entangled himself metaphorically in the life and character of his Old Testament namesake, an evil king; Ahab attempts to escape ethical responsibility for his actions by claiming to first mate Starbuck that

> "Ahab is for ever Ahab, man. This whole act's immutably decreed. 'Twas rehearsed by thee and me a billion years before this ocean rolled. Fool! I am the Fates' lieutenant; I act under orders."[60]

Accepting (at least ambiguously) the wicked heritage of his Old Testament prototype demonstrates how Ahab's human perceptions of reality may have been influenced by linguistic, historical, and metaphorical constructs. By appropriating the Old Testament's metaphorical construct into his reality, Ahab relaxes or ignores preexisting ethical boundaries of his existence. Although he is a learned captain, he not only rejects the objectivity required to see and distinguish metaphor's ethical limits, he also rejects any consideration of the degree to which the metaphorical construction is a valid and credible facsimile of reality. To borrow George Eliot's words, Ahab gets his thoughts "entangled in metaphor and act[s] fatally upon the strength of them."[61]

The paradigm of becoming entangled in metaphor and acting fatally, however, may be reserved for Satan in *Paradise Lost*. His kingdom of Hell, Pandemonium, is structured to mimic heavenly hierarchies. After being evicted from heaven, Satan waxes poetic over his new domain with a monomaniacal supremacy of mind over matter and an intent to confuse, through metaphor, divinity and hell: "The mind is its own place, and in itself / Can make Heav'n of Hell, a Hell of Heav'n."[62]

The kind of dialectical collision initiated by metaphor of which George Eliot speaks and from which the likes of Ahab and Satan suffer occurs in the psyche, where volatile, equivocal mixtures of truth and illusion, good and evil, power and impotence, and knowledge and ignorance are planted like land mines, awaiting fatal steps of ethical

---

[60]Herman Melville, *Moby-Dick* (Berkeley: University of California Press, 1979) 563 (chap. 134).

[61]George Eliot, *Middlemarch*, ed. W. J. Harvey (New York: Penguin, 1965) 111 (bk. 1, chap. 10).

[62]John Milton, *Complete Poems and Major Prose*, ed. Merritt Y. Hughes (Indianapolis: Odyssey Press, 1957) 217 (*Paradise Lost*, bk. 1, ll. 254-55).

transgression. Dialectic, according to Kierkegaard, "teaches caution in the handling of strong medicine, teaches one first to make it possible that it can be used without doing harm, and only then does one use it." But, he adds, "when extraordinariness is represented temptingly as a brilliant distinction, such an example can have a harmful influence."[63] Earnestness continues to be essential to avoid fatal steps in the midst of the equivocation that dialectical collision presupposes: "Once the requisite earnestness takes hold," Kierkegaard writes, "it can also solve [such equivocation], but always in such a way that the earnestness itself vouches for the correctness."[64]

Soskice cites Marc Belth, who claims that " 'not to recognize metaphors . . . is to be used by those metaphors. . . . To recognize them is to use them, consciously alert to the influence and consequences of their use.' "[65] At face value, Belth suggests that meaningful or consequential metaphors may entangle a person if he is not aware of their ethical ramifications. His statement echoes Sontag's thesis in *Illness as Metaphor*, namely, that disclosing or seeing through the illusory poetization of metaphor to envision ethical truths suggested by metaphor will free the interpreter of metaphor from entanglement. Anxiety-ridden, self-conscious questions such as the one posed by Leopold Bloom in Joyce's *Ulysses* ("Art thou real, my ideal?"[66]) become moot, for such ethical objectivity breaks through the mask of such a person's fixed esthetic persona.

Belth's statement also elucidates Constantin Constantius's farcical entanglement in metaphor. In *Repetition*, Constantius consciously attempts through esthetic means to manipulate and conjure up an actual reality from an ideal reality. Gouwens writes that Constantius, living only through imagination,

> fixes upon a recollected ideal picture of the esthetic state to be repeated, a remembered image of the past that becomes his measure for testing, and finding wanting, the present external reality. Mired in recollection, Constantin gives up hope and ultimately ends in despair at the contradiction between his imagined ideal and the actual result. . . . Constantin's conclu-

---

[63]*Adler*, 170.

[64]*Point of View*, 34.

[65]Janet Soskice, *Metaphor and Religious Language* (Oxford: Clarendon Press, 1985) 79.

[66]Joyce, *Ulysses*, 298.

sion: in life there is no satisfaction, so better to opt for an esthetic self-sufficiency that recognizes repetition's impossibility.[67]

Constantius fails for *consciously* trying. He willfully attempts to catch the butterfly whose sole possibility to alight upon his shoulder exists only if he, in earnestness, lets well enough alone. But Constantius's intelligence cannot let well enough alone. The more he tries esthetically to mimic or be like his ideal, the farther from his ideal he becomes. Constantius fails at repetition because the scene desired to be repeated never can be repeated unless his intellectual acuity and will to repeat are negated and an unpretentious faith is posited. Irony (something in which Constantius is highly invested, despite his knowing that it is merely a negative relation to reality) must be rejected if he is even to consider the possibility of gaining repetition. In his journal, Kierkegaard writes that Constantius "is clever, an ironist, battles the interesting—but is not aware that he himself is caught in it . . . —therefore Constantin is wrecked on what he himself has discovered."[68] Meanwhile, according to Kierkegaard, the young man whom Constantius observes (and observes in contradistinction to his own existence) goes further.[69] Gouwens again brings into relief the Constantius/young man diptych. He states that the young man is oriented to feeling, not irony, and although he cannot match Constantius in terms of dialectical prowess, he goes beyond Constantius's imagination in terms of existence. "Instead of the category of jest Constantin exhibits, the young man possesses that category of earnestness Constantin describes but does not embody," Gouwens notes. "Like Constantin he withdraws into imagination, yet unlike Constantin the young man seeks repetition by serious imaginative reflection upon his ethical existence rather than mere manipulation of his environment."[70]

The young man succeeds in appropriating Job as metaphorical vehicle not only because he claims to understand Job's "tormented . . . powerful

---

[67]David J. Gouwens, "Understanding, Imagination, and Irony in Kierkegaard's *Repetition*," in *Fear and Trembling and Repetition*, International Kierkegaard Commentary 6, ed. Robert L. Perkins (Macon GA: Mercer University Press, 1993) 291.

[68]*Journals*, III, IV A 169, n.d. [1844], 764.

[69]*Journals*, III, IV A 169, n.d. [1844], 764. Note: see *Repetition*, Supplement, 326, for corrected version of the *Journals* entry.

[70]Gouwens, "Understanding, Imagination, and Irony in Kierkegaard's *Repetition*," 292, 293, 294.

cries" but because he makes Job's words his own and takes responsibility for such appropriation.[71] By such appropriation, freely born of an ethical suffering, the young man does what Constantius cannot. Gouwens adds that the young man's imagination considers possibilities by realizing them in the movement of freedom (*kinesis*) beyond reflection[72]:

> The model of Job's ordeal shapes his own existence, and thus he gains understanding of himself, and even a "consciousness raised to the second power," available only to those who in suffering relate possibilities to their lives. While he may lack Constantin's dialectical self-consciousness, the young man stands at the "Archimedean point," with an inwardness of understanding that is beyond Constantin and which, ironically, judges Constantin's limits. . . . The young man finally stands above Constantin—as the fruit of cultivated trees is more fragrant than the flower of wild trees (*Repetition*, 127)—precisely because the young man's passionate imagination and understanding are a decisive advance over the ironist's despairing imagination and understanding, opening the way to the religious spheres of existence.[73]

With respect to metaphor, what is important here is the ability that both Constantius and the young man have in entangling themselves in metaphor if ethical-religious qualifications do not exist. The young man maintains the possibility of ethical-religious qualifications because of the model he chooses (Job)—a role model of an ideal figure who, according to Gouwens, metaphorically provides new categories for self-illumination: "Constantin imagines the categories of the ethical and religious spheres descriptively, but the young man uses his imagination in concrete exploration of these categories—and of himself."[74]

Gouwens' assessment of the young man informs a reader's subtle understanding of the influence that a model or prototype may have if ethically appropriated as a metaphorical vehicle to a reader's life. The young man does not deny that he walks a thin line between the positive therapeutic effect that such a metaphor may have upon him and the dangers that await him if he, denying an ethical posture and romantically and demonically acting like Captain Ahab, willfully manifests his own

---

[71]*Repetition*, 205-206.
[72]Gouwens, "Understanding, Imagination, and Irony in Kierkegaard's *Repetition*," 300. See also *Repetition*, 149, and Supplement to *Repetition*, 310, 322.
[73]Ibid., 300-301, 305.
[74]Ibid., 296.

destiny. He writes: "anxiety comes over me, as if I still did not understand what someday I would come to understand, as if the horror I was reading about was waiting for me, as if by reading about it I brought it upon myself, just as one becomes ill with the sickness one reads about."[75]

Contrary to the young man in *Repetition*, Johannes the Seducer is the imaginary character who, in the most extreme flight of self-deception in Kierkegaard's esthetic *dramatis personae*, attempts to push Constantius's own desire for repetition into actuality while ignoring all ethical avenues by which the actualization of such desire may be made possible. In the penultimate journal entry of his diary, Johannes the Seducer, like a vampire or one of the witches in *Macbeth* that inspire demonic doubleness and dark ambiguity, evokes the midnight powers of erotic love in himself, before intoxicatingly asserting his own esthetic ideality and immortality:

> Everything is metaphor; I myself am a myth about myself, for is it not as a myth that I hasten to this tryst? Who I am is irrelevant; everything finite and temporal is forgotten; only the eternal remains, the power of erotic love, its longing, its bliss. How responsive is my soul, like a taut bow, how ready are my thoughts, like arrows in my quiver, not poisoned, and yet able to blend with blood. How vigorous, sound, and happy is my soul, as present as a god.[76]

Gouwens cites Ronald Grimsley:

> "As [Johannes] gazes steadfastly at the image mirrored in his own consciousness, . . . the dividing line between reality and imagination becomes blurred. . . . " Johannes's imagination becomes completely enclosed within itself. . . . In a complex hierarchy of imaginative irony, Johannes hovers completely above not only his own but also his victim's emotions in a complicated dance of deception.[77]

Johannes the Seducer and Constantius meet on the level of consciously attempting to force the ideal into the actual. Where they differ is how they respond to such an ethical breach: Constantius despairingly resigns

---

[75]*Repetition*, 206.

[76]*Either/Or* I, 444.

[77]Gouwens, *Kierkegaard's Dialectic of the Imagination*, 176. Perhaps Joseph Conrad's narrator in *Lord Jim* has a similar sentiment in mind when he describes imagination as "the enemy of men, the father of all terrors." See Joseph Conrad, *Lord Jim* (Garden City NY: Doubleday, Page & Co., 1924) 11.

the task by suggesting that repetition is impossible, while Johannes the Seducer simply ignores the breach, plunging himself headlong into self-deception and emptiness. Like Kierkegaard's lover of the Greek mode of architecture,[78] Johannes the Seducer tries to acquire life through an idealized form instead of allowing such a form to be acquired through humble striving in life; he consciously attempts (like any of Kierke-gaard's romantic esthetes) to compose himself poetically instead of allowing himself to become poetically composed.[79] By consciously willing himself to be a myth (that is, that which is not himself) he despairs by not willing to be himself; by choosing not to be himself, he partakes in an egoistic self-deception that avoids the ethical demands of accepting one's own humanity and human limitations. He becomes lost in abstraction and does not honestly attend to himself. His love is purely reflective, thus, according to Judge William, it "consumes itself and . . . arbitrarily takes one position then another";[80] he thereby avoids any and all ethical commitments to himself.

Esthetic hiddenness and self-deception also are transferable to historical characters, and Kierkegaard took issue (especially in his later writings) with such characters. Adolph Peter Adler is a case of someone who willfully imposed an apostolic ideality upon his own actual existence, thereby entangling himself in metaphor. "Carried away into religious eccentricity," Kierkegaard writes, Adler "mistakes himself for an apostle."[81] Adler is no Johannes the Seducer, and although Kierkegaard treats Adler with some diplomatic sympathy, his reason for writing about Adler is to point out, once again, the danger of misappropriating—either romantically or otherwise—a metaphorical vehicle by self-consciously or willfully constructing that vehicle in one's own image.

Adler was deeply moved by something higher, Kierkegaard writes,

> but now when he wants to express his state in words, wants to communicate, *he confuses the subjective with the objective, his altered subjective state with an external event,* the dawning of a light upon him with the coming into existence of something new outside him, *the falling of the veil from his eyes with his having had a revelation.* Subjectively his emotion is carried to the

---

[78]*Early Writings,* 47.
[79]See *Irony,* 280-81.
[80]*Either/Or* II, 30.
[81]*Adler,* 132.

extreme; he wants to select the most powerful expression to describe it and by means of a mental deception grasps the objective qualification: having had a revelation.[82]

Kierkegaard's assessment of Adler articulates a theme evident in his entire authorship, namely, that the need to distinguish dialectically between categories—between, e.g., what is subjective from what is objective—is essential to becoming fully human.[83] His assessment further intimates George Eliot's notion of how a human being may become romantically or esthetically entangled in metaphors and act fatally upon the force of them, especially when such subjective/objective categories distinguishable in the metaphoric instead become blurred:

> So Magister Adler was deeply moved. That in the first moment of being deeply moved one easily runs the risk of a mistake, that of mistaking one's own change for a change outside oneself, that of mistaking the perception of everything as changed for the coming into existence of something new— that is familiar enough. I do not need to dwell on such things. If Magister Adler for some time has continued to be ensnared by this mistake, it would be foolish to censure him, partly because it is nobody's business, and partly because it is human. . . . The question is only about expressing oneself if one is ensnared in this self-redoubling. The more fantasy one has in this case, the more easily it goes with continuously having revelations. It is reflection that makes manifest the redoubling, and fantasy then fantastically steps over to the side of the apparent self and dramatically gives support.[84]

Later, Kierkegaard discusses Adler as a reflective individual. The discussion is not unlike his assertions about the romantic esthete as one who, in a state of reflection, fails to see that the dialectical tension experienced by the individual is best treated through resolution and action instead of becoming "productive about his state in tension."[85] Bereft of such resolve, an esthetic hiddenness or self-deception ensues and overwhelms the individual by diverting his mind with the fragmentary details of reflection: "The more richly thoughts and expressions offer themselves, the more briskly the productivity advances—in the wrong

---

[82]*Adler*, 117; see also 119.
[83]See 65-67, above.
[84]*Adler*, 118, 119.
[85]*Adler*, 127.

direction—the more dangerous it becomes and the more it hides from the person concerned that his work, his extremely strenuous work, his very interesting (perhaps also for a third party who has a total view) work, is a work of bogging himself down deeper and deeper," Kierkegaard writes. "That is, he does not work himself loose but works himself fast and becomes interesting to himself by reflecting on the tension [*deleted in version IV*: and diverts himself with an utterly piecemeal productivity about detached details]."[86] Kierkegaard suggests here that Adler does not treat himself nor his reflection ethically. Lacking ethical earnestness, Adler hides himself from the rigors of the ethicist seeking to determine the truth. "Even to the most earnest ethicist who is out upon the waters of reflection," Kierkegaard writes, "it can happen that he at some time makes a mistake for a moment."[87] But unlike Adler, the ethicist "will quickly discover it, because he tests his life in order to see where he is. Even to the most earnest ethicist it can happen that he is at some time ensnared in a self-deception for a moment, but [unlike Adler] he will soon discover it."[88]

The link between a person like Adler as a self-professed apostolic "truth-witness" and the hiddenness of the esthetic poet perhaps is most directly illuminated by Kierkegaard in his attack on corrupt pastors in Christendom. Such pastors are those who dilute the message of Christianity while simultaneously inferring that they themselves are truth-witnesses. In one article in *The Moment*, Kierkegaard asserts that "the poet is, in a godly sense, the most dangerous of all just because people love the poet above all."[89] Kierkegaard then links esthetic poetry to hypocritical words of Christendom's less discriminating pastors. Such pastors, like the poet, cling to the seductive powers of the imagination with no earnest intention of transferring those ideas into the spheres of actuality and ethics. Kierkegaard writes:

> Christianity is renunciation of this world. The professor lectures on this and then makes lecturing on this his career, without ever admitting that this actually is not Christianity—if this is Christianity, where then is the renunciation of this world? No, this is not Christianity; it is a poet-rela-

---

[86]*Adler*, 127.
[87]*Adler*, 128.
[88]*Adler*, 128.
[89]*Late Writings*, 225.

tion.—The pastor preaches, he "witnesses" (well, thanks for that!) that Christianity is renunciation, and then makes preaching this his livelihood, his career; he does not himself ever admit that this actually is not Christianity—but where then is the renunciation? Is this then not also a poet-relation?

. . . Thus the title to this piece is not altogether true, that the poet, in a godly sense, is the most dangerous of all. The poet claims only to be a poet. *What is much more dangerous is that the person who is only a poet, by being, as it is called, a pastor, passes himself off as being something much more earnest and true than the poet, and yet is only a poet. This is hypocrisy to the second power.*[90]

The esthetic poet, Adler, and corrupt pastors hide behind or within mansions of metaphoric constructs in which they wittingly or (more often) unwittingly pretend to be something that they are not. They lack a certain earnestness, not so much because they lack a longing for the religious, but because they lack the courage to disclose themselves ethically and thereby honestly—a disclosure that not only would illuminate a truer version of their own limitations and possibilities, but one that also would befit religious earnestness.

---

[90]*Late Writings*, 226.

Chapter 3

DISCLOSING COLLISIONS OF THE SELF: THE ETHICAL ANALYSIS OF METAPHOR

A. From Concealment to Disclosure

Karsten Harries maintains it is easy to show the pervasiveness of the esthetic approach in art and poetry. He suggests it is equally easy to point to attempts to restore to poetry the ontological significance that is sacrificed by the esthetic approach. He cites T. S. Eliot, who insists that reading poetry should be "'not merely an experience, but a serious experience.' Such an experience, Eliot explains, cannot have its value solely in itself; it cannot be merely esthetic. A poem should reveal what matters and thus help the individual to determine what his place in the world is to be."[1] Harries's assertion informs a contemporary reader of Kierkegaard about Kierkegaard's intentions for the imagination and metaphorical constructions. Gouwens speaks similarly in reference to Kierkegaard, stating that "the remedy for losing oneself in imagination—in whatever form, as esthete or speculative philosopher—is not to suppress or leave the imagination, but rather to grasp the true extent and power of the imagination in the higher spheres of the ethical and the ethicoreligious life."[2] Gouwens implies that the imagination (and, by extension, the metaphoric) so celebrated by romantic and esthetic strains may be redeemed by ethics:

> the refinement of one's imaginative abilities in the direction of ethical action is fundamental to the personal development an ethical life offers. Lacking the ethical, the imagination must soon become abstract in a Romantic or speculative fashion; lacking the imagination, the ethical must soon become

---

[1]Karsten Harries, "Metaphor and Transcendence," *On Metaphor*, ed. Sheldon Sacks (Chicago: University of Chicago Press, 1979) 86.

[2]David J. Gouwens, "Kierkegaard on the Ethical Imagination," *The Journal of Religious Ethics* 10 (Fall 1982): 205.

vacuous. Kierkegaard's turn to the ethical is the imagination's redemption, and in redeeming the imagination, Kierkegaard redeems the ethical as well.[3]

The ethical intent of Kierkegaard's metaphors resembles the intent of Plato's parable of the cave in book 7 of *The Republic*: to draw the reader from a state of ignorance to a state of understanding and knowledge, from a state of darkness to a state of light. Metaphor for ethicists like Kierkegaard carries the reader over from an esthetic state where it is possible to seduce and be seduced by a language that wittingly or unwittingly *hides* something (namely, the ethical-religious and its difficult demands upon existence) to an ethical state where the disclosure of formerly concealed knowledge renders the reader responsible for discriminating between the bogus and the true, for judging what is real and what is not, for obliging to choose either/or instead of both-and. " 'That it is every man's duty to become revealed,' "[4] which Kierkegaard quotes from *Either/Or* II, in one journal entry, "actually says the opposite of what the whole first part [*Either/Or* I] says. . . . The esthetic is always hidden: if it expresses itself at all, it is exploitive."[5] In *Fear and Trembling*, Johannes de Silentio writes similarly:

> The single individual, qualified as immediate, sensate, and psychical, is the hidden. Thus his ethical task is to work himself out of his hiddenness and to be disclosed to the universal. Every time he desires to remain in the hidden, he trespasses and is immersed in spiritual trial from which he can emerge only by disclosing himself. . . . Esthetics, then, demand[s] the hiddenness and reward[s] it; ethics demand[s] the disclosure and punish[es] the hiddenness.[6]

Just as the esthetic employs metaphor to conceal (thereby denying the potential for existential collisions to become manifest in actuality), so too the ethical reveals—in the context of *revelation*, as it were—and thereby exposes an individual to collisions in actuality that existentially are capable of developing resolve and commitment within an individual. "At every moment you live existence is judging you, since to live is to judge oneself, to become disclosed," Kierkegaard writes in *Works of Love*.

---

[3]Ibid., 214.
[4]See *Either/Or* II, 322: "it is every human being's duty to become open."
[5]*Journals* V, IV A 234, n.d. [1843], 222-23.
[6]*Fear & Trembling*, 82, 86.

"This is why existence must be arranged in such a way that you do not, with the aid of a reliability of knowledge, sneak out of disclosing yourself in judging or in the way you judge."[7] For the sake of such ethical development, the papers of B compiled in *Either/Or* II explode myths and metaphors developed in the papers of A in *Either/Or* I. Just as pseudonymous writer Vigilius Haufniensis in *The Concept of Anxiety* maintains that esthetically "the demonic is inclosing reserve," so too he writes that, ethically, "disclosure is the good, for disclosure is the first expression of salvation." He adds: "There is also an old saying that if one dares to utter 'the word,' the sorcery's enchantment is broken, and therefore the somnambulist wakes up when his name is spoken."[8] The fragmentary romantic-esthetic practices hiddenness and mystification, making life a masquerade. Contrarily, as Walsh writes, "the [integrated] ethical-esthetic requires revelation of oneself and openness to others as well as transparency to oneself."[9] Unless all existence is a medium of revelation, William Temple has maintained, no particular revelation is possible.[10]

A scene from Shakespeare's *A Midsummer Night's Dream* contrasted with Shakespeare's sonnet 130 offers a graphic example of how the use of metaphor by an esthete is defined by hiddenness while metaphorical use by an ethicist is defined by disclosure or revelation. Approximately twenty lines after Puck's famous quip ("Lord, what fools these mortals be!"[11]), the young lover Demetrius wakes to the sight of Helena, his nemesis *d'amore*. However, since he has just been drugged by the aphrodisiacal juice of "a little western flower" called "love-in-idleness,"[12] he

---

[7]*Works of Love*, 227-28.

[8]*Anxiety*, 126, 127. In this context, King makes an astute contradistinction between Kierkegaard and Nietzsche: "While the 'shadow-existence' for Kierkegaard has been seen as having a thoroughly negative character, Nietzsche's ideal thinker is 'like a shadow.' For Kierkegaard it is the personal 'disclosure' that is to be actualized, for Nietzsche 'concealment.' " G. Heath King, *Existence, Thought, Style: Perspectives of a Primary Relation Portrayed through the Work of Søren Kierkegaard* (Milwaukee: Marquette University Press, 1996) 80. (King refers to Nietzsche's *On the Genealogy of Morals*, trans. Walter Kaufmann and R. J. Hollingdale [New York: Vintage Books, 1967] 110.)

[9]Sylvia Walsh, *Living Poetically: Kierkegaard's Existential Aesthetics* (University Park: Pennsylvania State University Press, 1994) 115.

[10]See epigram to Loren Eiseley, *The Immense Journey* (Alexandria VA: Time-Life Books, 1962).

[11]*A Midsummer Night's Dream* 3.2.115.

[12]*A Midsummer Night's Dream* 2.1.166, 168.

is romantically overcome with love for her. He waxes poetic-erotic, his intoxicating enthusiasm reflected not only by his repeated use of conventional couplets but also by his repeated use of the same rhyme in the second and third couplets (poetically rendering the lyricism even more conventional by portraying it as more banal):

> O Helen, goddess, nymph, perfect, divine!
> To what, my love, shall I compare thine eyne?
> Crystal is muddy. O, how ripe in show
> Thy lips, those kissing cherries, tempting grow!
> That pure congealed white, high Taurus' snow,
> Fann'd with the eastern wind, turns to a crow
> When thou hold'st up thy hand. O, let me kiss
> This princess of pure white, this seal of bliss.[13]

Like Satan with Eve, Demetrius uses metaphor esthetically in his attempt to lure Helena to him, to flatter and seduce her by concealing (through gilding) her less than perfect mortal beauty. Yet, to his object of love and to the audience, the metaphors more poignantly display how Helena is rather *unlike* perfection. Pursuer now unnaturally turned pursued, Helena takes Demetrius's seductive flights of metaphorical fancy as a mockery. Self-conscious of what she considers as her average outward beauty, Demetrius's metaphors rot on the vine; Helena assumes that they attempt to conceal what she knows to be Demetrius's opinion of her beauty—an opinion based more on cold sense than hot fancy. In other words, the intent of metaphor in the hands of the (albeit drug-induced) esthete Demetrius here is to hide certain information that, when fully understood by the beloved, would foil the esthete's intention to seduce.

The intent of metaphor in the hands of an ethicist, however, is precisely the opposite. It is to disclose certain information that, if fully understood by the beloved, would not foil the ethicist's intentions but rather foster a clarity upon which an ethical response may be issued. Such disclosure informs the beloved of the need to judge and choose responsibly. The esthete exploits metaphor for his own purposes while the ethicist disengages, disarms, and disenfranchises metaphor's deceptive character to reach a certain ethical *telos*.

---

[13]*A Midsummer Night's Dream* 3.2.137-44.

Just as some of Kierkegaard's esthetes are not unlike Demetrius, so too his ethicists are not unlike the narrator of Shakespeare's sonnet 130, the latter of whom states:

> My mistress' eyes are nothing like the sun;
> Coral is far more red than her lips red;
> If snow be white, why then her breasts are dun;
> If hairs be wires, black wires grow on her head.
> I have seen roses damask'd, red and white,
> But no such roses I see in her cheeks,
> And in some perfumes is there more delight
> Than in the breath that from my mistress reeks.
> I love to hear her speak, yet I well know
> That music hath a more pleasing sound;
> I grant I never saw a goddess go,
> My mistress when she walks treads on the ground:
> > And yet, by heaven, I think my love as rare
> > As any she belied with false compare.

Here, the narrator attacks by parody conventional love lyrics like Demetrius's that (through a litany of metaphorical constructions) catalog feminine features as divine or otherworldly. The beloved of the sonnet is neither celestial nor pure nor ethereal; she is concretely flesh-and-bone, an actual human being who walks where all human beings walk—on earth. The sonnet's three quatrains thus may offend a purely romantic reader by rejecting metaphorical embellishments that otherwise would charge erotic love. More specifically, the quatrains may offend by their *seeming* harsh critique of the outer beauty of the beloved. In the concluding couplet (where many reversals of thematic fortune in Shakespeare's sonnets are evident), the narrator achieves two ethical goals: (1) he indicts all metaphor as "false compare," thereby disclosing the narrator's ethical responsibility and truer commitment toward his beloved; and (2) he more effectively praises his beloved by asserting her inward beauty over and against either the absence or presence of any outward beauty. The beloved is actual, concrete—"down-to-earth" as it were—and for all that even more beautiful in an ethical and more permanent sense. A balance between the esthetic and the ethical is achieved.

(Although the sonnet cursorily may offend by suggesting that the beloved could be as ugly as a witch in *Macbeth*, its ethical force resides in its deeper implication, which asserts that the beloved may still be as

outwardly beautiful as a Juliet, a Desdemona, or a Miranda—yet even
such beauty pales in the ethical actuality of inward beauty. Ethics, in
other words, asserts that inward beauty is the essential while outward
beauty is the accidental.)

Conventional esthetic or erotic poetry is conventional because it is
what people *want to hear*—echoing Kierkegaard's repeated assertions that
the world wants to be deceived.[14] Such poetry is thereby exploitive in that
it depicts only the ideality, outside the context of actuality. The position
Shakespeare assumes toward esthetic metaphorical construction in the
above sonnet is unconventional precisely because it is both ethical and,
by disclosing metaphor's ability to conceal, earnestly true. The romanti-
cist may find it unpoetical and thereby offensive in a strict esthetic sense
because it neither conceals, gilds, glosses, nor embellishes actuality—such
a person may not want to hear of it nor hear of any other unwelcome
truths made by such an ethicist and poet.[15] Nonetheless, such poetry redeems the imagination ethically by aspiring to an ethical commitment
based upon truth and honesty rather than illusion and deception.

How the beloved of the sonnet receives the ethical (yet still esthetically valid) message of love reflects the beloved's own degree of ethical
maturity. If the beloved recognizes the contradiction ethically put forth
by the narrator-lover—namely, that the beloved, expecting (like any
romantic reader) an erotic declaration of love in the esthetic context of
metaphorical conceit and embellishment, is instead startlingly confronted
with a rejection both of metaphor and outward beauty for the sake of an
ethical, inward validity of beauty—then the beloved's response to the
contradiction will reflect *her* own degree of earnestness. Anti-Climacus
writes of the ethical value of being confronted by such disclosure and
contradiction:

---

[14]See, e.g., *Irony*, 253-54; *Stages*, 340; *Judge for Yourself!*, 139-40; *Point of View*, 58;
Late Writings, 45; *Journals*, V, VII^1 A 147, September 7, 1846, 343; VII^1 A 148, n.d.
[1846], 345; VI, X^1 A 320, n.d. [1849], 151; X^3 A 450, n.d. [1850], 350-51.

[15]Often in his journals, Kierkegaard speaks of the ethicist as being not only undesir-
able but even hated, for he claims that the high standards to which the ethicist aspires are
also standards of which all striving human beings are capable. See, e.g., *Journals*, I, X^4
A 580, n.d. [1852], 376; VII^1 A 28, n.d. [1846], 408-09; VII^1 A 30, n.d. [1846], 409;
VIII^1 A 398, n.d. [1847], 417; VIII^1 A 671, n.d. [1848], 418-19; X^1 A 393, n.d. [1849],
424-25; X^3 A 104, n.d. [1850], 431-32; II, XI^2 A 271, n.d. [1855], 305; IV, VIII^1 A 160,
n.d. [1847], 290-91; VI, X^5 A 104, March 25, 1853 [Good Friday], 473.

A contradiction placed squarely in front of a person—if one can get him to look at it—is a mirror; as he is forming a judgment, what dwells within him must be disclosed. It is a riddle, but as he is guessing the riddle, what dwells within him is disclosed by the way he guesses. The contradiction confronts him with a choice, and as he is choosing, together with what he chooses, he himself is disclosed.[16]

An existential qualification of metaphor thus begins with full disclosure of the contradictory *collision* between tenor and vehicle and ultimately is manifested in how a person reacts to such disclosure. In the case of sonnet 130, the narrator defines both the truly outward finitude and truly inward infinitude of the beloved. Its message prompts the beloved to choose: Either reject the sonnet by placing sad longing for ideality promulgated by the esthetic-erotic on a higher plane than ethical actuality / Or welcome the sonnet and render beauty esthetically valid by qualifying it spiritually through ethical distillation.

The narrator-lover of sonnet 130 grounds love in ethics and finite human existence by disclosing and indirectly analyzing the limits and falsifications of metaphor. Similarly, Kearney suggests that existentialism in general and Kierkegaard's existentialist imagination in particular ground ethical imagination by revealing the shallowness of adhering to a strictly romantic imagination:

> Existentialism is, above all else, a philosophy of human finitude. It describes man in his concrete situation in the world. Thus while it inherits the romantic cult of subjectivity, it exposes the existential limits of man's creative powers. As such, existentialism tempers the initial optimism of romantic idealism. It clips the wings of the transcendental imagination and lays bare the everyday obstacles which obstruct its flight and fiats. Against romanticism's claim for the unlimited and quasi-divine potential of imagination, the existentialist sounds a note of irony—even pessimism. He brings imagination back to earth.[17]

Gouwens speaks in similar terms of the passion of existential imagination. For the Kierkegaardian ethicist, Gouwens notes, "imaginative passion

---

[16]*Practice*, 127.

[17]Richard Kearney, *The Wake of Imagination* (Minneapolis: University of Minneapolis Press, 1988) 196.

culminates in a descent back to finitude" at the "pinnacle of a proper abstraction in the ethical life."[18]

Against romantic imagination's transcendental emphasis that denies actuality for the sake of ideality, Walsh also develops the existentialist imagination of Kierkegaard further in the context of finitude's dailiness:

> When the esthetic ideal is portrayed existentially, the personal life itself becomes a mode of artistic representation, giving expression to those qualities of the spiritually qualified esthetic that other forms of poetic reproduction can only hint at—qualities such as constancy and faithfulness in love, which require daily repetition in existence to acquire. In this way the ethical mode of living poetically provides not merely a semblance of the ideal, as in the Platonic theory of imitation, but a reduplication of it in time and actuality.[19]

In other words, an existential imagination that appreciates the full scope of metaphor and acts ethically toward its usage does not denude esthetics from existence. Rather, it incorporates and validates esthetics by weaving esthetics into a practicable pattern within the greater context of ethics, into the ethical actuality of the daily, and into a striving to reduplicate the ideal in the actual.

B. Practicing What You Preach: Ethical Actuality's Terrifying, Matter-of-Fact Task

For Kierkegaard, "truly to apprehend ethical and ethical-religious truth means to reduplicate existentially what is known."[20] More simply put, "to reduplicate is to be what one says,"[21] or, as Anti-Climacus writes, "to exist in what one understands is to reduplicate."[22] According to Malantschuk, essential reduplication for Kierkegaard thus belongs to the ethical and ethical-religious sphere, for it presupposes reflection or knowledge of the good to be actualized—an activity not possible in the esthetic sphere of spontaneity.[23] Reduplication is not only ethically charged,

---

[18]Gouwens, "Kierkegaard on the Ethical Imagination," 209.

[19]Walsh, *Living Poetically*, 111.

[20]*Journals*, I, VIII² B 88, n.d. [1847], 297.

[21]*Journals*, VI, IX A 208, n.d. [1848], 37.

[22]*Practice*, 134.

[23]*Journals*, III, Commentary, 910.

however; it is also metaphysically charged, bound up as it is in a relationship between possibility and actuality. And it is Kierkegaard's idea of the leap—his most celebrated metaphor—that articulates the metaphysics of reduplication.

Malantschuk notes that Kierkegaard found the definition of the leap in Aristotle's theory of motion, movement, and change,[24] and understood it as "the transition from possibility" or from the sphere of thought "to actuality"[25] or existence:

> In itself possibility is only "a thought actuality" (*Postscript* I, 321) and as such still a nothing, because in order for possibility to become actuality there must also be a resolution, a movement. As an existential thinker, Kierkegaard particularly stresses the importance of moving possibility out into actuality. There are many reminders in Kierkegaard's writing that one must not merely experiment with possibilities but must actualize them.[26]

Indeed, there *are* many reminders of this inwardly dramatic ethical and ethical-religious mode of transition that "leap" invokes, of this essential of all existential movements, of this terrifying and anxiety-ridden shift from possibility to actuality, of this significant task by which the ethical and the ethical-religious individual is defined. What is curious, however, is that Kierkegaard's tone in these many reminders seldom is dramatic, terrifying, or anxiety-ridden. Rather, the tone is sober, earnest, matter-of-fact. Without dint of humor, for instance, Johannes Climacus writes: "The individual's own ethical actuality is the only actuality."[27] Without ambiguity or equivocation, Kierkegaard asserts in one journal entry: "If a man does not become what he understands, then he does not understand it either."[28] If there is no connection to actuality, Judge William maintains, "no ethical view of life can be put into practice."[29] The same message from various writing tables of Kierkegaard's authorship is simple: the ethicist practices what he preaches. Ethical activity reduplicates the sermon. Such a simple message, even for Kierkegaard himself, is never-

---

[24]*Journals*, III, Commentary, 794.
[25]*Journals*, I, IV C 47, n.d. [1842-43], 109.
[26]*Journals*, III, Commentary, 872.
[27]*Postscript* I, 327.
[28]*Journals*, IV, VII^1 A 72, n.d. [1846], 347.
[29]*Either/Or* II, 250.

theless not without dialectical knots. In one journal entry, for example, Kierkegaard asks:

> [T]o what extent should a person dare present the ideal of the Christian although he himself is so far from it? A poet-existence which is not at all related in striving to the ideal, but merely presents it, is one thing; it is something else actually to strive oneself, but then poetically to present the ideal which he himself is far from being."[30]

The simple message of ethical striving in actuality is universally knotty insofar as its terrifying content and matter-of-fact tone seem contradictory—a contradiction understandable by considering point of view.

From an esthete's view, the ethicists' claim to "just do it" (that is, "just do" the ethical, "just do" the good) is terrifying because ethical activity for the esthete is at best merely possible and not actual. Kierkegaard writes in one journal entry: "it is far easier and much less dangerous for understanding to admire the idea than to believe the actuality."[31] The esthete also wittingly or unwittingly knows that the ethicist champions ethical activities of which all humans are capable but few achieve without some ethical or ethical-religious transformation or "leap." "This is why all esthetic and sensuous men have anxiety about living contemporaneously with such an ethical individual," Kierkegaard writes in one journal entry, "simply because [the ethicist] transforms everything into actuality: what he understands, he does."[32] (Here is one instance where Kierkegaard as ethicist-poet distinguishes himself from the esthetic-poet, for he considers himself "unusually ethical . . . in the sense of an emphasis upon willing to be what is poetized."[33])

The esthete does not act because he continues to be fixated upon escaping *from* instead of *to* actuality—a reaction that nonetheless lacks a certain ethical will based upon courage and faith. Judge William writes in terms that may be offensive (if not frightening) to the esthete regarding the esthete's escapist tendencies that lead the latter away from actuality and himself—tendencies that instead lead him into esthetic imagination

---

[30]*Journals*, I, X1 A 502, n.d. [1849], 373.

[31]*Journals*, I, V A 35, n.d. [1844], 371.

[32]*Journals*, I, X^1 A 393, n.d. [1849], 425. See above, 102 and n. 15.

[33]*Journals*, VI, X^1 A 94, n.d. [1849], 112-13.

where metaphor is a poetic end in itself and not an ethical or religious means to understanding and appropriating what it means to be human:

> [T]he poet-existence as such lies in the darkness that is the result of the soul's continuing to quake in despair and of the spirit's inability to achieve its true transfiguration. The poetic ideal is always an untrue ideal, for the true ideal is always the actual. So when the spirit is not allowed to rise into the eternal world of spirit, it remains in transit and delights in the pictures reflected in the clouds and weeps over their transitoriness.

Judge William concludes this sentiment by stating that a poet-existence as such is an unhappy existence, higher than the finite and yet not infinite:

> The poet sees the ideals, but he must run away from the world in order to delight in them. He cannot carry these idols within him in the midst of life's confusion, cannot calmly go on his way unmoved by the caricature that appears around him, to say nothing of his having the strength to put on the ideals.[34]

Ethical imagination, on the other hand, functions concretely in existence by appropriating ethically charged metaphors. Timothy Polk writes that

> [I]mportant as decision making may be for an analysis of the ethical, such an analysis can only understand life as episodic, a collection of discreet moments. Insofar as our lives exhibit patterns of behavior and thus have an element of continuity, ethical analysis needs to attend to the formation of character, which includes the formation of the imagination and the role it plays in how we construe the world.[35]

In addition to suggesting that the ideal self intimates the ethicist's life, and that imagination orients the ethicist to sympathy, insight, and understanding, Gouwens notes how extensive and dialectical the role of imagination is in the ethical, how imagination "is a term for a medium of possibility, an activity of idealizing, a passion which contributes to reso-

---

[34]*Either/Or* II, 210.

[35]Timothy Polk, *The Biblical Kierkegaard* (Macon GA: Mercer University Press, 1997) 10. Polk's text asserts the importance of analogical narrative theology in both biblical and Kierkegaardian studies.

lution, an organ for the concrete, and a capacity or disposition which describes not only what the ethical person does, but how he does it. The imagination is central to Kierkegaard's picture of the moral life, for being imaginative is part of being ethical."[36]

Walsh further elucidates the vitality of imagination on the field of actuality:

> Philosophically, the category of actuality is of central importance for the young Kierkegaard, and the thrust of his esthetics in this place is to insist that we must properly relate ourselves and our poetic ideals to it. This does not mean, however, that he denies or denigrates the importance of change and possibility; rather, his point is that imagination must not cut itself loose from actuality but should serve as a medium through which a transformation and development of our given actuality within a religious orientation can take place.[37]

Ideality and possibility on the one hand and actuality on the other nevertheless remain polarized, united only under an auspicious and terrifying ethical requirement that demands an existential leap. In other words, the move from estheticism to ethics remains difficult, if for no other reason than, according to Kierkegaard in one journal entry, "that which in possibility stirs us, awakens our admiration, etc.—the same thing in actuality we hate, curse, persecute."[38] Elsewhere in his journal, Kierkegaard writes:

> The ideal is enmity toward the human.—Man naturally loves finitude. The introduction of the ideal is to him the greatest agony; of course, if it is introduced very poetically as fascinating make-believe, well, this he accepts with pleasure.
> But when the idea is introduced as the requirement, an ethical religious demand—it is the most terrifying agony for man. In the most agonizing way it slays for him everything in which he actually has his life. In the most agonizing way it shows him his own wretchedness. In the most painful way it keeps him in sleepless unrest; whereas finitude quiets him down in a life given over to enjoyment.[39]

---

[36]Gouwens, "Kierkegaard on the Ethical Imagination," 216.
[37]Walsh, *Living Poetically*, 62.
[38]*Journals*, I, X⁴ A 580, n.d. [1852], 376. See above, 102 and n. 15.
[39]*Journals*, II, XI² A 271, n.d. [1855], 305. See also 102 and n. 15.

Climacus minces no words in his own assessment of the difficult life-task of the ethical idealist in actuality: "To be an idealist in imagination is not at all difficult, but to have to *exist* as an idealist is an extremely rigorous life-task, because existing is precisely the objection to it."[40] To exist for the subjective thinker, therefore, becomes "an art" for Climacus: "The subjective thinker is esthetic enough for his life to have esthetic content, ethical enough to regulate it, dialectical enough in thinking to master it."[41] (No wonder that Kierkegaard saw in Socrates the ethical human prototype: "That Socrates belonged together with what he taught, that his teaching ended in him, that he himself was his teaching, in the setting of actuality was himself artistically a product of that which he taught—we have learned to rattle this off by rote but have scarcely understood it."[42])

Nonetheless, from the strict point of view of the ethicist (namely, the one who has achieved some success in practicing what has been preached), the ethical possibility already has become actual in its continued commitment to the process of ethical striving. Subsequently, anxiety is demythologized because it is being met and is being suffered, thus explaining the matter-of-fact tone. The ethicist "step[s] forth in character,"[43] which means, as Howard Hong notes, "to reduplicate an idea or vision in a personal act, which is qualitatively different from poetizing the vision."[44]

Like Thomasine Gyllembourg, author of *A Story of Everyday Life*, the ethicist at this juncture "lies on the boundary of the esthetic and in the direction of the religious." As Kierkegaard writes in his review of Gyllembourg's work,

> Where poetry to all intents and purposes stops, this author begins. For poetry does not essentially reconcile with *actuality*; by means of the imagination it reconciles with the ideality of the imagination, but this reconciliation in the actual individual is precisely the new split with actuality. . . . The lifeview is the way out, and the story is the way."[45]

---

[40]*Postscript* I, 353.
[41]*Postscript* I, 351.
[42]*Journals*, VI, X^1 A 146, n.d. [1849], 126.
[43]*Journals*, VI, X^1 A 273, n.d. [1849], 147.
[44]*Journals*, VI, Notes, 606.
[45]*Two Ages*, 14-15.

Ethical and ethical-religious transitions hinge upon such leaps into actuality. Significant human development rests upon such metamorphoses between the possible and the actual. Just as the story is the way for Gyllembourg, so too metaphorical construction is the way Kierkegaard prompts the reader to carry over his understanding from the idea of one sphere of existence to another, from abstraction to concretion—while simultaneously leaving the reader alone to venture the existential leap that makes manifest the metaphoric meaning in the reader's own life. No wonder, then, that so many of Kierkegaard's metaphorical constructions are issued matter-of-factly; they indirectly motivate an individual into a confidence that, in turn, will prompt the reader to address and carry over ethical or ethical-religious tasks that (externally) may be terrifying, anxiety ridden, replete with fear and trembling. Actuality for Kierkegaard is thus both a "gift that refuses to be rejected" and a "task that wants to be fulfilled."[46] Ethics requires that an individual take responsibility, not only for disclosing collisions in all their terror, but also for addressing collisions, for committing oneself to attend to the collision issued by metaphor.

Choosing neither-nor (that is, standing prior to choice) renders a person entangled like T. S. Eliot's J. Alfred Prufrock. Prufrock, in his private confession, is afraid, unable to force any moment—no matter how trivial or significant—to its crisis; he instead is left lingering "in the chambers of seas" until, ethically and metaphysically, he drowns. Choosing both-and (that is, feigning choice without suffering the loss implicit in choosing one thing and not another) renders a person like Ibsen's Peer Gynt. Such a Gyntian self is part human, part troll, with his ethical or ethical-religious self no more than imaginatively conceived (instead of ethically distilled in actuality) and thereby considered merely "enough."[47] The Gyntian self, in other words, "chooses everything" in the purely esthetic realm of imagination, which translates into choosing nothing (or, rather, standing prior to choosing) in the ethical realm of actuality. Striving to become more than simply "enough"—to become a

---

[46]*Irony*, 276.

[47]Henrik Ibsen, *Peer Gynt*, trans. Rolf Fjelde (Minneapolis: University of Minneapolis Press, 1980) 55 (act 2, sc. 6) and 113 (act 4, sc. 5). See also Kierkegaard on the concept of "enough" or "to a certain degree" in *Either/Or* I, 203; *Eighteen Discourses*, 21; *Various Spirits*, 64ff.; and *Judge for Yourself!*, 106-107.

human being in an ethical-religious context—is not compatible with the pure esthete's pattern of thought.

The terror of the ethical task, however, may not be met and suffered if readers fail to recognize how metaphors pointing to that task apply to them personally. The "dizziness of freedom"[48] that helps constitute being human by positing anxiety—anxiety that, according to Vigilius Haufniensis, "emerges when . . . freedom looks down into its own possibility"[49]— such "dizziness" may not be suffered if readers fail to recognize what it means to strive to appropriate metaphorical meaning into their lives. When such failure is the case, the ethicist's task is twofold, although both elements meet in mutual opposition: (1) to render the message of the metaphor unambiguous to readers, to somehow say to them that the person reading is the very one to whom the metaphor refers; and (2) to maintain a maieutic or indirect posture that does not condescend to readers, thereby allowing readers to recognize that they are the ones to whom the metaphor refers. Such a dialectical dance is not undertaken lightly by Kierkegaard.

C. "You Are the One"

Throughout his authorship, Kierkegaard continually intimates to the reader that the content of his work is for the reader because the subject of his thought is the reader. Metaphorical constructions are used by Kierkegaard because meanings mined from metaphor and appropriated inwardly are intended to develop the reader's own personal meaning and establish a basis for the reader's existential and spiritual upbuilding. And although a direct communicative approach by the author may let readers more easily know in what respect they are being addressed, Kierkegaard seldom breaks from his Socratic fidelity with the reader by assuming such an authorial or dogmatic stance evoked by direct communication. Instead, he continually seeks out new ways to prompt the reader into self-awareness. In effect, Kierkegaard offers direct assertions for a reader's consideration while persistently maintaining a maieutic distance from the reader. More often than not, metaphor plays a significant role, not only in communicating assertions but also in upholding his art of indirect communication.

---

[48]*Anxiety*, 61.
[49]*Anxiety*, 61.

Frater Taciturnus, for instance, considers how metaphor may help self-tormenting individuals return to a healthier, even comic, understanding of their existence, and thereby potentially mitigate their self-torment: "One of course does not bring the patient to laugh immediately at his own fixed idea but by means of analogies comes closer and closer to him."[50] Here, Taciturnus assumes that readers may recognize that metaphorical constructions in the form of analogies are meant for them *if* readers consider themselves such patients.

Elsewhere, Taciturnus is more direct with readers, yet he remains oblique enough to avoid presenting himself as presumptuous, authorial, or dogmatic. In his parable about a repentant gambler witnessing the corpse of another gambler (a suicide being drawn from the Seine), he writes: "my gambler is a man who has understood the old saying *de te narratur fabula* [the tale is told of you]; he is no modern fool who believes that everyone should court the colossal objective task of being able to rattle off something that applies to the whole human race but not to himself."[51] In this assertion, Taciturnus does not seem to be as confident as before of the reader's ability to take the hint that Taciturnus writes not only to the reader but *about* the reader. On the other hand, he may simply seek to relax the indirect method so that the reader may more readily take the hint. Either way, Taciturnus still does not directly state to readers that the parable is a tale told of *them*, and that humanity (readers included) generally may be divided into two categories: repentant and unrepentant gamblers. To be so direct would be presumptuous and thereby less effective than if readers were to come to the tale's moral on their own and strive to appropriate it personally. In both of Taciturnus's statements above, however, his issuance of ideas with the aid of metaphor once again prompts the reader to take to heart the metaphoric meaning instead of sloughing off the message onto humanity as a whole and thereby disengaging oneself from the essential rigor of personal self-examination.

Taciturnus arguably may be said to speak directly to the reader as the title of his epistle in *Stages*, "Letter to the Reader," claims. Nevertheless, he still maintains a sense of indirect communication through the parable of the gambler. So too Kierkegaard arguably speaks directly to his reader

---

[50]*Stages*, 466.
[51]*Stages*, 478.

in *Either/Or* II, yet he maintains his indirect communicative tactics by having Judge William speak directly to A about how A ought to approach metaphorical constructions. At the outset of Judge William's response to A's papers, he writes:

> You know how the prophet Nathan dealt with King David when he presumed to understand the parable the prophet had told him but was unwilling to understand that it applied to him. Then to make sure, Nathan added: You are the man, O King. In the same way I also have continually tried to remind you that you are the one who is being discussed and you are the one who is spoken to.[52]

In *Christian Discourses*, Kierkegaard cuts loose from the benefit of indirect communication-by-pseudonymity. He nevertheless continues to intimate the double movement that the passionate reader experiences when simultaneously listening objectively to a story or parable that has metaphoric value and becoming subjectively "deceived into the truth."

> One tells [a person] a story. This now puts him completely at ease, because he understands well enough that since it is a story the discourse is not about him. A few words are introduced into this story that perhaps do not immediately have their effect but sometime later are suddenly transformed into a question of conscience. In this way the matter becomes all the more inward.[53]

Readers may initially be distanced from the message of, for example, a parable, because the parable is not *directly* about them. But when conscientious readers establish a relation or similarity between themselves and a character or situation in the story either because of or despite the

---

[52]*Either/Or* II, 5. See also "simile and metaphor" in *Fowler's Modern English Usage* (2nd ed., 1965) 558: "The object of [allegory and parable] is, at least ostensibly, to enlighten the hearer by submitting to him a case in which he has apparently no direct concern, and upon which therefore a disinterested judgement may be elicited from him, as Nathan submitted to David the story of the poor man's ewe lamb. Such judgement given, the question will remain for the hearer whether Thou art the man: whether the conclusion to which the dry light of disinterestedness has helped him holds also for his own concerns."

[53]*Christian Discourses*, 235.

distancing effect of metaphor, then the metaphor may become very close, personal, and thereby potentially transformative for the reader.[54]

Near the outset of *Works of Love*, Kierkegaard says directly what he means about a proper relation between the Gospel and the reader:

> It is one thing to give a person sagacious counsel, to recommend caution against being deceived by others; another and much more important thing is the Gospel's summons to the single individual that he bear in mind that the tree is known by its fruits and that it is he or his love that in the Gospel is compared to the tree. It does not read in the Gospel that, as sagacious talk would say, "You or we are to know the tree by its fruits," but it reads, "The tree is to be known by its fruits." The interpretation is that you who read these words of the Gospel, you are the tree. The Gospel does not need to add what the prophet Nathan added to his parable, "You are the man," since it is already contained in the form of the statement and in its being a word of the Gospel. The divine authority of the Gospel does not speak to one person about another, does not speak to you, my listener, about me, or to me about you—no, when the Gospel speaks, it speaks to the single individual. It does not speak *about* us human beings, you and me, but speaks *to* us human beings, to you and me.[55]

Here, Kierkegaard's message of the power of metaphor becomes transparent. Likewise, Kierkegaard considers in direct fashion in *For Self-Examination* that the one requirement to see oneself in the context of sacred writing is to "*remember to say to yourself incessantly: It is I to whom it is speaking; it is I about whom it is speaking.*"[56] Such activity is authentic earnestness for Kierkegaard, without which, as Kierkegaard

---

[54]See above, 14. For an unorthodox approach to the same end, see *Works of Love*, 378. In a discussion of the Gospel story relating Jesus' talk with the centurion from Capernaum (Matthew 8:5-13), Kierkegaard exemplifies the limitations and the therapeutic possibilities of metaphor. He achieves this by radically negating any comparison between the centurion and the listener to prompt the listener to become rigorous like the centurion (instead of allowing the listener to misunderstand the message by passively assuming he is like the centurion simply by hearing the metaphor and sympathizing with the centurion). Kierkegaard addresses the reader directly: "How rigorous! From this story of the centurion, you find out that he had faith; this actually does not pertain to you at all. Then you find out something essentially Christian, that it was done for him as he believed—but you, after all, are not the centurion."

[55]*Works of Love*, 14.

[56]*Self-Examination*, 35; Kierkegaard's italics.

later notes, God's word becomes objectified the same way in which Taciturnus spoke—into an "impersonal something (the objective, an objective doctrine, etc.)."[57]

That readers ought to see themselves in a text is of course not limited to sacred (or secular) texts. Constructing and reading analogues from nature is also possible. Although Kierkegaard stresses that nature cannot speak to a person because nature does not understand the person "even though it continually seems that it might arrive at an understanding,"[58] nature at least offers situations in which the person may speak with himself: "Indeed, little by little he discovers that he is speaking about himself, that what he says about the lily he says about himself."[59]

(This sentiment, incidentally, is embraced by Emerson, among other transcendentalists, who writes that "man is an analogist, and studies relations in all objects"—thus "the world is emblematic. Parts of speech are metaphors, because the whole of nature is a metaphor of the human mind."[60] Nevertheless, Kierkegaard sets himself apart from Emerson by asserting that God is not to be found in nature, nor does nature even resemble God, although it "bears a little mark by which it reminds one of God," and thus "all nature is like the great staff of servants who remind the human being . . . about worshiping God."[61])

Despite hints, readers who still dismiss that they are the subject of certain metaphorical constructions are not unlike Judge William's depiction of the mystic, or one who continues to live in abstraction instead of the ethical concretion of actuality. By failing to attend to, appropriate, and "put on" ethical messages that the metaphoric promotes, the mystic fails to "put on" oneself, fails to choose oneself. Repentance, ethically understood, is the recognition that not "putting on" oneself is tantamount to existential atrophy:

---

[57]*Self-Examination*, 36.

[58]*Various Spirits*, 21.

[59]*Various Spirits*, 165.

[60]Ralph Waldo Emerson, *Essays and Lectures* (New York: Library of America, 1983) 21, 24.

[61]*Various Spirits*, 192, 193. Aside from setting himself apart from Emerson's way of thinking, Kierkegaard also sets himself apart from Schleiermacher's understanding of the romantic religious vision in which, according to Gouwens, the infinite is found within the finite (Gouwens, *Kierkegaard's Dialectic of the Imagination*, 73).

A person can choose himself according to his freedom only when he chooses himself ethically, but he can choose himself ethically only by repenting himself, and only by repenting himself does he become concrete, and only as a concrete individual is he a free individual. . . .

The mystic's error is that in the choice he does not become concrete either to himself or to God; he chooses himself abstractly and therefore lacks transparency. . . . Therefore, his love for God has its highest expression in a feeling, a mood; at twilight, in the time of mist, he blends with his God in indeterminate movements. But to choose oneself abstractly is not to choose oneself ethically. Not until a person in his choice has taken himself upon himself, has put on himself, has totally interpenetrated himself so that every movement he makes is accompanied by a consciousness of responsibility for himself—not until then has a person chosen himself ethically, not until then has he repented himself, not until then is he concrete, not until then is he in his total isolation in absolute continuity with the actuality to which he belongs.[62]

In keeping with Judge William, Frater Taciturnus can thus suggest that esthetic "poetry cannot use repentance; as soon as it is assumed, the scene is internal."[63] Johannes de Silentio might add here that "if poetry becomes aware of the religious and of the inwardness of individuality, it will acquire far more meaningful tasks than those with which it busies itself now."[64] Given that the esthete is inattentive to the ethical clockworks of the spirit, he remains ethically inattentive to metaphorical constructions that may mirror himself and subsequently may become a means by which awareness of a higher *telos* of the self may be prompted.

Ferriera discusses the need for attention (in the context of choice and will) and, by extension, attending to oneself and to metaphors that one may appropriate for personal and spiritual upbuilding:

William James, in his *Principles of Psychology* (1890), pointed to the importance of attention, seeing '*effort of attention*' as "*the essential phenomenon of will*", and concluding that "*the essential achievement of the will, in short, when it is most 'voluntary', is to* ATTEND *to a difficult object and hold it fast before the mind*'. Rollo May offers a contemporary reminder of James's explicit identification of "belief", "attention", and "will", suggesting that

---

[62]*Either/Or* II, 247, 248.
[63]*Stages*, 446.
[64]*Fear & Trembling*, 91.

James's contribution was to show that "The effort which goes into the exercise of will is really effort of attention; the strain in willing is the effort to keep the consciousness clear, i.e., the strain of keeping the attention focused."[65]

Judge William, Kierkegaard's champion of ethical resolve through will and spiritual faith, would not disagree with William James on the issue of attention. And although the former claims to hate metaphorical or imaginary constructing, he nonetheless recognizes that the ethical challenges metaphor invites can be upbuilding if those challenges are attended to. He writes to A:

> You know how I hate all imaginary constructing [*Experimenteren*], but all the same it may be true that a person can have experienced in thought much that he never comes to experience in actuality. Moments of dejection come sometimes, and if the individual does not himself evoke them in order voluntarily to test himself, this, too, is a struggle and a very earnest struggle, and through this an assurance can be gained that is very significant, even if it does not have the reality [*Realitet*] it would have had if acquired in a real life situation. There are occasions in life when it is a mark of something great and good in a person that he is as if mad, that he has not separated the world of poetry and the world of actuality but sees the latter *sub specie poeseos* [under the aspect of poetry].[66]

Judge William is far more aware of himself than any esthete in that he can recognize the limits of metaphorical usage, and thereby can entertain the ethical possibilities that metaphor also offers. In the midst of constructing a parable to instruct A in the ethical, he admonishes (with the help of another metaphor) not to fear nor distrust metaphor's powers to conceal, but rather to initiate the ethical capacity to distance oneself from the seductive quality of metaphor in which an esthete otherwise entangles himself:

> You know that I am not an unwilling participant in little imaginary constructions like that, and, God be praised, I am sufficiently a child so that when a princely carriage with four snorting horses drives by me I can imagine that I am sitting inside it, sufficiently innocent so that when I have

---

[65]M. Jamie Ferreira, *Transformion Vision: Imagination and Will in Kierkegaardian Faith* (Oxford: Clarendon Press, 1991) 51.

[66]*Either/Or* II, 123.

convinced myself that this is not the case I am able to be happy that someone else is doing it, sufficiently unspoiled not to want the maximum to be
to keep one horse that is both a driving horse and a riding horse because my
circumstances allow me only that.[67]

The idealist as well as the pragmatist in Judge William melds into
Judge William the ethicist. There are enormous possibilities for personal
transformation through metaphor, but without a coexisting awareness of
the limitations of metaphor the therapeutic thrust of metaphor may be
lost. Without such awareness, in other words, one may—as George Eliot
says—become entangled in metaphors and act fatally upon the strength
of them.[68] Like the mirror described by Anti-Climacus in the following
passage, metaphor does not nor cannot tell the whole truth:

> Even in seeing oneself in a mirror it is necessary to recognize oneself, for
> if one does not, one does not see oneself but only a human being. The
> mirror of possibility is no ordinary mirror; it must be used with extreme
> caution, for in the highest sense, this mirror does not tell the truth. That a
> self appears to be such and such in the possibility of itself is only a half-
> truth, for in the possibility of itself the self is still far from or is only half
> of itself. Therefore, the question is how the necessity of this particular self
> defines it more specifically.[69]

Nevertheless, metaphors informing the self are helpful "mirrors" in
arriving indirectly at an awareness of the self, especially given that, as
Kierkegaard claims, "most people are afraid to look at themselves":

> It is, after all, a hazardous sight; once one has seen it, he does not get over
> it very easily. . . . You must remember how you look in the mirror. . . . Yet
> not despair, no matter how ugly you look, but neither let your appearance
> remain just a matter of memory—but begin with the most important, the
> decisive thing—to change before the mirror in accordance with the
> requirement of the mirror.[70]

In *For Self-Examination*, Kierkegaard's famous "Mirror and Love
Letter" and "Royal Decree" parables speak both to existing fully as a

---

[67]*Either/Or* II, 105.
[68]See above, 87.
[69]*Sickness*, 37.
[70]*Journals*, IV, X⁴ A 283, n.d. [1851], 359.

human being *and* to how to regard metaphor, namely, by ultimately abandoning the metaphor to *live* the metaphor, to become the parable. In other words, instead of making passive, scholarly, critical observations upon information that individuals ought to act upon, individuals instead must passionately interest themselves in *acting* upon the information—in effect, to see themselves as the metaphor, as the representation of enactment:

> *What Is Required in Order to Look at Oneself with True Blessing in the Mirror of the Word? The first requirement is that you must not look at the mirror, observe the mirror, but must see yourself in the mirror. . . . The second requirement is that in order to see yourself in the mirror when you read God's Word you must (so that you actually do come to see yourself in the mirror) remember to say to yourself incessantly: It is I to whom it is speaking; it is I about whom it is speaking. . . . Finally, if you want to look at yourself in the mirror with true blessing, you must not promptly forget how you looked.*[71]

Nevertheless, metaphor, Cynthia Ozick writes, "is one of the chief agents of our moral nature, and that the more serious we are in life, the less we can do without it."[72] Kierkegaard speaks similarly in one journal entry when, in the context of one of Christ's parables, he writes: "one should never overlook the meaning of the [religious] metaphor. . . . One ought not play or *flirt with such metaphors.*"[73]

---

[71]*Self-Examination*, 25, 35, 44.
[72]Cynthia Ozick, *Metaphor and Memory* (New York: Knopf, 1989) 270.
[73]*Journals*, I, III C 15, n.d. [1840-41], 238; Kierkegaard's italics.

Chapter 4

ENACTING COLLISIONS OF THE SELF:
THE RELIGIOUS LITERALIZATION OF METAPHOR

A. Kierkegaard's "Concept" of Metaphor

In his "Commentary" to the *Journals and Papers*, Malantschuk states that
from Kierkegaard's earliest works to his latest there are many hundreds
of references to God, and that "to pursue this theme requires that one
read the entire authorship."[1] The same claim could be said of other
ubiquitous aspects and themes of Kierkegaard's writings, for example, his
existential esthetics, his complex pseudonymity, his overarching maieutic
or indirect method of communication, his philosophy of man—not the
least his usage of metaphor. In addition to the thousands of metaphorical
constructions themselves, Kierkegaard's many hundreds of indirect references and suggestive commentaries about his concept and usage of
metaphor persistently inform his imaginative and existential thought.

This being said, Kierkegaard nonetheless offers in a single paragraph
at the outset of the second series of his *Works of Love* a direct and
compact version of what loosely may be considered his concept of
metaphor. And although the concept cursorily may appear fundamental
and basic, it implies deeper and wider discussions of metaphor in the
context of much of Kierkegaard's thought and writings:

> All human speech, even the divine speech of Holy Scripture, about the
> spiritual is essentially metaphorical [*overført*, carried over] speech. And this
> is quite in order or in the order of things and of existence, since a human
> being, even if from the moment of birth he is spirit, still does not become
> conscious of himself as spirit until later and thus has sensately-psychically
> acted out a certain part of his life prior to this. But this first portion is not
> to be cast aside when the spirit awakens any more than the awakening of the

---

[1]*Journals*, II, Commentary, 566.

spirit in contrast to the sensate-psychical announces itself in a sensate-psychical way. On the contrary, the first portion is taken over [*overtage*] by the spirit and, used in this way, is thus made the basis—*it becomes the metaphorical*. Therefore, in one sense the spiritual person and the sensate-psychical person say the same thing; yet there is an infinite difference, since the latter has no intimation of the secret of the metaphorical words although he is using the same words, but not in their metaphorical sense. There is a world of difference between the two; the one has made the transition [*Overgang*] or let himself be *carried over* [*føre over*] to the other side, while the other remains on this side; yet they have the connection that both are using the same words. The person in whom the spirit has awakened does not as a consequence abandon the visible world. Although conscious of himself as spirit, he continues to remain in the visible world and to be visible to the senses—in the same way he also remains in the language, except that his language is the metaphorical language! But the metaphorical words are of course not brand-new words but are the already given words. Just as the spirit is invisible, so also is its language a secret, and the secret lies in its using the same words as the child and the simpleminded person but using them metaphorically, whereby the spirit denies being the sensate or the sensate-psychical but does not deny it in a sensate-psychical way. The difference is by no means a noticeable difference. For this reason we rightfully regard it as a sign of false spirituality to parade a noticeable difference—which is merely sensate, whereas the spirit's manner is the metaphor's quiet, whispering secret—for the person who has ears to hear.[2]

Generally, the paragraph considers two different kinds of people (sensate-psychical and spiritual) speaking a similar language—but because two qualitatively distinct orientations are imposed upon the same language, the language offers two radically different meanings to the two different groups of people: (1) a literal meaning for the sensate-psychical group; and (2) a figurative, carried over, or metaphorical meaning for the spiritual group.

Kierkegaard explains that language in the context of the divine speech "*becomes the metaphorical*" as spirit "takes over" language used by the sensate-psychical person. The awakened religious person nonetheless does not abandon actuality for an abstraction constructed by language—which is a critical position Kierkegaard as an ethical human being and an

---

[2]*Works of Love*, 209-10.

existentialist must take (for abandoning actuality is something that only the esthete would do).

What metaphor is capable of, in a Christian context, is to establish a "new acquaintance with the old and familiar"[3] uses of language. Metaphor creates a "fresh air and a prospect"[4] that "does not become weary"[5] of actuality, but rather charges actuality with an ethical and spiritual component. In other words, earnestly attending to a given metaphor with the prospect of appropriating it is not unlike seeing the world as new and as fresh as a child sees it. But just as, according to Kierkegaard, the vehicle of metaphor is easily understood by the child, it is "also difficult for the adult"—given the latter's ability to recognize potential contradictions between vehicle and tenor and subsequently to become lost in doubt.[6]

Kierkegaard's discussion of how the two different groups of people may speak the same language yet understand it differently is suggested elsewhere in his authorship. Vigilius Haufniensis, for example, writes:

> There is an old saying that to understand and to understand are two things, and so they are. Inwardness is an understanding, but *in concreto* the important thing is how this understanding is to be understood. To understand a speech is one thing, and to understand what it refers to, namely, the personal, is something else; for a man to understand what he himself says is one thing, and to understand himself in what is said is something else. The more concrete the content of consciousness is, the more concrete the understanding becomes.[7]

In other words, a person's concrete understanding that metaphor (as used by the likes of Kierkegaard) refers personally to oneself points to the ethical-religious, whereas a mere abstract understanding of a given

---

[3]*Works of Love*, 210.

[4]*Works of Love*, 246. On this and the following page of *Works of Love*, Kierkegaard offers numerous metaphorical constructions that either begin or end with directly referring to the notion that Christianity provides a "prospect by speaking metaphorically." In other words, the subject of these two pages is metaphor and how metaphor informs Christianity.

[5]*Works of Love*, 210.

[6]*Eighteen Discourses*, 133-34.

[7]*Anxiety*, 142. See also, e.g., *Christian Discourses*, 144-45, where Kierkegaard offers a detailed example of the radical confusion that metaphor can elicit when perceptions of two distinctly different personalities render antithetical understandings from the same metaphorical phrase.

metaphor takes a person no further than the esthetic. Thus the truth of human becoming, according to Manheimer, requires metaphorical speech or that "language that continually calls for interpretation in the plenitude of its meanings."[8] Manheimer elucidates Kierkegaard's discussion of metaphor in *Works of Love* relative not only to how the metaphorical evokes irony, pathos, and humor, but also to how Kierkegaard helps the reader understand metaphor religiously:

> Having accepted the linguistic limits of the inexpressible, Kierkegaard proceeds to set himself two further limits. He divides his readers into two groups: those who hear only what is literally said and cannot imagine that they mean more than what they literally say; and a second group who both hear and say beyond the literalness of language, even if they should be heard to utter statements otherwise identical to members of the first group. The difference between those who perceive an irony, recognize pathos and humor, in the tone of a statement, and those who do not is what is being distinguished. Kierkegaard explains this by saying that members of the second group have passed from the "sensuous-psychical" dimension of life experience to that of the "spiritual" in such a way that the former becomes a base for the latter. Language for the first group (earlier stage) seems to involve the univocal identity of word and thing. But members of the second group (later stage) have passed into a realm of equivocal language, a development ushering them into the world of ambiguity, abundance of meanings, and correspondingly, a recognition of the need to interpret the speech and manner of listening of others. If the reader understands how this distinction "makes a world of difference" then he belongs on the same side of the limit as the speaker Kierkegaard. This makes the reader now, perhaps unwittingly, what Kierkegaard would call himself: a witness.[9] In this way

---

[8]Ronald J. Manheimer, *Kierkegaard as Educator* (Berkeley: University of California Press, 1977) 206.

[9]Manheimer footnotes here the journal entry number from Kierkegaard's *Papirer* from which he formulates his discussion of Kierkegaard as witness. It is important to quote the entry here as well in its entirety, so as not to misinterpret Manheimer's—or Kierkegaard's—meaning. Neither Manheimer nor Kierkegaard mean here that Kierkegaard considers himself or members of the second group as "truth-witnesses" holding apostolic authority, as the journal entry makes clear: "WITNESSING is still the form of communication which strikes the truest meaning between direct and indirect communication. Witnessing is direct communication, but nevertheless it does not make one's contemporaries the *authority*. While the witness's 'communication' addresses itself to the contemporaries, the 'witness' himself addresses God and makes him the authority" (*Journals*, I, X^1 A 235,

Kierkegaard creates a limit by means of which he gets us to cross over to the side of the speaker who is also now an interpreter. Correspondingly, we are invited to cross the distinction between a world of speech in which things are simply what they are (necessity), and one in which they enter into becoming (possibility), calling us to choose, respond, and anticipate a world in process of becoming what it "ought" to be. And Kierkegaard says that the form of an ethical communication will be such that it promotes our "oughtness capability" (*Journals*, I, VIII^2 B 83, n.d. [1847], 281).

If this first additional limit tends, by means of our becoming "witnesses," to blur an assumed distinction between author and reader—one which, by the way, must be carefully maintained in purely ethical communications, which stand apart from the "ethico-religious" ones—then the second limit that Kierkegaard imposes on himself brings sharpness and rigor to the issues of speaking and listening.[10]

In addition, Manheimer notes the second (or religious) group's accountability to the metaphor by discussing Kierkegaard's use of the term *overført Tale* (transferred language) where he might have used the Danish *metaphørisk* (metaphorical):

In doing so, he emphasizes the significance of the original Greek *metapherein*, since *overført* means literally "carried over." He draws our attention to this linguistic act of movement by means of which certain ways of speaking actually transfer us beyond a world of limit. And he is also playing with a second sense of "transfer" which belongs to the world of bookkeeping. The bookkeeper "carries over" (*overfører*) figures of income and expenditure in order to maintain the balance in economy. In that sense, he renders an accounting, as Kierkegaard would later give an "accounting" (*Regnskabet*) of his intentions as author in *Point of View*.

By transferred language (*overført Tale*), then Kierkegaard is suggesting to those of us who are members of his "second group" a theory of metaphorical utterance.[11]

---

n.d. [1849], 314).

[10]Manheimer, *Kierkegaard as Educator*, 192-93. For an indirect discussion by Kierkegaard of *how* the metaphorical is made manifest to the uninitiated sensate-psychical person, see *Point of View*, 45-46.

[11]Ibid., 195. Although Manheimer does not take this metaphorical extension of accountability any further in his discussion, the notion of "accounting" and "carrying over" numerical value is evident (as has been noted earlier—see 42-43, above) in *Point of View* (46, 53) when Kierkegaard discusses the "number carried [*Mente*]," namely, the

According to Kierkegaard, then, sacred words become more glorious
when a deeper understanding of metaphorical utterance in religious
speech is revealed. It is in this context that Kierkegaard calls metaphor
a secret language, "a quiet, whispering secret."[12] Earlier in *Works of Love*,
Kierkegaard writes that sacred words "speak about two thoughts although
they hiddenly speak about only one; the statement manifestly contains
one thought but also hiddenly contains another."[13] Such "secret" language
is the best means (despite that it always remains for Kierkegaard a poor
means relative to the eternal) by which human beings may begin to
articulate not only the inexorable chasm between God and humans, but
also the inexpressible link between God and humans that existentially is
manifested by faith. Within the span of two dozen pages in *Christian
Discourses*, Kierkegaard offers variations on this theme:

> We speak this way [metaphorically] with you, O God; there is a language
> difference between us, and yet we strive to understand you and to make
> ourselves intelligible to you. . . . What a strange language a human being
> speaks when he is to speak with [God]. . . . When it comes to describing our
> relation to the Deity, this human language is certainly second-rate and half-
> true. . . . Great you are, O God; although we know you only as in an
> obscure saying and as in a mirror.[14]

---

idea that the religious must be "carried over" and brought into the forefront of a discourse
that otherwise might be interpreted as esthetic.

[12]*Works of Love*, 210.

[13]*Works of Love*, 8.

[14]*Christian Discourses*, 268, 275, 286, 289. While discussing a moment in the early
nineteenth century when various French, American, and German romantic and mystic
poetry was claiming to occupy the function of religion, Roger Shattuck notes that Swiss-
French belletrist Mme. de Staël "had not given up belief in a Creator and in an ethics
based on analogy." Shattuck then cites a passage from Mme. de Staël's *De l'Allemagne*
(1810): "They are no purposeless play of the imagination, these continual metaphors that
compare our sentiments to exterior phenomena: sadness with a cloud-covered sky. . . . It
amounts to a single thought process of the Creator translating itself into two different
languages. Almost all axioms of physics correspond to moral maxims." Roger Shattuck,
Candor and Perversion (New York: W. W. Norton & Co., 1999) 49.

Interlude. The Coming into Existence of Metaphor

The opening sentences of the second series of *Works of Love* require further special attention:

> All human speech, even the divine speech of Holy Scripture, about the spiritual is essentially metaphorical [*overført*, carried over] speech. And this is quite in order or in the order of things and of existence, since a human being, even if from the moment of birth he is spirit, still does not become conscious of himself as spirit until later and thus has sensately-psychically acted out a certain part of his life prior to this.[15]

This preamble to Kierkegaard's concept of metaphor accounts for both the metaphorical nature of human speech in general and religious speech in particular. More importantly, the two sentences intimately and substantively link such language to human existence, to metaphor's coming into human existence. Kierkegaard here does not *compare* (in a metaphorical sense) metaphorical language to existence, for plain analogue would accent *dissimilarities* between language and existence. Rather, he asserts that metaphorical language in and of itself is far closer to human existence than simple comparison otherwise would imply. Metaphorical language is (as a point of fact and not a point of metaphorical or imaginative fancy) "quite in order or in the order of things and of existence." His assertion radicalizes metaphor's more prolix definitions by rendering language on par with existence—involved as it is in a deeply intimate and personal relationship with existence—rather than having language simply inform existence on a strict and limited level of cognition.

The intimacy between metaphorical language and existence asserted above by Kierkegaard prompted an important footnote by Howard Hong in the notes of the Hongs' 1962 translation of *Works of Love*.[16] Hong writes that the above passage and the entire paragraph from which it is excerpted is concerned with the "double" or metaphorical use of

---

[15]*Works of Love*, 209.
[16]The footnote is not included in Hong's notes for the 1995 *Works of Love* edition in Princeton's Kierkegaard's Writings series.

language. In addition, he claims the passage "is developed against a summary background of Kierkegaard's philosophy of man":

> [I]t epitomises his central affirmation that man is an intended being (related to spirit), a becoming being who in freedom ought to become that which as a human being he is intended to be (spirit), and a being who in becoming lives in qualitative categories (esthetic, ethical, religious) which are displaced (esthetic and ethical) but which are subsumed in new relationships and under new orientation.[17]

Remarking upon the relationship of duality shared by metaphor and human existence, Hong concludes his note by quoting from Anti-Climacus's composite structure of a human being that he writes at the outset of *The Sickness unto Death*, namely, that a self is a "synthesis of the infinite and the finite, of the temporal and the eternal, of freedom and necessity."[18] Similarly, a presupposition of the present discussion suggests that the ontological structure of a human being is not unlike the fundamental structure of metaphor itself. As a synthesis, humans mimic in their ontological DNA the paradoxical tension of opposites evident between tenors and vehicles in metaphors.[19]

Such an intimate relationship between metaphor and existence that Kierkegaard directly puts forth at the outset of the "Second Series" of his *Works of Love* and indirectly elsewhere is provocative if not controversial. For example, Soskice (citing Thomas Fawcett) suggests that theologians require metaphorical " 'models which are primarily valuable for their existential contents' " and that such " 'religious models exist to give a symbolic picture of reality of such a kind as to provide man with a way of orienting his life in the world.' "[20] Nevertheless, she questions: Is all religious language in fact "essentially" metaphorical?

> The answer depends on what we take religious language to be. If one takes the Bible as a body of religious language, it is clear that by no means all, or even the greater part, of religious language is metaphorical; along with

---

[17]Søren Kierkegaard, *Works of Love*, trans. Howard Hong and Edna Hong (New York: Harper & Row, 1962) Notes, 370.

[18]*Sickness*, 13.

[19]See above, 10.

[20]Janet Soskice, *Metaphor and Religious Language* (Oxford: Clarendon Press, 1985) 110.

nearly every other trope, the Bible includes language of narrative, chronology, and description which is not figurative at all. But people who ask whether all religious language is metaphorical usually mean something more specific by "religious language" and something rather broad by "metaphor". By "religious language" they mean language which is specifically about God, and by "metaphorical"—pictorial language like those metaphors which . . . [spin] out the implications of a model, such as God as father.[21]

Soskice's skepticism challenges the more intense degree of intimacy that metaphor and existence enjoy under the auspices of Kierkegaard's thought. She apparently rejects the kind of existential primitivity toward which Kierkegaard's more radicalized discussion and use of metaphors point in the context of Christianity and of becoming a Christian through faith. Although Soskice asserts that "a strong metaphor compels new possibilities of vision,"[22] her own concept of metaphor apparently is reluctant to break from the strict linguistic structure of metaphor with which she begins her own discussion.[23] She thereby excludes to a large degree any radically intimate (that is, potentially dangerous *or* potentially fulfilling) relationship between metaphor and human existence. Consequently, any "new possibilities of vision" that her concept of metaphor otherwise could offer may only be of very limited scope.

Kierkegaard's metaphors, on the other hand (especially the bulk of his religious metaphors as opposed to most metaphors in his pseudonymous authorship), strive to compel truly new and original possibilities of vision by taking the figurative language literally. Kierkegaard literalizes religious metaphors in ways that evoke ultimate existential meaning—meaning bound up in ethical-religious practice, action, and actuality. In this sense, what Loren Eiseley writes of John Donne also may be said of Kierkegaard:

John Donne gave powerful expression to a feeling applicable . . . to literature when he said devoutly of certain biblical passages: "The literall sense is always to be preserved; but the literall sense is not always to be discerned; for the literall sense is not alwayes that which the very letter and

---

[21]Ibid., 63-64.
[22]Ibid., 58.
[23]See above, xv-xvi.

grammar of the place presents." A figurative sense, he argues cogently, can sometimes be the most "literall intention of the Holy Ghost."[24]

"New possibilities of vision" that Kierkegaard entertains in his religious authorship are (not coincidentally) derived from established and commonly known metaphors in biblical text. Use of metaphors from sacred text speaks initially to Kierkegaard's intent to establish a "new acquaintance with the old and familiar."[25] No less important to Kierkegaard in his religious authorship, however, is his intent to prompt readers to envision a simpler, more fundamental and unmediated relationship with God by readers' "new acquaintance with the old and familiar." Subsequently, he interprets the relationships between tenors and vehicles of the biblical metaphors that he uses in a more simple, fundamental, and unmediated way than in his pseudonymous authorship. Just as an absolute relationship with the absolute is simple but not easy to achieve in existence, however, so too the simplicity and greater intimacy between tenors and vehicles render Kierkegaard's religious metaphors more difficult to grasp than those evident in his pseudonymous authorship.[26] When, for instance, Kierkegaard considers the metaphorical implications

---

[24]Loren Eiseley, *The Star Thrower* (New York: Harvest/HBJ, 1978) 274.

[25]*Works of Love*, 210.

[26]In *Being and Time*, Martin Heidegger writes that "there is more to be learned philosophically" from the upbuilding writings in Kierkegaard's religious authorship "than from his theoretical ones" in his pseudonymous authorship. *Being and Time*, trans. John Macquarrie and Edward Robinson (New York: Harper & Row, 1962) 494n.vi. Heidegger draws this conclusion from his claim that, although Kierkegaard rightly considered the problem of existence an existential one, the "existential problematic was so alien to him that, as regards his ontology, he remained completely dominated by Hegel and by ancient philosophy as Hegel saw it" (ibid.).

Heidegger's argument in praise of Kierkegaard's religious authorship, however, appears to be made not so much on the merits of the religious authorship itself as upon criticism leveled toward Kierkegaard's presumably limited ontological vision in his pseudonymous authorship. Had Heidegger instead focused upon the religious authorship's own philosophical merits—merits that he rightly praises (although without actually considering them), merits that include the elegant existential simplicity *and* difficulty of Kierkegaard's religious metaphorical constructions within the strict context of existence—perhaps his claim that denigrates the scope of Kierkegaard's ontological vision might have been revised, if not deleted. As the remainder of this discussion suggests, the degree of intimacy Kierkegaard exposes between metaphor and existence in the sphere of the religious is both uncompromising and unparalleled.

of figurative speech like "God the Father" or the "finger of God," tenor and vehicle become reversed: tenor and vehicle, in effect, fuse.

Such a dialectical two-step effectively literalizes the metaphor in religious discourse. Kierkegaard collapses tenor into vehicle and, in the radical collision, renders the metaphorical literal. Unlike the esthetic stage in which the literalization of metaphor ends in an individual becoming egoistically lost in a strange dream world of possible self-images, however, the religious literalization of metaphor places the individual at the threshold of a proper relation with God. Kierkegaard does this by (1) disclosing the possibilities and limitations of metaphor, (2) helping the reader distinguish between what metaphor may mean externally as opposed to inwardly, and (3) deepening a linguistic understanding of what we think of when we think of God in the Western tradition:

> We call God "Father"; we rest happily and confidently in this name as the most beautiful, the most uplifting, but also the truest and most expressive of names, and yet this expression is a metaphorical expression drawn from earthly life. . . . But if the expression is figurative, metaphorical, does it actually reach up to heaven to describe what it is supposed to describe, or does it not dwindle away the higher it ascends, like an earthly longing, which always speaks only obscurely. Yes, to one who looks at the external, the expression remains figurative and unreal; if he thinks that God gives the good gifts as a father gives them, but yet in such a way that it is the gifts that demonstrate, so to speak, that God is our Father, then he is judging externally, and for him truth itself becomes figurative. But the inner being looks not at the gifts but the giver. For the inner being, the human distinction between what might be called gift and what language is not inclined to designate as gift vanishes in the essential, in the giver; for the inner being, joy and sorrow, good and bad fortune, distress and victory are gifts; for it, the giver is primary. Then the inner being understands and is convinced that God is a Father in heaven and that this expression is not metaphorical, imperfect, but the truest and most literal expression, because God gives not only the gifts but himself with them in a way beyond the capability of any human being. . . . Then you perceived that it is not because you have a father or because human beings have fathers, that it is not for this reason that God is called Father in heaven, but it is as the apostle says—from him all fatherliness in heaven and on earth derives its name. Therefore, even though you had the most loving father given among men, he would still be, despite all his best intentions, but a stepfather, a shadow, a reflection, a

simile, an image, a dark saying about the fatherliness from which all fatherliness in heaven and on earth derives its name.[27]

In upbuilding discourses of Kierkegaard's such as this, a reader begins to see how the language of a religious reality for Kierkegaard is carried over from the language of sensate-psychical realities. The metaphor ceases to be metaphor through its own literalization. The metaphor collapses under the earnest call of eternity for humans to believe that the figural is the literal, that God as *idea* is *actual*, is fully *real*: the God in time. Kierkegaard writes in a later upbuilding discourse: "even though in every other sense it is just a figurative expression to say that we see the finger of God in life, a person who is concerned about himself understands it quite literally, because all deeper and more inward self-knowledge is under divine guidance and continually sees the finger of God that points to him."[28]

In a section of his discussion about what can be learned from the lily and the bird, Kierkegaard literalizes and thereby collapses metaphorical speech when he repeatedly states that the lily and bird take Peter's words—"Cast all your sorrows upon God"—literally.[29] In other words, the literalization of metaphoric speech becomes the essential means by which the Christian existing in time strives toward the religious *telos*, namely, the unmediated, original, primitive, absolute relationship with God—this despite the terror of radical collision between time and eternity in actuality.

In his discussions of Christian ethics—especially his most renowned discussions found in the first series of *Works of Love*, where he considers neighborly love—Kierkegaard mimics such a striving for an absolute relationship with God. His ideas on neighborly love, as his ideas on an absolute relationship with God, emerge organically from the same terminology of likeness and unlikeness that informs his thoughts on metaphor at the outset of the second series of his *Works of Love*. Manheimer writes that an upbuilding speech

> awakens the listener by evoking a sense of contrast between the relative density or magnitude of two dimensions of meaning. And just as metaphor,

---

[27] *Eighteen Discourses*, 98-99, 100.
[28] *Eighteen Discourses*, 276.
[29] *Without Authority*, 41.

by creating a field of contrast, releases us from the captivity of confined meanings to the surprise of new ones, so an [upbuilding] discourse has the capacity to renew our concern for what is of ultimate value, that we may once again (or even for the first time) arrive at a threshold of choice. Having brought the reader to this threshold, Kierkegaard then "reaches through" this metaphorical utterance become symbol, finding in that symbol a comparison to Christian love, the love of the neighbor, the love in which the familiar and the strange draw closer together in establishing affinities, as a person goes over to encounter a stranger.

In the self-neighbor relationship metaphorical speaking becomes metaphor in the flesh: first, because in the love of the neighbor like and unlike are united, and second, this reaching out to the stranger (as to oneself) reveals the hidden meaning of Christ's life. The individual enacts a likeness to the Divine Presence corresponding to the divine having become humanlike in the God-Man. To find oneself where one least expected, in the unfamiliar, the neighbor who is simply "nearby," is a lesson in surprises transcending the idea of development as self-discovery, self-identity, or self-improvement. The real test of love consists in the response to the call of likeness in the most unlike, the neighbor.[30]

Expressions of the self-neighbor relationship and the self-God relationship are similar metaphoric expressions, then, insofar as they both demand awareness and acceptance of the unlikeness or the dissimilar upon which metaphoric expression builds.

In his various yet not unrelated discussions of religious metaphors such as "God the Father" or "finger of God" or "neighborly love," then, Kierkegaard ultimately suggests that religious figures of speech are not figures of speech at all to the true believer. Rather, they are speech to be taken literally. Far from thinking that the metaphorical equation is contradictory ($X=Y$), the believer draws comfort from the essential similarity yielded by the conjoined dissimilarities in a metaphor. "The metaphorical language could become even more comforting," Kierkegaard writes, "when actuality also [begins] to explain . . . the metaphors of earthly life, that the conclusion of the words could become even more firmly set when reversed—something [a] soul would need when life had reversed everything for him."[31]

---

[30]Manheimer, *Kierkegaard as Educator*, 198.
[31]*Eighteen Discourses*, 129-30.

Yet another aspect of Kierkegaard's treatment of metaphor and religious language is worth mentioning here, especially given that Kierkegaard claims all of his works point to the spiritual.[32] If a reader agrees with Kierkegaard that "all human speech, even the divine speech of Holy Scripture, about the spiritual is essentially metaphorical speech,"[33] and if all metaphors in religious discourse are literalized, then religious language is the greatest agent to render much metaphorical language into dead metaphor. In other words, while religious texts collapse tenor-vehicle distinctions implicit in much metaphorical meaning, the metaphor becomes commonplace or "dead." The tenor-vehicle construct, which is a logical contradiction based upon dissimilarity, may come to show little if any sign of contradiction to the religiously minded reader. The implications (already intimated above) are provocative: God literally *is Father*, while God's *finger* literally *points* at the worshiper. The paradox of religious language here is that its total usage of metaphor annuls metaphor totally, literalizes metaphor literally, and thereby makes the analysis of metaphor and religious language far more difficult if for no other reason than because particular metaphorical constructions become virtually impossible to detect. Just as there is no law when "all is law," metaphor ceases to exist in religious discourse when all religious language is considered metaphorical. The literalization of metaphor toward which Kierkegaard strives ultimately cancels out esthetic, sensate-psychical distinctions between what is and what is not metaphor, offering the reader opportunities to stand unmediated in existence before eternity. Just as Johannes Climacus writes that "doubt is a protest against any conclusion that wants to go beyond immediate sensation and immediate knowledge" while "belief is a sense for coming into existence,"[34] so too the paradox of religious language offends the doubter as much as it empowers the believer.

It should be noted again here that the degree of tension that Kierkegaard maintains in his dialectics—the absolute distinction between what is relative and what is absolute, what is finite and what is infinite, what is earthly and what is heavenly—remains intact. The last thing Kierkegaard wants to do is shut out the absolute distinction between God and

---

[32]*Journals*, II, X[1] A 646, n.d. [1849], 283. See also 31n.11, above.

[33]*Works of Love*, 209.

[34]*Fragments*, 84.

humans. He is aware of the potential backlash of such primitive relationships between metaphor and existence—evidenced, for example, by his discussion of Adler misconstruing himself as an apostle.[35] Nonetheless, he also is aware of such fulfillment in the context of what he considers to be an existential need for a primitive relationship with Christ—a relationship derived from a radical faith that imaginatively presupposes a collapse of time and space between the historical existence of any human being and the historical existence of Christ.[36] In the moment of such faith, as Gouwens notes,

> the imagination more positively allows one to apprehend Christ as *contempo-*
> *raneous with the believer*. The believer's new possibility is grounded in
> Christ; therefore, to obtain that new possibility, it is necessary to become
> contemporaneous with Christ. Whereas Kierkegaard earlier affirms Christ's
> historical actuality against those who would reduce him to a mere ideal or
> mythic figure, directly graspable by the imagination, Kierkegaard can now
> grant that the imagination may secure an "understanding" of Christ in
> contemporaneity.[37]

An intimate relationship between metaphor and existence nevertheless has the ambiguous potential of producing anything from an earnest religious enthusiast (that is, a true religious disciple, an actual knight of faith) to a mad religious fanatic who pathetically and pathologically has lost or abandoned part of his humanity by rejecting reason for some dubious, narcissistic, or self-aggrandizing end (á la Melville's Ahab). Kierkegaard's Christian idealism nonetheless indicates such risk and venture to the earnest in order to establish an absolute relationship with the absolute. (The problem with Adler, for instance, was not that the pastor attempted to become contemporary with Christ but that he attempted to assume apostolic authority that, in the end, rendered him disingenuous. Adler was not earnest with his own existence—subsequently, he could not be earnest with metaphors of apostolic virtue that he attempted to appropriate to guide his life.)

---

[35]See above, 92-95.

[36]See *Fragments*.

[37]David J. Gouwens, *Kierkegaard's Dialectic of the Imagination* (New York: Peter Lang, 1989) 250.

In the following passage about the life of John Brown from Russell Banks's historical novel, *Cloudsplitter*, the famous abolitionist's relationship to Scripture goes beyond simple mining for and appropriation of metaphorical meaning for personal existence to a radical religious collision between biblical language and personal existence. John Brown

> didn't read the Bible like a man who thought he was *like* the ancient Israelites; he read it as if he were an Israelite himself, as if he, too, were receiving instructions from the Lord. The man did not simply *remember* the Bible, as a person remembers the alphabet or even as he remembers old injuries or triumphs. No; for the Old Man, the Bible *was* his memory.[38]

There is of course great risk and danger in such a total appropriation of sacred text (another example may be Brigham Young's appropriation of the Exodus story for his and his fellow Mormons' exodus). Similarly, however, there also *may be* great potential for striving toward an absolute relationship with the absolute. Soskice dismisses on rational grounds narrative, chronological, and descriptive biblical language as being metaphorical because it is not strictly "pictorial language like those metaphors which . . . [spin] out the implications of a model"[39]; Kierkegaard's unified conception of metaphor and human existence, on the other hand, does not exclude prosaic language of narrative, chronology, and description. Such language informs the likes of Adler, Brown, Young, and Abraham (despite that any or all of them may be attacked as hypocrites and madmen or praised as prophets or knights of faith). In the case of John Brown and his ultimate violent attack on Harpers Ferry that helped lead an entire nation into civil war, some critics understandably charge that Brown was an insane religious fanatic. Supporters such as Henry David Thoreau (despite his aversion to violence) proclaimed him a martyr and compared his death to Christ's crucifixion. The issue here is not whether John Brown was as disingenuous a man as Adler in his personal relationship to imaginative constructions that he appropriated to develop his religiosity. Neither does this discussion mean to conclude that Brown was as pure in his belief and principles as a knight of faith—that he was a leader and harbinger of a new nation like Abraham who, in what Johannes de Silentio calls a teleological suspension of the ethical, intended to

---

[38]Russell Banks, *Cloudsplitter* (New York: HarperFlamingo, 1998) 373.
[39]Soskice, *Metaphor and Religious Language*, 63-64.

suspend worldly tribal laws in this case and kill his son to affirm his faith in his God. Rather, the issue in the present discussion suggests that a saintly apostle as much as an insane imitator of an apostle both radically collapse metaphorical language and existence into each other, thereby suspending the ethical for the sake of some higher *telos* or goal.

The difference between such extreme personalities resides in the degree of personal earnestness and honesty such individuals have toward collisions from which they suffer in human existence between the infinite and the finite, the temporal and the eternal, and freedom and necessity.[40] Despite the difficulty (if not impossibility) of any observer judging the authenticity of such deep acts of subjectivity, Kierkegaard treats Adler in *The Book on Adler* as one who willfully imposes an apostolic ideality upon his own actual existence, and thereby entangles himself in metaphor. Just as effectively, Kierkegaard treats Abraham as a genuine knight of faith in *Fear and Trembling*. As Kierkegaard writes, "everything depends upon how the relationship is viewed"[41]—the relationship in this context is reflected in the degree of earnestness by which metaphor is appropriated. Alberto Manguel cites German critic Hans Blumenburg: " 'Metaphors are no longer considered first and foremost as representing the sphere that guides our hesitant theoretic conceptions, as an entrance hall to the forming of concepts, as a makeshift device within specialized languages that have not yet been consolidated, but rather as the authentic means to comprehend contexts.' "[42] An ecstatic admiration for how metaphor develops mere theoretic conceptions in the strict contexts of existence and actuality is not earnest, while an understanding of how metaphor fits into and aids in the comprehension of the context of human existence is earnest.

In *Practice in Christianity*, Anti-Climacus pits "the supreme upbringing in the school of life: becoming and being a Christian" against the upbringing of a quixotic young man whose powerful imagination is

---

[40]Weighing personal, social, and religious collisions in his own life, Kierkegaard reflects upon the value of collision, that it led him to "recognize at once my identity, my personal peculiarities." He claims that for every one of his own collisions "there is also a collision with God or a struggle with God. It is precisely this aspect of the collision which makes my suffering so frightfully earnest" (*Journals*, VI, X^1 A 260, n.d. [1849], 141, 142).

[41]*Christian Discourses*, 126.

[42]Alberto Manguel, *A History of Reading* (New York: Viking Penguin, 1996) 168.

judged by his contemporaries as having become "overwrought and ridiculous" and unfit for the actual world.[43] This same situation may be said of Adler, John Brown, Brigham Young, or Abraham. Yet whereas some or all of the above historical figures may have been seduced by worldly power, ambition, or self-aggrandizement, Anti-Climacus maintains that human life ultimately is governed not by such power but by love, and even

> Loving Governance does not judge this youth unlovingly, as the world judges, but says: Good for you! Now the earnestness of life is beginning for you; now you have come out so far that it will become a matter of earnestness for you that to live is to be examined. The earnestness of life is not all this pressure of finitude and busyness with livelihood, job, office, and procreation, but the earnestness of life is to *will* to be, to *will* to express the perfection (ideality) in the dailiness of actuality, to *will* it, so that one does not to one's own ruin once and for all busily abandon it or conceitedly take it in vain as a dream—what a tragic lack of earnestness in both cases!—but humbly wills it in actuality.[44]

Of the four figures mentioned, Adler or Brown or Young either may or may not fall short of such rigorous earnestness to which Abraham universally (and thereby, in the Judeo-Christian canon, unambiguously) ascribes. Mackey notes that, although belief is a resolution of the will, "it is also the supreme effort of the imagination"[45] (an assertion that at least conditionally sympathizes with Adler or Brown or Young, however misguided each ultimately may or may not have been). One believes as he thinks, imaginatively and metaphorically: "Poetry, the imaginative cultivation of multiple perspectives, is the condition, the environment, and the source of belief."[46] Anti-Climacus notes similarly that "in order for a person to become aware of his self and of God, imagination must raise him higher than the miasma of probability."[47] The upshot is that metaphor becomes something different in the religious sphere, something more, something transformed, something concrete through imagination instead

---

[43]*Practice*, 186, 189.

[44]*Practice*, 189-90.

[45]Louis Mackey, *Kierkegaard: A Kind of Poet* (Philadelphia: University of Pennsylvania Press, 1971) 293.

[46]Ibid., 293.

[47]*Sickness*, 41.

of simply linguistic. Metaphor becomes existence, and thereby metaphor ceases to be metaphor.

> Why become concrete at once [an ironic Johannes Climacus goads], why begin at once to construct imaginatively [*experimentere*] *in concreto*, or could not this question be answered in the dispassionate brevity of abstraction, which has no means of distraction or enchantment? What does it mean that the idea becomes concrete, what is coming into existence, how is one related to that which has come into existence, etc.?[48]

The remainder of the discussion considers how Climacus's ponderings apply religiously to metaphor.

B. Rejecting or Annulling Metaphor to Embrace It Existentially

Soskice rightly considers that if Jesus' contentious phrase "this bread is my body" is critiqued as if it were a metaphorical issue instead of a metaphysical issue, neither metaphor, metaphysics, nor Jesus' phrase would be well served. Linguistically, she notes, the phrase is metaphorical, yet

> the point at issue is not really whether we have metaphor here, but what the metaphor is doing: is it simply ornamental redescription, so that Jesus has redescribed bread in an evocative way? or is the metaphor genuinely catachretical, not a redescribing but a naming or disclosing for the first time? It is one's metaphysics, not metaphor, which is at issue. To put is another way, the question is not simply whether we have a metaphor here or not, but what, if anything, the metaphor refers to or signifies.[49]

Harries extends Soskice's point about signification in religious language to the sphere of esthetics by concluding that even the poet's own attempt to escape from the referentiality of language finally cannot succeed:

> The attempt to use metaphor to establish the poem as an autonomous esthetic object must fail, and this failure can open us to the mysterious presence of the things to which the poem obliquely refers. Nor should this

---

[48]*Fragments*, 78.
[49]Soskice, *Metaphor and Religious Language*, 90.

reversal, which endows the esthetic project with an ontological significance, surprise us.[50]

Similarly, Ferreira writes:

> If, as one recent analysis of metaphor claims, the "distinctive metaphorical move" is "the perspectival shift" or "jump" across semantic fields, then metaphor may well provide a very helpful perspective on such qualitative transitions, including the transition to faith.[51]

Here, Ferreira, Harries, and Soskice distinguish between metaphor in the context of linguistics and metaphor in a "carried over" context to metaphysics or religion. "Carrying over" metaphor to a sphere other than linguistics nevertheless implies at least the linguistic annulment of metaphor.

Even in an ethical sphere, metaphor and imaginative constructions (that is, those imaginative constructions that are put forth ethically to offer humans possibilities) must ultimately be renounced by the reader to choose and appropriate the good. Not to set metaphor aside, but instead to be overwhelmed by the possibilities of imaginary constructions to the point of existential paralysis, may lead an individual to the esthete's hallmark signature, namely, to refrain from choosing. Judge William maintains that

> the inner working of the personality has no time for imaginary constructions in thought, so that it continually speeds ahead and in one way or another posits either the one or the other, whereby the choice is made more difficult in the next moment, for that which has been posited will be withdrawn.[52]

Judge William then seals the idea by analogy:

> Imagine a captain of a ship the moment a shift of direction must be made; then he may be able to say: I can do either this or that. But if he is not a mediocre captain he will also be aware that during all this the ship is

[50]Karsten Harries, "The Many Uses of Metaphor," in *On Metaphor*, ed. Sheldon Sacks (Chicago: University of Chicago Press, 1979) 171.

[51]M. Jamie Ferreira, *Transforming Vision: Imagination and Will in Kierkegaardian Faith* (Oxford: Clarendon Press, 1991) 72. The "recent analysis" to which Ferreira refers is Eva Feder Kittay, *Metaphor: Its Cognitive Force and Linguistic Structure*, Clarendon Library of Logic and Philosophy (London: Oxford University Press, 1987) 4, 28.

[52]*Either/Or* II, 163-64.

ploughing ahead with its ordinary velocity, and thus there is but a single moment when it is inconsequential whether he does this or that. So also with a person—if he forgets to take into account the velocity—there eventually comes a moment where it is no longer a matter of an Either/Or, not because he has chosen, but because he has refrained from it, which also can be expressed by saying: Because others have chosen for him—or because he has lost himself.[53]

Of metaphor and imaginative constructing, Judge William stresses that "as soon as the ethical person's gymnastics become an imaginary constructing he has ceased to live ethically. All such imaginary gymnastic constructing is equivalent to sophistry in the realm of knowledge."[54] In other words, metaphor dictated solely by esthetics ultimately must be revoked so that actuality, and not simply an *image* of actuality, may honestly be gained. Kierkegaard writes:

> In the knowledge, as contemplation and deliberation, that is, the distance of eternity from time and actuality, there presumably is truth, and the knower can understand the truth in it, but he cannot understand himself. It is true that without this knowledge a person's life is more or less devoid of thought, but it is also true that this knowledge, because it is in a counterfeit eternity for the imagination, develops double-mindedness if it is not honestly gained slowly through purity of the will.[55]

---

[53]*Either/Or* II, 164. Just as Judge William subordinates imagining to acting, Emerson (perhaps more judiciously) subordinates reading books to "reading God directly":

> Undoubtedly there is a right way of reading, so it be sternly subordinated. Man Thinking must not be subdued by his instruments. Books are for the scholar's idle times. When he can read God directly, the hour is too precious to be wasted in other men's transcripts of their readings. But when the intervals of darkness come, as come they must,—when the sun is hid, and the stars withdraw their shining, we repair to the lamps which were kindled by their ray, to guide our steps to the East again, where the dawn is. We hear, that we may speak. The Arabian proverb says, "A fig tree, looking on a fig tree, becometh fruitful." (Ralph Waldo Emerson, *Essays and Lectures* [New York: Library of America, 1983] 58.)

Similarly, Kierkegaard writes elsewhere: "[A] man of prayer does not pore over scholarly books but is the wise man 'whose eyes are opened—when he kneels down' (Numbers 24:16)" (*Various Spirits*, 26); and Climacus: "But one does not prepare oneself to become aware of Christianity by reading books or by world-historical surveys, but by immersing oneself in existing" (*Postscript* I, 560).

[54]*Postscript* I, 253.

[55]*Various Spirits*, 74.

In the religious sphere, metaphor also is not simply a trope for esthetic poetization; but neither is it simply an ethical tool to disclose deeper levels of the self. In the context of religious existence, metaphor becomes even more radicalized, literalized, and thereby must be said to annul itself completely. In at least one instance,[56] Kierkegaard even considers indirect communication in the form of storytelling and metaphorical constructions still a form of impersonal and direct communication that must be sloughed off, annulled, abandoned, in order to develop one's personality to enact existentially the story that is told. Despite metaphor's great service to Christianity, if metaphor is not eventually annulled it ultimately disparages Christianity by mediating between the existing individual and absolute faith in the paradox of Jesus Christ, which Kierkegaard calls "the absurd." In one journal entry, Kierkegaard writes:

> Earlier the Bible was reflected imaginatively in imagination: here is the whole range of allegorical interpretation. It is really an expression of the inability to comprehend how the infinite descends to the ordinary, the historical. Allegory as the primary interpretation is really an indirect attack upon Christianity. . . . Christianity is not allowed to be the paradox—this is not regarded as sufficient—so the imaginary is to be substituted, which, however, it should be noted, is not Christianity. . . . This is a fundamental confusion which appears again and again. Men simply refuse to be satisfied with acknowledging the absurd.[57]

Metaphor and imagination, then, are necessary but not sufficient conditions for becoming human, for in and of themselves they do not meet existential requirements for becoming fully human in a religious context. "There no doubt must be something poetic in the religious domain, mainly just to get hold of existential ideals again and to encounter the existential ideals," Kierkegaard writes in one journal entry. But he adds in the same entry: "Then it will become apparent whether a new generation will get the power to make an attempt again to *actualize* the ideals existentially."[58] Similarly, pseudonymous writer H. H. writes: "All thinking draws its breath in immanence, whereas paradox and faith constitute a separate

---

[56]See *Self-Examination*, 39.

[57]*Journals*, IV, X² A 548, n.d. [1850], 462; and X² A 549, n.d., 563.

[58]*Journals*, II, X³ A 576, n.d. [1850], 289; my emphasis.

qualitative sphere."[59] Thus, he suggests, if the apostle Paul is to be praised for his "brilliance, profundity," his "beautiful metaphors,"[60] then such praise for such *thinking* smacks of estheticism and scholarship, not Christianity. Paul becomes misinterpreted as a genius instead of an apostle who, by divine authority, offers the actual, literal, living word for human beings to consume like bread, to internalize, and to be nourished by in order to become that to which the word refers.[61] Words and metaphors pale, become "something vanishing"[62] compared with the earnest sustenance of apostolic news. So Paul writes:

> [1]Do we begin again to commend ourselves? Or need we, as some others, epistles of commendation to you, or letters of commendation from you? [2]Ye are our epistle written in our hearts, known and read of all men: [3]forasmuch as ye are manifestly declared to be the epistle of Christ ministered by us, written not with ink, but with the Spirit of the living God; not in tables of stone, but in fleshy tables of the heart. [4]And such trust have we through Christ to God-ward: [5]Not that we are sufficient of ourselves to think any thing as of ourselves; but our sufficiency is of God; [6]Who also hath made as able ministers of the new testament; not of the letter [i.e., the Law], but of the spirit: for the letter [i.e., the Law] killeth, but the spirit giveth life.[63]

As much as Kierkegaard wants to secure metaphor as an esthetic construction throughout his authorship, then, he equally wants ethically and

---

[59]*Without Authority*, 94.

[60]*Without Authority*, 93.

[61]George Steiner also comments on the *physical* internalization or consumption of sacred text:

> Man's relation to written texts has always been complicated and always charged with emotions and metaphoric associations which go right back to the origins of man and to that Hebraic formula—but not exclusively Hebraic, for we find it also in other Middle Eastern languages—the Book of Life. Life itself is in some manner to be imaged as a book which we read. We think of the great passage of Ezekiel 3, when the divine voice bids the prophet, the reluctant prophet, to consume physically, to put in his mouth, the scroll of the law, to appropriate, to embody, to incorporate, the text in his body. (George Steiner, "Books in an Age of Post-Literacy," *Publishers Weekly* [24 May 1985]: 44.)

See also Timothy Polk, *The Biblical Kierkegaard* (Macon GA: Mercer University Press, 1997) 65.

[62]*Without Authority*, 94.

[63]Second Corinthians 3:1-6 KJV.

religiously to eliminate it, to kill it before it kills us. Just as Kierkegaard claims that Christianity "seems to be working against itself by establishing sin so securely as a position . . . and [yet] it is this very Christianity that . . . wants to eliminate sin,"[64] so, too, he persistently posits metaphor in his writings as an esthetic vehicle for the sake of ethical understanding before ultimately dispensing with metaphor in the religious sphere for the sake of faith. "Although it is the utmost strenuousness," Kierkegaard writes, "imitation should be like a jest, a childlike act—if it is to mean something in earnest, that is, be of any value before God."[65] And although Kierkegaard perhaps only could arrive at this thought through metaphor, he nonetheless understands an essential imperative for any human being: Because of one's understanding of metaphor and after one has used metaphor in the context of religious upbuilding, metaphor (and the imitation to which it ethically points) ultimately must be cast out by the existing individual—abandoned, negated, annihilated, reduced back to airy nothingness, made an impression of a silhouette upon the very center of being—all for the human being to appropriate and atone for the possibility of standing at the "coming into existence" of the truest impression, namely, the time when "the single individual who as the single individual stands in an absolute relation with the absolute."[66] If the task (as Johannes Climacus suggests) is to strive toward an absolute relation with God, "then existence becomes exceedingly strenuous because a double movement is continually being made."[67] The double movement here is a striving that, paradoxically, works against itself, for

> every striving which does not apply one-fourth, one-third, two-thirds, etc. of its power to systematically *working against* itself is essentially secular striving, in any case unconditionally not a *reforming* effort.
>
> Reduplication means to work against oneself while working; it is like the pressure on the plow handles, which determines the depth of the furrow—whereas working which does not work against itself is merely a superficial smoothing over.[68]

---

[64]*Sickness*, 100.

[65]*Journals*, II, X^4 A 491, n.d. [1852], 353.

[66]*Fear & Trembling*, 56.

[67]*Postscript* I, 409.

[68]*Journals*, VI, X^2 A 560, n.d. [1850], 294.

Before offering at one point in *Postscript* the application of a few metaphorical constructions from minor situations in life, Johannes Climacus warns the reader of the limits of analogy in the sphere of the religious: "continually bear in mind the absolute difference that there is no analogy to the sphere of the paradoxically religious, and thus the application, when it is understood, is a revocation."[69] Revoking metaphor is central to Climacus's concept of the religious. By revoking that which rationale uses to evoke the paradoxical, rationale also is revoked: "the difficulty is not to understand what Christianity is but to become and be a Christian."[70] Subsequently, the existing individual is prepared for that which is beyond understanding, namely, faith in the absurd, faith in the paradox of Jesus Christ. Climacus writes: "Faith belongs essentially in the sphere of the paradoxical-religious. . . . All other faith is only an analogy that is no [analogy], an analogy that can serve to make aware, but no more, the understanding of which is therefore a revocation."[71] The eternal life, Kierkegaard writes elsewhere, is "beyond all comparison."[72] And again: "To need the Holy Spirit is a perfection in a human being, and his earthly need is so far from illuminating it by analogy that it darkens it instead."[73]

It cannot be stressed enough, however, that Kierkegaard does not become undialectical or dogmatic in his religious writings by his revocations. To the contrary, as Gouwens asserts, "just as the imagination takes on many dialectical forms in the intellectual and esthetic realm of possibility, so too the imagination becomes dialectical in the ethical stage and, even more so, in the religious stages of existence."[74] Nor does Kierkegaard deny the need for metaphor in the composition of his religious authorship.[75] Rather, metaphor ultimately becomes an essential foil or a

---

[69] *Postscript* I, 567.

[70] *Postscript* I, 560.

[71] *Postscript* I, 569.

[72] *Christian Discourses*, 16.

[73] *Eighteen Discourses*, 139.

[74] Gouwens, *Kierkegaard's Dialectic of the Imagination*, 191.

[75] In *Self-Examination*, Kierkegaard defends metaphor's necessary imperfections when comparison is made with the perfect or the divine. He writes in his introduction to the renowned parable in which God's word is compared to a mirror and a love letter (25ff.):

jesting means for apprehending God, if only in negative terms that none-theless indicate the *possibility* of ultimately apprehending God positively in existence. In a journal entry discussing his composition of forthcoming discourses on the lilies and the birds,[76] Kierkegaard states that

> there will be a development of the conflict between poetry and Christianity, how in a certain sense Christianity is prose in comparison with poetry (which is desiring, charming, anesthetizing and transforms the actuality of life into an oriental dream, just as a young girl might want to lie on a sofa all day and be entranced)—and yet it is the very poetry of the eternal.
>
> Of course the lilies and the birds, that is, the sketching of nature will this time have an even more poetic tone and richness of color, simply to indicate that the poetic must be put aside, for when poetry in truth shall fall . . . , it ought to wear its party clothes.[77]

Nature and the metaphors it may inspire become even further re-moved from a religious individual's perspective, for the religious indi-vidual focuses more on spirit (which is invisible) than on what is visible:

> When a person sees his image in the mirror of the ocean, he sees his own image, but the ocean is not his image, and when he departs the image dis-appears. The ocean is not the image and cannot keep the image. Why is this, except for the reason that the visible form by its very visibility is powerless (just as the physical presence makes it impossible to be omnipresent); there-fore it cannot reproduce itself in another in such a way that the other keeps the image when the form departs.[78]

My listener, how highly do you value God's Word? Now, do not say that you value it so highly that no expression can describe it, for one can also speak so loftily that one says nothing at all. Therefore, in order to make something out of this, let us take a simple human situation [metaphorically]; if you value God's Word higher, so much the better. (26)

[76]See *Various Spirits*, 155ff.

[77]*Journals*, II, VIII¹ A 643, n.d. [1848], 377.

[78]*Various Spirits*, 192. Of Christ's invisibility and his vanishing after his last meeting with the apostles (Luke 24:31), Kierkegaard writes: "The very fact that he becomes invisible to me is the sign that I recognize him: he is indeed the object of faith, a sign of contradiction, in a certain sense must become invisible before I recognize him. He is the prototype, must therefore become invisible so that the imitator can be like him" (*Journals*, VI, X² A 40, n.d., 222). Invoking Paul's notion of the eternal and unchangeable reality of things unseen and the temporal mutability of things seen (2 Corinthians 4:18), Kierke-gaard maintains that "faith always relates itself to what is not seen" (*Works of Love*, 294).

Kierkegaard thus maintains that human consciousness is "the place where the eternal and the temporal continually touch each other, where the eternal is refracted in the temporal."[79] Metaphor, then, is tantamount to the imperfect translation or refraction of the eternal. The "wing-stroke of faith," for instance, is in the divine sense perfect, whereas "the bird's wing-stroke [is] a feeble and metaphorical suggestion."[80]

Just as James Joyce's poet-hero, Stephen Dedalus, considers himself a "priest of eternal imagination,"[81] so too Kierkegaard would consider himself a poet of eternity.[82] Nevertheless, the respective descriptors for Dedalus and Kierkegaard must be considered metaphorical, for the poet Dedalus is no priest in a purely religious sense and the Christian existentialist Kierkegaard is no poet in the purely esthetic sense. As such, the descriptors must eventually be shed, like a snake its skin or a man his party clothes, to get to a purer apprehension of a Dedalus or a Kierkegaard—an apprehension that nevertheless is born of and shaped by the shell or costume of a metaphor that ultimately is discarded and revoked. Metaphor, in other words, must eventually be cast away—must eventually fail—in order to witness or existentially experience its full referentiality. So too, in apprehending the God-incarnate, Gouwens writes that analogies finally fail:

> [T]he Incarnation is not directly imaginable or conceivable, yet in the use of disanalogy, a kind of *via negativa* is envisioned that, grounded in passionate interest, allows one to apprehend if not comprehend the God-incarnate. Thus it is that the examples Johannes Climacus gives in *Philosophical Fragments* to illustrate (not explain) the Absolute Paradox are appeals to the imagina-

---

[79]*Works of Love*, 195.

[80]*Works of Love*, 194.

[81]James Joyce, *A Portrait of the Artist as a Young Man*, ed. Chester G. Anderson (New York: Penguin, 1977) 221.

[82]For, as Manheimer notes, "Kierkegaard is focusing upon the power of the Word, the *logos*, to make us visible to ourselves. But it is his own language that serves as the background for its effect. His language, which is to a significant degree poetical, aims to facilitate this meeting of the human spirit with the *logos*. The effort is paradoxical since the success of his own art would mean the overshadowing of divine language. Yet he finds that he must speak, that he must take the chance that the sensuous medium of language may conceal that which is purely spirit. Even though his subject is Christian ethics, Kierkegaard's problem lies in the meeting of the esthetical and the religious" (Manheimer, *Kierkegaard as Educator*, 187).

tion to see analogies in disanalogies. The illustration of the king and the maiden, is, Climacus admits, disanalogous and inadequate: "no human situation can provide a valid analogy, even though we shall suggest one here in order to awaken the mind to an understanding of the divine" [*Fragments*, 26]. The disanalogy is that while the king is incognito in order to win the maiden's love, the God's servant-form is the God's true form: "this form of a servant is not something put on like the king's plebeian cloak, which just by flapping open would betray the king; . . . it is his true form" [*Fragments*, 31-32]. Grasping at disanalogies, the imagination has a place in the apprehension of the God in time.[83]

Thus the operative advantage of being sensitive to metaphor is in appreciating not so much the *similarities* between tenor and vehicle (without which there would be no metaphor at all) as their *dissimilarities*, the radical distinctions between tenor and vehicle. For, after comparisons are made, for example, between God and humans (that is, Christ looking *like* a man, man made in the *image* of God)—in order to initiate the reader into the nature of God by operating within sensate-psychical language and images—a reader ultimately must *renounce* the similarities to appreciate the radical, absolute contrast between God and human, between infinitude and finitude. Ethically, the existing individual has no other choice but to renounce the metaphor for this very reason, for only by such renunciation comes the possibility in existence of a primitive, original faith or an absolute relationship with the absolute while existing in the world. Only by such renunciation, according to Johannes Climacus,

---

[83]Gouwens, *Kierkegaard's Dialectic of the Imagination*, 249-50. Soskice writes: "To dissuade us from probing the Divine mysteries, Francis Bacon says: '*there is no proceeding in invention of knowledge but by similitude*: and God is only self-like, having nothing in common with any creature, otherwise than as in shadow and trope.' It is now becoming apparent that, to speak somewhat paradoxically, the task of saying the unsayable is aligned to that of knowing the unknowable. This has been judged to be particularly, and some say exclusively, so in religious matters and yet there has been an equally common assumption that figures and tropes and, in particular, metaphors somehow give us a means of speaking of God" (Soskice, *Metaphor and Religious Language*, 63). Although Soskice may be taken at her word that Bacon's statement is meant to "dissuade us from probing the Divine mysteries," such a statement does not stop the likes of Kierkegaard to attempt to probe (by way of similitude through metaphor) if not the Divine mysteries then at least to probe the very significance of the claim of Bacon that Kierkegaard shares.

can the absolute be practiced, despite that the "task is ideal and perhaps is never accomplished by anyone."[84]

(In *Point of View*, Kierkegaard speaks similarly, although he more convincingly accentuates the need to attend to the task of relating oneself to the absolute despite impossible odds of actually achieving such a state: "To live only in the unconditional, to breathe only the unconditional—the human being cannot do this; he perishes like the fish that must live in the air. But on the other hand a human being cannot in the deeper sense *live* without relating himself to the unconditional; he expires, that is, perhaps goes on living, but spiritlessly."[85])

In addition, Climacus states that "the task is to practice the absolute distinction, it does not necessarily mean that the existing person becomes indifferent to the finite."[86] Rather, to apprehend a God-relationship or apprehend the multifarious contradictions, collisions, and tensions of a religious metaphorical construction, "the appointed task is simultaneously to relate oneself absolutely to the absolute *telos* and relatively to relative ends."[87] In the scope of religious metaphor, the task is to understand the contradictions implicit in the metaphor in relative terms while simultaneously embracing existentially the paradox to which metaphor refers for the goal of believing. Religious metaphor, like Christianity, does not tolerate mediation, but instead collides ideality and actuality as a matter of course. A reader must at least momentarily *imagine, believe, and have faith* that—despite logical contradictions—X=Y for the metaphor to achieve its end and adhere to its single hidden meaning (bound up as the metaphor's meaning is in the implicit or explicit tenor or referent); further, by the reader believing X to equal Y, the metaphor ultimately then must be revoked. Religious metaphor is a paradoxical agent in that its mission is to cancel itself upon the advent of faith (otherwise faith is not faith, but something remaining within the sphere of human ingenuity and understanding)—a process that Kierkegaard knew only too well: "As long as I live," Kierkegaard writes in one journal entry,

> I live in contradiction, for life is contradiction. On the one side I have eternal truth, on the other side manifold existence, which human beings as

---

[84]*Postscript* I, 431.
[85]*Point of View*, 20.
[86]*Postscript* I, 413.
[87]*Postscript* I, 431.

such cannot penetrate, for then we would have to be omniscient. The uniting link is therefore faith.[88]

Just as a synthesis does not make a self out of a human being,[89] so too metaphor offers building blocks for—but cannot offer a copestone to place atop of—a complete architecture of the self. Malantschuk notes that Kierkegaard's concept of the self constitutes the highest form of being, namely, a conscious, personal, and altogether independent being:

> Understood this way, only God is a self in the genuine sense. Of all created beings, only man has the possibility of becoming a self, which is the very goal of human existence. But man can never become an independent self, only a "derived self" (*Sickness*, 69), consequently a self indebted to God for its being.[90]

Faith is posited through divine providence—not through human ingenuity—to clear the air of the smoke of finitude's ambiguities and contradictions, to distinguish between what is absolute and what is relative, all in the service of rendering the self concrete. Kierkegaard writes:

> There at the boundary where human language halts and courage fails, there revelation breaks forth with divine origination and proclaims what is not difficult to understand in the sense of profundity or human parallels but which did not arise in any human being's heart. It actually is not difficult to understand once it has been expressed; indeed, it wants only to be understood in order to be practiced, but it did not arise in any human being's heart.[91]

C. Enacting and Literalizing Metaphor through Imitation, Suffering, and Atonement

Kierkegaard asks in one journal entry: "Is there, then, no eternal agreement (*harmonia præstabilita* [preestablished harmony]) concluded between the heavenly and the earthly?"[92] Throughout his authorship, Kierke-

---

[88]*Journals*, I, V A 68, n.d. [1844], 329.
[89]See *Sickness*, 13.
[90]*Journals*, IV, Commentary, 634.
[91]*Works of Love*, 24-25.
[92]*Journals*, I, V A 41, n.d. [1844], 355.

gaard's metaphors originate from this fundamental question—at least they indirectly respond to it. His metaphors are attempts (no matter how inadequate Kierkegaard claims them to be when pitted against eternity) to reconcile heaven and earth—God and humans—by articulating relative and absolute disparities to "find an expression for the divine in the most beautiful relation in earthly existence."[93] In this context, Kierkegaard is witness to and confessor of such disparity, and his metaphors are evidence of that disparity. They indicate the human, ethical-religious need to repent of the fundamental disparity of ignorance which, according to Anti-Climacus, is sin.[94]

As noted earlier, Kierkegaard uses the metaphoric to "make a truer impression" upon his reader regarding the significance of the religious.[95] Elsewhere, however, he notes that "only in the situation of actuality is it possible to get the true impression of the essentially Christian."[96] In other words, "a truer impression" of the religious may be afforded by metaphor when it is imaginatively appropriated, but the *true* impress of Christianity is manifested existentially and in actuality, not linguistically and solely in the imagination. The communication of the true impress is an *existence*-communication,[97] not a verbal-linguistic communication. Existence-communication, in turn, is predicated upon existential appropriation of meaning, a reduplication of idea in actuality. Kierkegaard writes: "In the realm of spirit a victory is not possible in any accidental and external way but is possible only in an *essential* way; but the essential way is neither more nor less than the reduplication of the victory, just as in the world of spirit the form is the reduplication of the content."[98] Practiced existentially (that is, first imaginatively, then in actuality), Kierkegaard's metaphors are composed to help humans imagine an elemental, fundamental, primitive relationship with and practice of "original" Christianity (that is, Christianity that, according to Kierkegaard, is meant to collide in dead earnest with this world[99]). In addition, metaphors help humans strive in actuality toward a concrete unification of the self. Such unification is evi-

---

[93]*Eighteen Discourses*, 130.

[94]See *Sickness*, 87ff.

[95]See 5, above.

[96]*Journals*, IV, X^2 A 13, n.d. [1849], 122.

[97]See *Postscript* I, 560.

[98]*Adler*, 160.

[99]*Late Writings*, 206.

dent when metaphor is literalized in earnest, when idealities and actualities—or, to use Mackey's words, the *signum* (significance) and *res* (thing) implicit in being human—collide and synthesize, and the self both reposes ontologically in itself and points beyond itself to its divine referent.[100]

Just as collision is the first condition of repose, so too, according to Anti-Climacus, imagination—or the ability to construct human ideas and situations metaphorically—is the "first condition" for becoming a unified person,[101] the capacity *instar omnium* [for all capacities].[102] Gouwens exposes the religious underpinnings of Anti-Climacus's high designation for the imagination by considering imagination in the scope of both the possible and the actual. In a discussion of the distinctions between Johannes Climacus's levels of the religious (Religiousness A—religiousness that approaches Christianity, and Religiousness B—religiousness in a purely Christian sense), Gouwens writes:

> One must have the esthetic ability to dream of another self if one is to acquire the God-relationship of [Religiousness] A; and a religious person must relate to God in suffering and hope if one is to approach Christ as the Absolute Paradox. . . . Without imagination there is mere spiritlessness; with imagination there is life. . . .
>
> In [Religiousness] B Kierkegaard reverses the entire pattern he has developed in the ethical sphere and in [Religiousness] A of how one relates "actuality" and "possibility." In the ethical sphere and in [Religiousness] A the imagination raises one's own actuality to possibility as an ideal task; whatever another person does, that is, another person's "actuality," is irrelevant to whether I can or ought to do something. But in the encounter with Christ, actuality is higher than possibility; one can no longer generate a possibility for one's own life, and furthermore, it is only another person's actuality—that of Christ as an historical figure in time—who can reopen possibility for the disciple. In relying on God for possibility, one relies on the

---

[100]See 24, above. Thoreau offers a more concrete, but not dissimilar, formula: "The fall of each humblest flower marks the annual period of some phase of human life, experience. I can be said to note the flower's fall only when I see in it the symbol of my own change. When I experience this, then the flower appears to me" (*The Journals of Henry David Thoreau*, II, ed. Bradford Torrey and Francis H. Allen [Salt Lake City: Gibbs M. Smith, Inc., 1984] 431).

[101]*Practice*, 186.

[102]*Sickness*, 31.

God in time. Christ and the atonement he offers relieve one of the burden of an independent quest for wholeness by way of the imagination; to appropriate the atonement one needs to accept the forgiveness of the Teacher and reverse one's self-understanding, seeing oneself as a sinner, without possibility, before one can regain possibility.[103]

Here, metaphor used in the sphere of the religious that approaches Christianity (Religiousness A) removes a person from the actual by allowing him the ability to envision the possible, the ideal, the best for which he may strive. Metaphor used in the sphere of the purely Christian (Religiousness B) returns one from the purely imaginative-ideal by placing one back into actuality. Metaphor becomes literalized by *imitating* the ideal within the context of actuality and existence. " 'Imitation,' " Kierkegaard writes in one journal entry, "really provides the guarantee that Christianity does not become poetry, mythology, and abstract idea. . . . 'Imitation' places 'the single individual,' every one, in relationship to the ideal."[104] "The existential is the characteristic that distinguishes between poetry and mythology—and Christianity," Kierkegaard writes elsewhere in his journals. "Indeed, the reason Christ proclaimed Christianity is discipleship or imitation was to prevent a merely imaginary relationship to the essentially Christian."[105]

In the act of becoming human within the realm of the religious, then, the imagination functions as a primer (not a substitute) for suffering and faith in the forgiveness of sins.[106] The existential religious imagination

---

[103]Gouwens, *Kierkegaard's Dialectic of the Imagination*, 277, 236-37.

[104]*Journals*, II, X⁴ A 354, n.d. [1851], 348.

[105]*Journals*, III, XI¹ A 217, n.d. [1854], 238.

[106]Although *imagination* and *faith through suffering* are radically distinct, they are not wholly dissimilar. They both stand apart from the common. They both are, according to Kierkegaard, strangers and alien to actuality. In distinguishing between esthetic imagination and religious faith relative to actuality, Kierkegaard writes: "Esthetically the individual is led away from actuality and translated into the medium of imagination; religiously, the individual is led away and translated into the eternity of the religious: in both instances the individual becomes a stranger and an alien to actuality. Esthetically the individual becomes an alien to actuality by being absent from it; religiously the individual becomes an alien and a foreigner in the realm of actuality" (*Two Ages*, 20). Kierkegaard's sentiment here—linking the esthetic with the religious via linking the imagination with faith—is supported elsewhere in his writings. In one journal entry, for instance, he fuses the esthetic and the ethical in the religious with language that invokes both the imaginative-metaphoric (that is, the discovery of likeness in unlikeness) and faith (that is, the

moves a person *toward* suffering and faith in the requirement of *imitatio Christi* (the imitation of Christ). Metaphor becomes Kierkegaard's workshop for *imitation* so as to conceive how one thing (the actual) can be like another (the ideal) despite overt dissimilarities. In the sphere of the religious, metaphor prompts the individual to strive to meet the ideal in the actual. As Kierkegaard writes of the namesake of one of his more celebrated pseudonyms and of the saintly imitation of that namesake: "The actual Johannes Climacus (author of *Scala Paradisi*) says: There are few saints; if we wish to become saintly and saved, we must live as do the few."[107] Regarding the scope and importance of imitation in Kierkegaard's religious authorship, Howard Hong similarly notes that "The [second authorship] is marked by a heightened level of ideality in the requirement of *imitatio Christi* and in the venture into the second danger, possibly martyrdom, entailed by witnessing to the faith."[108] In *Late Writings*, Kierkegaard invokes Christ's admonition: "Christ has asked for imitators and has very exactly defined what he meant: that they should be salt, willing to be sacrificed, that to be a Christian is to be salt and the willingness to be sacrificed."[109] And it is within such a metaphor of salt that Christian imitation and Christian atonement meet. Gouwens writes:

> The primary distinction to keep in mind in approaching this dialectic [between imitation and atonement] grows out of the centrality of grace: it is the distinction between Christ as atoner and Christ as prototype. While Kierkegaard stresses discipleship in imitation of Christ as prototype for the follower—directed against a misuse of the Lutheran emphasis on faith as opposed to works—he still insists that the atonement is primary: "Although the present situation calls for stressing 'imitation' . . . the matter must above all not be turned in such a way that Christ now becomes only prototype

---

establishment of likeness through absolute unlikeness): "The esthetic-sensuous man admires the strange, that which has no relation to himself; the ethical man admires what has an essential likeness to himself—the great, that which can be the prototype of what he himself ought to be; the religious man admires God, who is of course the absolutely different but still is that with whom he ought to have likeness through the absolute unlikeness" (*Journals*, IV, VI A 123, n.d. [1845], 287).

[107]*Journals*, VI, X¹ A 151, n.d. [1849], 128.

[108]*Late Writings*, Historical Introduction, xxiii. Hong notes the following examples: *Various Spirits*, 217-29, 240, 245; *Christian Discourses*, 181-87, 278; *Practice*, 106, 206-209, 233, 237-57; *Self-Examination*, 67-70; *Judge for Yourself!*, 136-38, 187-204.

[109]*Late Writings*, 42.

[*Forbillede*] and not Redeemer, as if atonement were not needed, at least not for the advanced. No, no, no—for that matter the more advanced one is, the more he will discover that he needs atonement and grace. No, the Atonement and grace are and remain definitive" [*Journals*, II, X⁴ A 491, n.d. (1852), 353]. Kierkegaard further separates the atonement from the ideal by stressing how the atonement refers to the sinner's past, whereas the prototype refers to the future: "Christ is the Atoner. This is continually in relation to the past. But at the same moment he is the Atoner for the past he is "the prototype" [*Forbilledet*] for the future" [*Journals*, II, X⁵ A 44, n.d. (1852), 360]."[110]

The end of religious imitation for Kierkegaard, then, is in actual suffering implied in Christian sacrifice. In *Judge for Yourself!*, Kierkegaard moves the reader from the esthetic to the religious, from poetic imitation to Christian suffering and atonement—all in the context of the metaphor of the lily of the field and the bird of the air:

> The lily and the bird certainly can with truth be said to serve only one master, but this is still only metaphorical and here a person's obligation *to imitate* is a poetic expression. . . . Moreover, if a person, with the lily and the bird as prototypes, lived . . . so that he thought the thought of God in everything, this is indeed piety, and a piety, entirely pure, that surely is never seen among men. But in the strictest sense this is still not Christianity. . . . What is crucial in Christianity is not manifested here at all; to suffer because one adheres to God—or, as it is called, to suffer for the doctrine— the true imitation of Christ.[111]

Less poetically developed than the parable of the lily and the bird (which is evoked in various religious discourses of Kierkegaard's), although more ethically developed, is Anti-Climacus's parable of the imaginative youth in *Practice in Christianity*.[112] This particular figurative construction, in other words, comes closer to depicting the ethical-religious relationship *in existence* between imagination and metaphor on the one hand and actuality and suffering on the other. Kierkegaard asks his reader to imagine a youth who "perceives some image of perfection (ideal),"[113] either a historical actuality or imaginatively formed. Given that

---

[110]Gouwens, *Kierkegaard's Dialectic of the Imagination*, 247-48.

[111]*Judge for Yourself!*, 187.

[112]*Practice*, 186-92.

[113]Unless otherwise indicated, quoted material in the next several pages is from *Practice* and will be cited below on 158.

the image is only at this time imaginatively constructed "in the imagination's infinite distance from actuality, is the image of complete perfection," it is "not the image of struggling and suffering perfection." The image of the youth's ideal, which he does not abandon, "becomes his love, his inspiration, for him his more perfect (more ideal) self." Kierkegaard then suggests Christ to be the youth's image of perfection and focuses on the youth's imitation of Christ. He first addresses, however, the limitations of the imagination without neglecting the need for imagination:

> However great the efforts of imagination to make this imagined image [of perfection] actual, it cannot do it. If it could do that, then with the help of the imagination a person could experience exactly the same as in actuality, could live through it in exactly the same way as if he lived through it in actuality, could learn to know himself as accurately and fundamentally as in the experience of actuality—then there would be no meaning in life. . . . In turn the image produced by the imagination is not that of true perfection; it lacks something—the suffering belonging to actuality or the actuality of suffering. True perfection is that it is this perfection—but the suffering is actual, that it is this perfection that day after day, year after year, exists in the suffering belonging to actuality—this frightful contradiction, not that the perfection exists in something more perfect but that the perfection exists in something infinitely less perfect. And this is precisely the imperfection of the image belonging to the imagination—that the imperfection is not depicted. Alas, and this is what is tragic, that in actuality, the only place where true perfection can truly be, it is so rare, because there it is so hard and exhausting to be that, so hard, yes, so hard that to be that is for that very reason true perfection.

Kierkegaard then returns to the youth, who continues to seek only the image: "he walks like a dreamer, and yet one can see by the fire and flame in his eyes that he is wide awake; he walks like a stranger, and yet he seems to be at home, for through the imagination he is always at home with this image, which he desires to resemble." Here, Kierkegaard describes the transformation of the youth from a world of imagination to a world of actuality. Just as a tenor and a vehicle that otherwise are radically dissimilar begin to resemble each other in an engaging metaphor, the youth begins to resemble, both because of and despite his metaphoric-imaginative powers, his ideal. A "truer impression" is forged ("forged" not only in the sense of "imitation" by a kind of deception, but "forged" also in the sense of earnestly "shaping" or "moulding" one's self existentially):

> And just as it so beautifully happens with lovers that they begin to resemble each other, so the young man is transformed into the likeness of this image, which imprints or impresses itself on all his thought and on every utterance by him, while he, to repeat, with his eyes directed to this image—has not watched his step, has not paid attention to where he is. He wants to resemble this image; he is already beginning to resemble it—and now he suddenly discovers the surrounding world of actuality in which he is standing and the relation of this surrounding world to himself.

Kierkegaard is quick to suggest at this point that "in a certain sense the youth's imagination has deceived him." But, as Kierkegaard has repeatedly suggested elsewhere, the deception deceives into the truth of actuality,[114] into the suffering implicit in actuality, and into becoming fully human in a Christian sense:

> The imagination has deceived the youth, has by means of that image of perfection made him forget that he is, after all, in actuality, and now he is standing there—in exactly the right position. A shudder, it is true, may go through him for a moment as he now considers the matter, but abandon the image—no, that he cannot persuade himself to do. On the other hand, if he cannot persuade himself to abandon the image, he cannot escape the suffering either, because, since the image he wants to resemble is the image of perfection and since the actuality in which he is and wants to express the resemblance is anything but perfection, suffering is in store and is not to be avoided. He is, then, God be praised!—away with cowardly talk and cursed be the mockery of wretchedness here, where in truth there can be only a question of congratulations—he is, then, God be praised, in a tight corner.

Given that the youth chooses not to abandon the image of perfection but rather "cheerfully enters the suffering into which he is being led," he now "loves that image of perfection twice as much, for one always loves more something for which one has suffered. Wonderful! But something has escaped him; no help arrived as he had hoped; only in one sense has he been helped, for he has become stronger." Kierkegaard concludes:

---

[114]See 44-46, above.

This is how Governance deals with him many times, and every time helps him further and further out into suffering, because the youth does not want to abandon that image he so desires to resemble. Then comes a moment when everything becomes clear to him; he understands that that hope belonged to youth, he understands now that suffering cannot be avoided and that it will increase with every step he goes forward. Now existence has turned the screws as tight as it can tighten the screws on a human being; to live under or to endure life under this pressure [*Tryk*] is what we call with emphasis [*Eftertryk*]: to exist as a human being. If existence had done this at the outset, it would have crushed him. Now he is probably able to bear it—yes, he must be able to, since Governance does it with him—Governance, who is indeed love. But still he shudders; the tempter whispers to him that he should abandon that image. But he cannot persuade himself to abandon it; and then he cries out: I cannot do otherwise, God help me. Let us assume that he perseveres until he dies: then he passed his test. He himself became the image of perfection he loved, and the imagination has truly not deceived him any more than Governance.[115]

The "true impression" of metaphor places the opposites of tenor and vehicle together and collides them existentially into a synthesis. Similarly, the young man's ideal collides with the actual in the form of Christian suffering that manifests profound joy of the eternal in the fear and trembling of the actual—for, according to Kierkegaard "the essentially Christian always places opposites together, so the glory is not directly known as glory but, just the reverse, is known by inferiority, debasement—the cross that belongs together with everything that is essentially Christian is here also."[116]

The imaginative young man's life thus suggests that his act of literalizing or annulling the Christian metaphor of the exalted suffering of the cross in effect is an act of existence-communication that "speaks" the language of God. For even though Kierkegaard writes that all divine speech is metaphorical speech,[117] such speech remains only a medium, an approximation. The real language of God is not linguistic for an individual but existential, namely, the appropriation of the metaphorical speech, the literalization of the speech, *the activity to which the speech*

---

[115]*Practice*, 186-91.
[116]*Judge for Yourself!*, 161.
[117]*Works of Love*, 209.

points, which subsequently cancels the metaphoric in the strict linguistic sense of the word. Metaphor nevertheless serves the significant function of bringing an individual to the point where full existential appropriation may occur.

D. The Woman Who Was a Sinner

Kierkegaard's imaginative construction of the youth in *Practice* ostensibly ends with the youth having "passed his test"[118] and having become transformed into the image of perfection that he loved. The youth as metaphor *in and of himself* is complete: he has become the very tenor to which he himself also was vehicle. The youth as metaphor *for* Kierkegaard's readership, however, has just begun. After Kierkegaard states that the youth passed his test, he addresses readers directly regarding why and how they ought to imitate and thereby transform themselves into the likeness of the youth:

> In order to enter into the kingdom of heaven a person must become a child again, but in order that his life can express that he has entered into the kingdom of heaven he must become a youth a second time. To *be* a child and to *be* a youth when one is a child or a youth is easy enough, but a *second time*—the second time is what is decisive. To become a child again, to become nothing, without any selfishness, to become a youth again (although one has become sagacious, sagacious from experience, worldly-wise), to disdain acting sagaciously, to *will to be* the youth, to *will* to preserve youth's enthusiasm, rescued in all its original character, to *will* to struggle to the end . . . yes, that is the task.[119]

When metaphor—in this case the parable of the youth—is literalized by the youth in the parable, it becomes annulled or absent as a metaphor in the consciousness of the youth. Metaphor as a construct, however, is not thereby entirely annihilated. When the youth appropriates the metaphor in such a way as to literalize it *for himself*, he annuls it for himself *but not for others*, not for readers. By literalizing it for himself he becomes a metaphor for others to examine and appropriate. "The task" with which Kierkegaard ultimately ends this parable, then, is not the youth's task, for the youth already has accomplished his task through an earnest

---

[118]*Practice*, 191.
[119]*Practice*, 191-92.

alliance between his metaphoric imagination and will. Rather, "the task" is for individual readers to transform themselves existentially into the youth.

In a symposium addressing what it means to be human, Boris Pasternak states that a person becomes fully human when he is portrayed essentially in metaphorical terms *for* the upbuilding of others:

> A human being achieves his utmost when he, when his physical being, his life, his activity becomes a symbol, a master-concept. . . . Every human being, every single individual is a rarity, a singularity. Because his consciousness forms a world. Because this world completes itself in the *unity* of the idea and brings it to a conclusion.[120]

By transforming himself into his ideal, the young man in *Practice* becomes an ideal, a symbol, a master-concept for others to emulate—even as blood courses through his veins and he continues to live out his actual life. What an ironically "leaden-witted" G. K. Chesterton says of St. Francis of Assisi on the issue of the saint *qua* metaphor also could be said of the youth:

> There does indeed run through the whole of his life a sort of double meaning, like his shadow thrown upon the wall. All his action had something of the character of an allegory; and it is likely enough that some leaden-witted scientific historian may someday try to prove that he himself was never anything but an allegory. . . . He was a poet whose whole life was a poem.[121]

As Kierkegaard, Pasternak, and Chesterton all suggest, the life of the person who becomes fully human by striving for, imitating, and appropriating an ideal—and thereby becoming fully human—is part and parcel of a singular, personal, particular, *actual* life. But as poem, metaphor, allegory, symbol, the life of one who becomes fully human is also thereby universalized for those willing to see and hear of ideality for the sake of striving to become fully human themselves. Such a personality is what

---

[120]From a contribution of Boris Pasternak to a symposium addressing the question "What is man?" which appeared in *Magnum* (Cologne, December 1959). Translated by Howard Hong.

[121]G. K. Chesterton, *St. Francis of Assisi*, An Image Classic (New York: Image/Doubleday, 1990; orig., 1923) 58, 89.

Howard Hong calls "the universal singular."[122] In this context, the parable of the young man in *Practice* may be considered the most developed of Christian metaphors in Kierkegaard's writings for becoming fully human—save one.

The woman who was a sinner in *Without Authority* offers a more compact and direct collision of image and actuality and, as such, may be said existentially to go beyond the example of the young man. This more unmediated collision may be explained in part by the viscerally (as opposed to imaginatively) driven sin-consciousness of the woman, a consciousness more "primitive" in the sense that the woman lacks the potentially self-deceptive encumbrance of *self*-consciousness with which the imaginative youth in *Practice* is endowed. Whereas the youth, through a self-conscious and imaginatively initiated metaphorical transfer, consciously shifts from imagining the idea of Christian suffering to experiencing actual Christian suffering, the woman in her elemental sin-consciousness apparently makes no self-conscious transfer at all. The youth self-consciously places himself, "God be praised, in a tight corner,"[123] by having deceived himself into the truth of Christian suffering. On the other hand, the woman, as simply a self-confessed sinner, *de facto* manifests all the elements of a parable or symbol for all who look upon her.

> "She sits at [Christ's] feet, anoints them with the ointment, wipes them with the hair of her head, kisses them—and weeps." She says nothing and therefore is not what she says, but she is what she does not say, or what she does not say is what she is. She *is* the symbol, like a picture. She has forgotten speech and language and the restlessness of thoughts, has forgotten what is even greater restlessness, this self, has forgotten herself—she, the lost woman, who is now lost in her Savior, who, lost in him, rests at his feet—like a picture.[124]

---

[122]Howard Hong, "Trying to Do the Right Thing," *Reece Report* 7/1 (January 1992): 18: "the view of the person as the universal singular presupposes the universally human, but for the person in the ethical process of becoming, the movement is not from the universal to the individual, but from the individual, through the universal, to the individual, the universal singular. The given of the universally human is normative, and it is the task of the individual to realize the universal in his actuality."

[123]*Practice*, 190.

[124]Unless otherwise indicated, quoted material in the remainder of this section that is not footnoted is from *Without Authority* and will be cited on 163, below.

By describing the silent woman as a picture, Kierkegaard hones the central meaning of Luke's narrative of the sinner sitting at Christ's feet, namely: Christ uses the woman as a metaphor of sin-consciousness *for* those present to witness the "actual" (a universally singular) face of sin-consciousness. The woman, Kierkegaard notes in one journal entry, "is present almost as if only in effigy, and yet she is the one around whom the action centers—the one who is present."[125] She indeed is the center of attention, if only for the observers' gazes upon her to be mirrored and reflected back upon themselves and to illuminate their own sin-consciousness. After all, by her own recognition and acceptance of her sin-consciousness, she has become one who (like the youth) has "passed the test," has become saved, and therefore has become transformed into an image—a picture, a parable, a metaphor—of a saved sinner for others to see and potentially appropriate. Achieving her utmost as a human being in this way, she now serves Christ as a living metaphor "to make the application" of sin-consciousness "more impressive to those present," to offer a *truer impression* of a saved sinner *for* others who have not manifested the essentially Christian existence of sin-consciousness.

As Kierkegaard's version of the woman who was a sinner develops, Kierkegaard depicts Christ *seemingly* treating the woman before his audience as coldly and objectively as an anatomy professor might treat a cadaver before medical students—"as if she were not an actual person." Christ knows, however, who has been saved (the woman) and who needs to be saved (his audience). His attention thereby already has shifted from the needs of the woman (which have been met) to the needs of each contemporary reader-witness (which have not been met). Christ's mission here (as everywhere in his parables) is to help each audience member see himself metaphorically through a picture—"not," as Johannes Climacus writes, as "an eyewitness (in the sense of immediacy), but as a believer [that] he is a contemporary in the *autopsy* of faith."[126] The saved sinner is portrayed by Christ as a picture or a parable for an audience of witnesses to see, read, and appropriate into their own lives:

---

[125] *Journals*, IV, X³ A 566, n.d. [1850], 118.

[126] *Fragments*, 70. "Autopsy," Howard Hong notes, literally means "the personal act of seeing" (Gk. *autos*, self + *optos*, seen) (*Fragments* and *Climacus* [*KW* VII], Notes, 296).

It is almost as if the Savior himself momentarily looked at [the woman who was a sinner] and the situation that way, as if she were not an actual person but a picture. Presumably in order to make the application more impressive to those present, he does not speak *to* her; he does not say, "Your many sins are forgiven you, because you loved much." He speaks *about* her; he says: Her many sins are forgiven her, because she loved much. Although she is present, it is almost as if she were absent; it is almost as if he changed her into a picture, a parable. It is almost as if he said, "Simon, I have something to tell you. There was once a woman. She was a sinner. When the Son of Man was at a dinner one day in the house of a Pharisee, she, too, came in. The Pharisees mocked her and judged her, that she was a sinner. But she sat at his feet, anointed them with ointment, wiped them with her hair, kissed them, and wept. Simon, I want to tell you something: her many sins were forgiven her, because she loved much." It is almost like a story, a sacred story, a parable—and yet at the same moment the same thing was actually taking place on the spot.

This explosive, unmediated collision of such an actual situation—this fusion of ideal sinner and actual sinner, of esthetic beauty and religious pathos—is not accidental by the metaphorist Kierkegaard. The hope of changing the actual into the ideal, the vehicle into the tenor, becomes the very transformative power of metaphor—not only for the woman, but also for the audience.

But "*her many sins were indeed forgiven her*"—and how could this be expressed more strongly, more truthfully, than by this, that it is all forgotten, that she, the great sinner, is changed into a picture. When it is said, "Your sins are forgiven you"—oh, how easy the recollection of herself returns to her if she was not first strengthened by this infinite oblivion: her many sins were forgiven her. "She loved much"; therefore she forgot herself completely; she forgot herself completely—"therefore her many sins were forgiven her." Forgotten, yes, they were drowned with her, so to speak, in oblivion. She is changed into a picture; she becomes a recollection, yet not so that it reminds her of herself. No, just as she forgot it by forgetting herself, so also, not eventually but immediately, recollection forgot what she is called. Her name is: the woman who was a sinner, neither more nor less.[127]

---

[127]*Without Authority*, 141-42. The parable of the woman who was a sinner is not unlike the wonder of the wishing person in *Three Discourses*. While discussing the wishing person in a spiritual context, Kierkegaard again reverses and collapses tenor and

The woman (in words that describe the *telos* of the imaginative youth in *Practice* after a certain sagacious self-consciousness had been shed from him) has "become a child again . . . become nothing, without any selfishness."[128] In her honest repentance, she does not "remind . . . herself of herself." Her sin-consciousness is precisely what makes her a child again—a selfless being, a significant "nothing"—because sin-consciousness makes her ignorant a second time. To invoke Franz Kafka's famous parable on parables, she lost in worldly reality because of her sins and her sin-consciousness, but she has won in parable—parable that exists on the very borderline of eternity.[129] Such *learned ignorance* is the lesson here and elsewhere in Kierkegaard's writing of religious suffering and sin-consciousness. It is what Kierkegaard comes to describe as "dying to

---

vehicle in his metaphorical speech to lay the groundwork for a God-relationship: "Indeed, what more powerful expression of wonder is there than for the wonderer to become as if changed, than for the wisher to change color; what more powerful expression than this, that he *actually* becomes changed! And so it is with this wonder—it changes the seeker; and so it is with this change—it seeks to become something else, indeed, become the very opposite: to seek means that the seeker himself is changed. He is not to look for the place where the object of his seeking is, because it is right with him; he is not to look for the place where God is, he is not to strive to get there, because God is right there with him, very near, everywhere near, at every moment everywhere present, but the seeker must be changed so that he himself can become the place where God in truth is" (*Three Discourses*, 23).

[128]*Practice*, 192.

[129]"Many complain that the words of the wise are always merely parables and of no use in daily life, which is the only life we have. When the sage says: "Go over," he does not mean that we should cross to some actual place, which we could do anyhow if the labor were worth it; he means some fabulous yonder, something unknown to us, something too that he cannot designate more precisely, and therefore cannot help us here in the very least. All these parables really set out to say merely that the incomprehensible is incomprehensible, and we know that already. But the cares we have to struggle with every day: that is a different matter.

"Concerning this a man once said: Why such reluctance? If you only followed the parables you yourselves would become parables and with that rid of all your daily cares.

"Another said: I bet that is also a parable.

"The first said: You have won.

"The second said: But unfortunately only in parable.

"The first said: No, in reality: in parable you have lost." Franz Kafka, *Parables and Paradoxes* (New York: Schocken Books, 1975) 11.

the world"—a fundamental metaphor of Christian suffering and redemption and one on which the present discussion concludes.

E. Epilogue. Metaphor and Dying to the World

Kierkegaard maintains that a person becomes "and remains ignorant by having become aware of something else totally different (because by becoming aware of something else one *becomes* ignorant of what one knew)."[130] In the cases of the woman who was a sinner and the young man in *Practice*, becoming ignorant a second time is tantamount to becoming Christianly aware of God: "This knowledge totally engages the Christian's mind and thought, blots out everything else from his memory, captures his heart forever, and thus he becomes absolutely ignorant."[131]

No small attribution to metaphor exists—as both a linguistic and existential prompter—for an individual's religious becoming in such a way. Metaphor ushers a person into a second ignorance by depicting opposites (that is, "something else totally different") in close relation to each other: to imagine or conceive of the ideal, the reality of finitude in a vacuum is negated, excluded, becomes nothing in the moment of imagining.[132] Once a person appropriates the religious metaphor fully, all aspects of the world that do not directly inform the individual's religiosity dies away, is blotted out—allowing an individual to escape into the religious by dying to the world.

To aid in manifesting such a "death" and escape, the gift of metaphor helps individuals first imagine and then become something that they, through grace, may become only in profound inwardness. A person "does not reflect oneself into Christianity," Kierkegaard writes, suggesting that mind and imagination alone cannot achieve personal religiosity. Nevertheless, one "reflects oneself out of something else and becomes more and more simple, a Christian."[133] Although the initial attraction toward appropriating metaphor (toward, for example, imitating Christ as the young man does in *Practice*) initially may appear esthetically interesting, donning the actual costume of Christian suffering ethically requires the shedding of metaphor's romantic script. After all, "the movement" of the

---

[130]*Christian Discourses*, 31.
[131]*Christian Discourses*, 33.
[132]See above, 81n.45.
[133]*Point of View*, 7.

religious, according to Kierkegaard, "is not from the simple to the interesting, but from the interesting to the simple—becoming a Christian."[134] Just as metaphor must eventually be sloughed off and annulled to make way for the actual and the religious, so all indirect (maieutic) communication must be abandoned, for "the communication of the essentially Christian," Kierkegaard writes in one journal entry, "must end finally in 'witnessing.' The maieutic cannot be the final form, because, Christianly understood, the truth doth not lie in the subject (as Socrates understood it), but in a revelation which must be proclaimed."[135]

When Kierkegaard Socratically suggests that ignorance is sin,[136] he indirectly ushers the usage of metaphor into the realm of the religious as the vehicle by which individuals not only envision sin but also claim it. The believer is not simply *like*, for example, a prisoner in Socrates' "Allegory of the Cave."[137] Rather, the believer *is* a prisoner because of ignorance (sin). Metaphor appropriated religiously becomes a signpost of grace by illuminating the possibility of faith, redemption, and an ideal life after death through the contrasts of opposites. The woman who was a sinner becomes the parable, not by virtue of the parable itself, but by virtue of God's grace that allows her—and readers—to see herself as something dialectically opposite. The woman, in effect, dies to the world by "fleeing" to grace, for she learns the divine language of grace through sin-consciousness. The young man in *Practice* also becomes a parable for readers because he corners himself in such a way (through suffering) as to need grace to fulfill his own religious *telos*. The woman and the young man become existentially contemporaneous with Christ, and, as Kierkegaard notes in one journal entry, "by becoming contemporaneous with Christ (the prototype), you simply discover that you are not like it at all, not even in what you call your best moment; for in such a moment you are not in the corresponding tension of actuality but are spectating. The result is that you effectively learn to flee to faith in grace."[138]

Not until an individual appreciates how unlike he is to the prototype can that individual begin to see similarities (ethical similarities through

---

[134]*Point of View*, 94.

[135]*Journals*, II, IX A 221, n.d. [1848], 383. Revelation here embodies an earnest confession of sins and a yielding to divine grace.

[136]See *Irony*, 61, 149, 211, 230-31; *Christian Discourses*, 61, 63, 67; *Sickness*, 87ff.

[137]See *Dialogues of Plato* I, 773-78 [*Republic*, 514-19].

[138]*Journals*, I, IX A 153, n.d. [1848], 324.

imitation) surface amid radical dissimilarities. The dialectical tension between the need to see both how dissimilar one *is* relative to the prototype and how similar one *can be* to the prototype always must exist to become fully human in a Christian sense. Walsh suggests that

> as Kierkegaard sees it, Christ never appears simply as the prototype but incorporates with this the grace whereby real imitation is made possible. For the gift of grace does not mean that imitation is thereby dispensed with; no, Kierkegaard says, "the prototype remains with his demand that there be a striving to be like him" (*Journals*, II, X⁵ A 23, n.d. [1852], 138).[139]

To exist on the cusp of such grace means to die to the world, to appropriate a second ignorance, to recognize Socratically not only the limits of knowledge, but also the boundaries of ignorance and the border of language where epistemological contraband must be surrendered if one is to travel beyond language to faith. Here, many of Kierkegaard's parables are not unlike the parables of Jesus—especially in that, according to Donahue,

> the most fundamental message of Jesus' parables is that things are not as they seem, that you must be open to having your tidy vision of reality shattered. By their paradoxical qualities the parables become metaphors of the transcendent. Only when one stands before the limits of language is one able to accept the advent of God's kingdom as gift.[140]

As with a Socratic understanding of the limits of knowledge, such an understanding of the limits of language by appropriating metaphor's paradoxical nature illuminates Kierkegaard's own conception of dying to the world. In one journal entry, Kierkegaard discusses a lover who, unable to speak the beloved's language, must learn the unknown language for the sake of a happy relationship. Then he states: "It is the same with dying to the world in order to be able to love God. God is spirit—only one who has died to the world can speak this language at all."[141] Here, one's understanding of God's language and dying to the world intersect where the language of religious suffering ends and actual religious suffering begins.

---

[139]Sylvia Walsh, *Living Poetically: Kierkegaard's Existential Aesthetics* (University Park: Pennsylvania State University Press, 1994) 238.

[140]John R. Donahue, *The Gospel in Parable* (Philadelphia: Fortress Press, 1988) 16.

[141]*Journals*, I, X⁴ A 624, n.d. [1852], 219. Cf. *Self-Examination*, 26-32.

Kierkegaard writes elsewhere in his journal: "Really and truly, anyone who has the remotest idea of what it actually is to die to the world also knows that this does not take place without frightful agonies."[142]

Of the language of religious suffering, little else other than metaphor can be used to describe the indescribable and incommunicable nature of *actual* suffering—language that even then falls short of the mark. Nevertheless, metaphor is used in the spirit of maieutic or indirect communication to point to and promote religious suffering. And it is in this spirit that the rustic response of Diggory Venn to Clym Yeobright's consideration of religion, suffering, and the metaphoric prove to be words of great wisdom in Thomas Hardy's *Return of the Native*. When Yeobright suggests through metaphor how mortal death *is* eternal life, Venn replies: "You say right, nó doubt. Trouble has taught you a deeper vein of talk than mine."[143] Venn suggests here that metaphor is the deeper and more substantive vein of communication than direct communication. The choice of using the metaphoric is derived as much from actual suffering as from the inability to speak effectively about suffering in any other way.

It is no wonder, then, that Kierkegaard "masks" himself with so many rich personae. The masks challenge his readers by suggesting that metaphor, as a primary means to address the absolute and the specific simultaneously, ought to be used as imaginative constructions to prompt, promote, and actualize inward religious suffering *for* all readers, even Kierkegaard himself: "If no one else wants to try to present the absoluteness of the religious placed together with the specific, a combination that in existence is the very basis and meaning of suffering, then I will do it, I who am neither a religious speaker nor a religious person, but just a humorous, imaginatively constructing psychologist."[144] Whether he writes under the pen of religious humorist, imaginatively constructing psychologist, seducer, judge, editor, silent brother, or any number of other pseudonyms—even including (in a Nabokovian sense) his own name—Kierkegaard always and everywhere is committed as a writer to vanish, to be at most a silhouette or an insignificant epigram or an absentee or a non-

---

[142]*Journals*, II, X³ A 373, n.d. [1850], 125.

[143]Thomas Hardy, *The Return of the Native* (New York: Signet, 1959) 318. The third epigram of the present discussion seems an appropriate companion piece to Clym Yeobright's notion.

[144]*Postscript* I, 483.

person, to become at best nothing—like the darkened figure in the *Corsair* caricature[145]—so that all readers *qua* human beings may inwardly examine and read themselves. Even Kierkegaard himself looks upon himself as more reader than writer: "I regard myself as a *reader* of the books," Kierkegaard writes in *Point of View*, "not as the *author*."[146]

Personae and pseudonyms aside, Kierkegaard is ostensibly considered in the present discussion as both philosopher *and* poet. The art of his poetry is intent upon grounding his philosophical and religious ideas in the actual. Metaphor is the "art" that must be created *in order* to be forgotten for the actual.[147] Such metaphorical art for Kierkegaard ultimately may be considered a work of art in the promotion of worldly ignorance for the sake of eternal grace:

> To be ignorant is no art, but to *become* ignorant and to be ignorant by having become ignorant—that is the art. . . . The Christian becomes ignorant . . . [and] ends with being ignorant—and Christianly the question is never asked about what a person was but about what he became, not about what he was like, but about what sort of person he became, not about the beginning but about the end. Yet to become ignorant in this way can take a long time, and it is a difficult task before he succeeds, little by little, and before he finally succeeds in really becoming ignorant of what he knows, and then in remaining ignorant, in continuing to be that, so he does not sink back again, trapped in the snare of knowledge.[148]

Such metaphorical art also may be considered an ultimate work of art in the spirit of what Richard Shiff considers an ultimate work of art to be. Shiff writes that such art, "applying its metaphoric power to its limit, would indeed cause a leap rather than a gradual passage from one level of reality to another. The experience of such a work of art would be analogous to the revelation of absolute truth, as opposed to the attainment of relativistic knowledge which further experience might modify; transported to an entirely new reality, our old identities would die with our old world."[149]

---

[145]See title page (iii) and 1-5, above.

[146]*Point of View*, 12. Cf. above, 15, and *Journals*, VI, X^2 A 281, n.d. [1849], 268.

[147]See the second epigram of the present discussion (xi) (from *Eighteen Discourses*, 130-31).

[148]*Christian Discourses*, 25-26.

[149]Richard Shiff, "Art and Life: A Metaphoric Relationship," in *On Metaphor*, ed.

Transported to an entirely new reality through the course of his life and authorship, even Kierkegaard's old identities ultimately die with his old worlds. The esthetically interesting transforms into the religiously simple. There was a time in his past when Kierkegaard, embarking upon his brief but incomparably full and intense writing career, required and quickly achieved a multifaceted and metaphoric literary persona

> as piercing as the glance of *Lynceus*, as terrifying as the groan of the giants, as sustained as a sound of nature, extending in range from the deepest bass to the most melting high notes, and modulated from the most solemn-silent whisper to the fire-spouting energy of rage . . . in order to breathe, to give voice to what is on [his] mind, to make the *viscera* of both anger and sympathy tremble.[150]

But for his literary voice to breathe the clean air of honesty, Kierkegaard knew that he also had to breath the vivifying air of the religious, transfiguring into a beautiful and amiable jest whatever metaphor that his poetry created.[151] Through the voice of Johannes Climacus, Kierkegaard writes:

> For immediacy, poetry is the transfiguration of life; but for religiousness, poetry is a beautiful and amiable jest, whose consolation religiousness nevertheless rejects, because it is precisely in suffering that the religious breathes. Immediacy expires in misfortune; in suffering the religious begins to breath.[152]

Sheldon Sacks (Chicago: University of Chicago Press, 1979) 106.

[150]*Letters & Documents*, 54. See also above, 36.

[151]In Kierkegaard's preface to "An Occasional Discourse," the diligent needlewoman about whom he writes hopes that her needlepoint points to the religious instead of the esthetic, becomes a religious jest instead of an esthetic production to be lauded. The needlewoman's hope, like Kierkegaard's hope for his own work, is that no one will "make the mistake of seeing her artistry instead of the meaning of the cloth or were to make the mistake of seeing a defect of the cloth instead of seeing the meaning of the cloth. She could not work the sacred meaning into the cloth; she could not embroider it on the cloth as an additional ornament. The meaning is in the beholder and in the beholder's understanding when, faced with himself and his own self, he has in the infinite remoteness of separation infinitely forgotten the needlewoman and her part" (*Various Spirits*, 5).

[152]*Postscript* I, 436.

In the end, Kierkegaard knows that it is one thing to compose metaphor and another thing to be composed (in part) by metaphor. The artist *composes* metaphor while the fully human *becomes composed* (in part by metaphor) in the religious: "it is indeed one thing to compose oneself poetically; it is something else to be composed poetically. The Christian lets himself be poetically composed, and in this respect a simple Christian lives far more poetically than many a brilliant intellectual."[153]

It is no wonder, then, that something Kierkegaard was reported to have said near the end of his life has significant metaphorical and literal value both in regard to his life and his thought. Dissimilar even to an absentee or a nonperson or a silhouetted figure in caricature, his words remark of dying to the world, of ultimately becoming nothing in this life in order to express fully his worship of God. To invoke an idea of Johannes Climacus, his words play out of the "wondrousness" of God's creation by suggesting that a human being can *become something* (a self dependent upon his Creator) that, through the true worship of God and by the power of freedom that is given by God, is able to *become nothing* before God.[154] Kierkegaard's words uttered near his life's end suggest the coming into existence of metaphor in his own personal life, which, at the time he uttered them, he himself was on the border between the finite and the infinite, the physical and the spiritual. The sentiment of his words is not unlike the trivial degree to which Socrates thinks about his own body when asked by Crito what the bereaved should do with the sage's body upon his death (namely, that the body is nothing to Socrates, that it means nothing when compared with the soul).[155] Finally, the sentiment of his words is not unlike the trivial degree that Paul values the visible and the material when compared with the invisible and the heavenly.[156] After falling at a party near the end of his life, his fragile body now crooked on the floor, Kierkegaard utters with a wink: "Oh, leave it—let—the maid—sweep it up—in the morning."[157] Given that Kierkegaard's life at this time existed upon the border region between mortal death and eternal life, upon the crossroad of the actual and the ideal, this last recorded

---

[153]*Irony*, 280-81.
[154]*Postscript* I, 246.
[155]See *Dialogues of Plato* I, 499 (*Phaedo*, 115).
[156]See 2 Corinthians 4:18.
[157]*Journals*, VI, Notes, 647.

statement of his in which he depicts himself as refuse—as nothing other than physical waste, which effectively represents nothing—is perfectly appropriate. His utterance is a metaphor of his ideal literary persona. What is more significant is that it is a metaphor of his ultimate, humbling prayer to and worship of God: to become nothing before God.

Works Cited

Banks, Russell. *Cloudsplitter*. New York: HarperFlamingo, 1998.

Booth, Wayne C. "Metaphor as Rhetoric: The Problem of Evaluation." In *On Metaphor*, edited by Sheldon Sacks. Chicago: University of Chicago Press, 1979.

Chaucer, Geoffrey. *Chaucer's Major Poetry*. Edited by Albert Baugh. Englewood Cliffs NJ: Prentice-Hall, 1963.

Chesterton, G. K. *St. Francis of Assisi*. An Image Classic. New York: Image/Doubleday, 1990.

_____. *The Man Who Was Thursday*. London: Penguin, 1986.

Cohen, Ted. "Metaphor and the Cultivation of Intimacy." In *On Metaphor*, edited by Sheldon Sacks. Chicago: University of Chicago Press, 1979.

Conrad, Joseph. *Lord Jim*. Garden City NY: Doubleday, Page & Co., 1924.

Davidson, Donald. "What Metaphor Means." In *On Metaphor*, edited by Sheldon Sacks. Chicago: University of Chicago Press, 1979.

De Man, Paul. "The Epistemology of Metaphor." In *On Metaphor*, edited by Sheldon Sacks. Chicago: University of Chicago Press, 1979.

Donahue, John R. *The Gospel in Parable*. Philadelphia: Fortress Press, 1988.

Eiseley, Loren. *The Immense Journey*. Alexandria VA: Time-Life Books, 1962.

_____. *The Star Thrower*. New York: Harvest/HBJ, 1978.

Eliot, George. *Middlemarch*. Edited by W. J. Harvey. New York: Penguin, 1965.

Eliot, T. S. *Complete Poems and Plays*. New York: Harcourt, Brace and World, 1971.

Elrod, John. *Being and Existence in Kierkegaard's Pseudonymous Works*. Princeton: Princeton University Press, 1975.

Emerson, Ralph Waldo. *Essays and Lectures*. New York: Library of America, 1983.

Evans, C. Stephen. *Kierkegaard's Fragments and Postscript: The Religious Philosophy of Johannes Climacus*. Atlantic Highlands NJ: Humanities Press, 1983.

Ferreira, M. Jamie. *Transforming Vision: Imagination and Will in Kierkegaard-ian Faith*. Oxford: Clarendon Press, 1991.

Fowler, H. W. *Fowler's Modern English Usage*. Second edition. New York: Oxford University Press, 1965. Third edition. Edited by R. W. Burchfield. Oxford: Clarendon Press, 1996.

Gouwens, David J. "Kierkegaard on the Ethical Imagination." *The Journal of Religious Ethics* 10 (Fall 1982).

_____. "Understanding, Imagination, and Irony in Kierkegaard's *Repetition*." In *Fear and Trembling and Repetition*. International Kierkegaard Commentary 6. Edited by Robert L. Perkins. Macon GA: Mercer University Press, 1993.

_____. *Kierkegaard's Dialectic of the Imagination*. New York: Peter Lang, 1989.

Hardy, Thomas. *The Return of the Native*. New York: Signet, 1959.

Harries, Karsten. "Metaphor and Transcendence." In *On Metaphor*, edited by Sheldon Sacks. Chicago: University of Chicago Press, 1979.

_____. "The Many Uses of Metaphor." In *On Metaphor*, edited by Sheldon Sacks. Chicago: University of Chicago Press, 1979.

Heidegger, Martin. *Being and Time*. Translated by John Macquarrie and Edward Robinson. New York: Harper & Row, 1962.

_____. *Poetry, Language, Thought*. Translated by Albert Hofstadter. New York: Harper & Row, 1971.

Hong, Howard V. "Tanke-Experiment in Kierkegaard." In *Kierkegaard: Resources and Results*, edited by Alistar McKinnon. Montreal: Wilfrid Laurier University Press, 1982.

_____. "The Comic, Satire, Irony, and Humor: Kierkegaardian Reflections." *Midwest Studies in Philosophy* 1 (1976).

_____. "Trying to Do the Right Thing." *Reece Report* 7/1 (Northfield MN: Richard Reece, January 1992).

Ibsen, Henrik. *Brand*. Translated by Michael Meyer; with a foreword by W. H. Auden. Garden City NY: Anchor Books, 1960.

_____. *Peer Gynt*. Translated by Rolf Fjelde. Minneapolis: University of Minneapolis Press, 1980.

Joyce, James. *A Portrait of the Artist as a Young Man*. Edited by Chester G. Anderson. New York: Penguin, 1977.

_____. *Ulysses*. Edited by Hans Walter Gabler et al. New York: Random House, 1986.

Kafka, Franz. *Diaries 1914–1923*. New York: Schocken, 1965.
_____. *Parables and Paradoxes*. New York: Schocken Book, 1975.
Kearney, Richard. *The Wake of Imagination*. Minneapolis: University of Minneapolis Press, 1988.
Keats, John. *Selected Poems and Letters*. Edited by Douglas Bush. Boston: Houghton Mifflin, 1959.
Kern, Edith. *Existential Thought and Fictional Technique*. New Haven: Yale University Press, 1970.
Kierkegaard, Søren. *Kierkegaard's Writings*. Twenty-five volumes. Howard V. Hong, general editor. Edited and translated with introduction and notes by Howard V. Hong and Edna H. Hong and others (others are noted below). Princeton NJ: Princeton University Press, 1978–1998. The twenty-five volumes are as follows.

I. *Early Polemical Writings*. Edited and translated with introduction and notes by Julia Watkin. 1990.

II. *The Concept of Irony*. 1989.

III. *Either/Or* I. 1987.

IV. *Either/Or* II. 1987.

V. *Eighteen Upbuilding Discourses*. 1990.

VI. *Fear and Trembling* and *Repetition*. 1983.

VII. *Philosophical Fragments* and *Johannes Climacus*. 1985.

VIII. *The Concept of Anxiety*. Edited and translated with introduction and notes by Reidar Thomte in collaboration with Albert B. Anderson. 1980.

IX. *Prefaces; Writing Sampler*. Edited and translated with introduction and notes by Todd W. Nichol. 1997.

X. *Three Discourses on Imagined Occasions*. 1993.

XI. *Stages on Life's Way*. 1988.

XII. *Concluding Unscientific Postscript to* Philosophical Fragments I-II. 1992.

XIII. *The* Corsair *Affair*. 1982.

XIV. *Two Ages*. 1978.

XV. *Upbuilding Discourses in Various Spirits*. 1993.

XVI. *Works of Love*. 1995.

XVII. *Christian Discourses* and *The Crisis and a Crisis in the Life of an Actress*. 1997.

XVIII. *Without Authority: The Lily in the Field and the Bird in the Air; Two Ethical-Religious Essays; Three Discourses at the Communion on Fridays; An Upbuilding Discourse; Two Discourses at the Communion on Fridays*. 1997.

XIX. *The Sickness Unto Death*. 1980.

XX. *Practice in Christianity*. 1991.

XXI. *For Self-Examination* and *Judge for Yourself!* 1990.

XXII. *The Point of View: On My Work as an Author; The Point of View for My Work as an Author; Armed Neutrality.* 1998.

XXIII. *The Moment and Late Writings: Articles from* Fædrelandet, *The Moment; This Must be Said, So Let it be Said; Christ's Judgment on Official Christianity; The Changelessness of God.* 1998.

XXIV. *The Book on Adler.* 1998.

XXV. *Kierkegaard: Letters and Documents.* Translated with introduction and notes by Henrik Rosenmeier. 1978.

_____. *Søren Kierkegaard's Journals and Papers.* I-VII. Edited and translated with notes by Howard V. Hong and Edna H. Hong. Commentary by Gregor Malantschuk. Bloomington: Indiana University Press, 1967–1978.

_____. *Works of Love.* Translated by Howard Hong and Edna Hong. New York: Harper & Row, 1962.

Kittay, Eva Feder. *Metaphor: Its Cognitive Force and Linguistic Structure.* Clarendon Library of Logic and Philosophy. London: Oxford University Press, 1987.

King, G. Heath. *Existence, Thought, Style: Perspectives of a Primary Relation Portrayed Through the Work of Søren Kierkegaard.* Milwaukee: Marquette University Press, 1996.

Kirmmse, Bruce H. *Encounters with Kierkegaard.* Princeton: Princeton University Press, 1996.

Locke, John. *An Essay Concerning Human Understanding.* Edited by Peter Nidditch. London: Oxford University Press, 1975.

Mackey, Louis. *Kierkegaard: A Kind of Poet.* Philadelphia: University of Pennsylvania Press, 1971.

Manguel, Alberto. *A History of Reading.* New York: Viking Penguin, 1996.

Manheimer, Ronald J. *Kierkegaard as Educator.* Berkeley: University of California Press, 1977.

Melville, Herman. *Moby-Dick.* Berkeley: University of California Press, 1979.

Milton, John. *Complete Poems and Major Prose.* Edited by Merritt Y. Hughes. Indianapolis: Odyssey Press, 1957.

Oden, Thomas C. *Parables of Kierkegaard.* Princeton: Princeton University Press, 1978.

Ozick, Cynthia. *Metaphor and Memory.* New York: Knopf, 1989.

Pasternak, Boris. Contribution to a symposium on "What is man?" in *Magnum* (Cologne, December 1959).

Perkins, Robert L. "Abraham's Silence Aesthetically Considered." In *Kierke-gaard on Art and Communication*, edited by George Pattison. New York: St. Martin's Press, 1992.

Plato. *The Dialogues of Plato*. I-II. Translated by B. Jowett. New York: Random House, 1937.

Polk, Timothy Houston. *The Biblical Kierkegaard*. Macon GA: Mercer University Press, 1997.

Sacks, Sheldon, editor. *On Metaphor*. Chicago: University of Chicago Press, 1979.

Sartre, Jean Paul. *The Psychology of Imagination*. A Citadel Press Book. New York: Carol Publishing Group, 1991.

Schleifer, Robert, editor. *Kierkegaard and Literature*. Norman: University of Oklahoma Press, 1984.

Shakespeare, William. *The Riverside Shakespeare*. Boston: Houghton Mifflin Company, 1974.

Shattuck, Roger. *Candor and Persuasion*. New York: W. W. Norton & Company, 1999.

_____. *Forbidden Knowledge*. New York: St. Martin's Press, 1996.

_____. *Proust's Binoculars*. Princeton NJ: Princeton University Press, 1983.

Shaw, George Bernard. *Seven Plays by Bernard Shaw*. New York: Dodd, Mead and Company, 1967.

Shiff, Richard. "Art and Life: A Metaphoric Relationship." In *On Metaphor*, edited by Sheldon Sacks. Chicago: University of Chicago Press, 1979.

Soskice, Janet. *Metaphor and Religious Language*. Oxford: Clarendon Press, 1985.

Steiner, George. "Books in an Age of Post-Literacy." *Publishers Weekly* (24 May 1985).

Stoppard, Tom. *Rosencrantz and Guildenstern are Dead*. New York: Grove Press, 1967.

Swenson, David. *Something about Kierkegaard*. Revised and enlarged edition. Minneapolis: Augsburg Publishing House, 1945. Reprint: Reprints of Scholarly Excellence 5 (ROSE 5). Edited by Lillian Marvin Swenson. Foreword to the ROSE edition by Mary Carman Rose. Macon GA: Mercer University Press, 1983.

Taylor, Mark. "Reinventing Kierkegaard." *Religious Studies Review* 7/3 (July 1981).

Thomas, Owen. *Metaphor and Related Subjects*. New York: Random House, 1969.

Thoreau, Henry David. *The Journals of Henry David Thoreau.* I-XIV. Edited by Bradford Torrey and Francis H. Allen. Salt Lake City: Gibbs M. Smith, Inc., 1984.

_____. *Walden.* Edited by Walter Harding. New York: Houghton Mifflin Company, 1995.

Walsh, Sylvia. *Living Poetically: Kierkegaard's Existential Aesthetics.* University Park PA: Pennsylvania State University Press, 1994.

Wheelwright, Philip. *Metaphor and Reality.* Bloomington: Indiana University Press, 1962.

Wordsworth, William. *Selected Poems and Prefaces.* Edited by Jack Stillinger. Boston: Houghton Mifflin Company, 1965.

Index

gambler, 112
giants, 66
Hercules, 30
king and maiden, 148
kite-flying child, 83-84
leap, 37
light, 30
lilies and the birds, 49,
    115, 132, 146, 155
looking at the sun, 47-48
lover of Greek architec-
    ture, 92
man standing on one leg,
    15
map of the country, 52
medicine, strong, 88
mirror, 103, 118
mirror and love letter,
    118-19, 167
mirror of ocean, 146
mock and real turtle, 32
Mohammed's coffin, 24
moving one's eyes, 49
music, 33n.16
mussels hawked, 57
mutiny, 56
natural science, 31n.11
needlewoman, 170n.151
number carried, 42-43,
    125-26n.11
party clothes, 146
passing the test, 158-59,
    162
pavement commission,
    59, 60
Phalaris's bronze bull,
    69, 69n.2
physiology, 71
plain dress, 58
plant world, 71
plow handles, 144
preface writing, 36n.28
priming powder, 66
prose, 146
rowboat, 17, 20
royal coachman, 34-35
royal decree, 118-19
salt, 154
sermon, 54
shrimp hawked, 57, 60

sneeze, 72
somnambulist, 99
staff of servants, 115
theatergoer, 65
toothless old man, 57, 60
topographical map, 52
tree known by its fruits,
    114
two kingdoms, xi
wardrobe, 60-61
web, 31n.11
wet bowstring, 66
wings, 10, 12, 147
wishing person, 163-
    64n.127
woman who was a sin-
    ner, 159-66
wreaths of woodruff
    hawked, 57
Middle Ages, 56
Milton, John, 25
mind, 57
    diverting one's, 49
    God and, 115
    nature and, 115
"mine" and "thine," 53
mirror, 103, 118
    love letter and, 118-19
    metaphor as, 118
    of ocean, 146
    of possibility, 117
    of the Word, 119
misrelationship, 13
    between self and poet-exis-
        tence, 75
    ethical, 13
    metaphors pointing to, 13
mistaking categories, 58-59,
    92-94
mock turtle, 32
Mohammed's coffin, 24
Monday-Christianity, New
    Testament, 58-59
monism, 12
mood, 116
morality, the moral
    life of, 108
    modern statistical approach
        to, 59
    tension and, 85

Mormons, 136
motion, linguistic, 8, 125
Murdoch, Iris, 42, 44
music, the musical, 33n.16
mussels hawked, 57
mutiny of words, 56
mystery and imagination, 47
mysticism, the mystic, 99,
    115-16, 126n.14

Nabokovian, 168
narcissism, 82, 135
narrative
    metaphor. *See* metaphor
    theology, 107n.34
Nathan, 113, 113n.51, 114
natural science, 31n.11
    as coordinate with theology,
        32-33
    details of, 33
nature, 21, 146
    God and, 115
    mind and, 115
    as staff of servants, 115
necessity, the necessary, 125
    of imagination, 64
needlewoman, 170n.151
negation, the negative, nega-
    tivity, 2, 33, 34, 85, 165-72
    illuminating the eternal
        through, 34, 145, 147
    Kierkegaard n. positioning
        himself, 3, 5, 168-71
    positive and, 64
    of reality, 81n.45, 89
neighbor, the, 53, 132-33
neither-nor, 110
New Testament
    Monday-Christianity, 58-59
    See also Bible
newspaper, reading the ex-
    traordinary in, 65
Nicholas of Cusa, 35
Nietzsche, Friedrich, 99n.7
nobody, teacher as, 3
nonperson, teacher as, 3
normative ethics, 12, 37,
    161n.122
nothing, Kierkegaard becom-
    ing, 2